SUNY Series on Sport, Culture, and Social Relations

Cheryl L. Cole and Michael A. Messner, Editors

PLAYING TO WIN

SPORTS AND THE AMERICAN MILITARY, 1898-1945

WANDA ELLEN WAKEFIELD

STATE UNIVERSITY OF NEW YORK PRESS

Cover photo credit to: US Army Military History Institute
Cover Design credit to: Charles Martin

Published by
State University of New York Press, Albany

© 1997 State University of New York

All rights reserved

Printed in the United States of America

For information, address State University of New York Press,
State University Plaza, Albany, NY 12246

Production by M. R. Mulholland
Marketing by Bernadette LaManna

Library of Congress Cataloging-in-Publication Data

Wakefield, Wanda Ellen, 1953–
    Playing to win : sports and the American military, 1898–1945 /
Wanda Ellen Wakefield.
        p.   cm. -- (SUNY series on sport, culture, and social
    relations)
    Includes bibliographical references and index.
    ISBN 0-7914-3313-7 (hc : alk. paper). -- ISBN 0-7914-3314-5 (pb :
alk. paper)
    1. Military sports--United States--History.   2. Sociology,
Military--United States--History.   3. Masculinity (Psychology)-
-United States.   I. Title.   II. Series.
    U328.U5W35   1997
    306.2 '7 '0973--dc20   96-19224
                                                                                              CIP
                                                                                              Rev.

10 9 8 7 6 5 4 3 2 1

THIS IS FOR

MY GRANDFATHER, LEONARD WAKEFIELD, DOUGHBOY,
WHO EARNED A SILVER STAR ON THE WESTERN FRONT

MY FATHER, DALE WAKEFIELD, SAILOR FROM 1941–1948,
WHO ONCE TOLD ME PLAYING FOOTBALL "DOESN'T HURT"

AND FOR PAM

CONTENTS

ACKNOWLEDGMENTS

No project such as this can succeed without strong financial support. I would like to begin by recognizing the contribution of the Mark Diamond Research Fund of the State University of New York at Buffalo, which supported me during my research trip to the Military History Institute. I would also like to thank the Monroe County, New York, Historian's Office, Dr. Kenneth P. O'Brien, historian, for the opportunity to work at public history while completing this book.

My everlasting gratitude goes to the history faculty at SUNY, College at Brockport, for rescuing me from the law business, and embracing me first as a student and then as a colleague. Special thanks to Bruce "Reading List" Leslie, Kathleen Kutolowski, Steve Ireland, Joan Rubin, Jim Horn, Robert Marcus, Robert Smith, Arden Bucholz, Ron Herlan, and extraspecial thanks to Lynn Parsons, who reminded me to get rid of all of that elaborate graduate school language, and write for real people. Thanks also to Colleen Donaldson, who taught me to write grant proposals which I worked at Brockport.

I also owe a tremendous debt of gratitude to those teachers at SUNY, University at Buffalo, who helped me mold and shape my thinking about this project, especially Susan Cahn and Nory Baker. Likewise, I can never thank Don Sabo of D'Youville College enough for his kind help and careful attention to this manuscript.

We students of history always need the chance to bounce our ideas off of friends and colleagues. While developing my thoughts about war and sports I was especially lucky to have Tom Bolze around to remind me that, after all, not everyone cares as passionately about these matters as do I. I can never thank my dear friend and writing partner, Carolyn S. Vacca, enough for helping me in my struggle for clarity of thought and language. Nor can I adequately express my gratitude to the novelist and writer, Anne Norton, for her help support and encouragement.

Historians also need a physical outlet and distraction from the hours spent in libraries and in front of computers. I want to take this time to recognize all of the women who came to my water aerobics classes at Fairport, Gates, and Brighton and worked out with me. And, of course, I cannot forget my pals

22*Acknowledgments*

and buddies at the U.S. Luge Association. There is nothing so physically demanding or distracting as to climb Mt. Van Hoevenberg at Lake Placid to officiate at a luge race. So special thanks to those who've frozen with me since the beginning—Gary Cichowski, John Bologna, Ellie Edwards, Rene Lebreque, and Carolle Gregory.

But we are not born anew at graduate school. I have been blessed with superb teachers since my childhood, all of whom influenced me in my decision to study history. First of all, let me thank Professor Ronald Rotunda of the University of Illinois law school, who did not think I was crazy to leave the law and return to school. Likewise, Father Robert McNamara of the Diocese of Rochester, New York, was quite an inspiration. One time at Grinnell College my teacher, Don Smith, commented on a paper that I wrote like a "real historian"—thanks Mr. Smith. Thanks also to Shirley Leffler, who never met a high school student she couldn't teach to write a coherent sentence, and to Florence Sears, who loves history as much as anyone I have ever known, and has never stopped studying it. Finally, I would like to take a moment to remember Jim Martin, my history teacher from seventh grade, who died way too young.

For those who helped me with my research—thanks always. I want to give special thanks to the fantastic staff at the Military History Institute at Carlisle Barracks, especially director Dr. Richard J. Sommers and David Keough. The librarians at Brockport and Buffalo were always helpful with my interlibrary loan requests. And I was very lucky to have available to me the extraordinary Rundel Public Library in Rochester, New York. Everyone in Rochester should cherish this library.

And finally I would like to thank my family. My uncles, Eldon Wakefield and Drexel McCormack, talked with me about their wartime experiences, and my Uncle Drexel shared with me his present thoughts on what leadership meant to members of a rifle company in the cold woods of the Ardennes in December, 1944. My mother, Eileen Wakefield, and my brother, Robert Wakefield, have always supported me in my endeavors—even when they must have seemed a tad odd. My two late cats, P.K. and Hershey, provided purrs and kisses when I needed them most (as do my present cats, especially the many-toed Jack). Thanks to all!

1

WAR AND SPORTS:
FROM THE SPANISH-AMERICAN WAR TO 1917

For the United States, as for the rest of the Western world, a sporting culture developed in the late nineteenth century benefiting from improvements in transportation, the growth of mass media, particularly cheap newspapers, urbanization, and industrialization. By 1898, athletic contests were a regular part of the national calendar. Baseball in America had developed sufficiently to support popular interest in a World's Series that would begin within five years to be played between teams from the two major professional leagues. Intercollegiate rivalries in football and other sports had been established that promised to endure for future generations believing in the importance of athletic competitions. But sports had not yet become a part of military life, and only with the entry of the United States into war with the Spanish over Cuba would a critical mass of men be gathered together in the armed services to justify the creation of a formal sports program.

After the defeat of the Spanish, military commanders intentionally created opportunities for soldiers and sailors in Cuba and in the Philippines to play baseball, to run track, and to experience other types of athletic competitions. National leaders such as President Theodore Roosevelt and Gen. Leonard Wood provided personal examples of the advantages derived from physical fitness. And General Wood began the process of ensuring that Regular Army units as well as National Guard outfits engaged in physical training commensurate with the demands to be placed on the country's soldiers in the future.

For those European-American men anxious for the United States to acquire its own Empire, events in the last years of the nineteenth century posed a unique opportunity to do so. With Frederick Jackson Turner having declared the frontier closed, and with the huge growth in American population due to immigration from Europe, empire-builders argued for the urgent need to expand America's role. The overthrow of the Hawaiian government provided an excuse to annex those islands as a site for expansion further into the Pacific. Then the struggle by Cuban rebels to establish their island's independence, with the consequent threat to American business interests on that island, and with the reports of the hideous conditions in which many in the Cuban population were living due to Spanish policies, led to a demand for the United States' involvement in the struggle against Spain. Despite substantial opposition among some in Congress, the press, and the general populace, in 1898 those who wanted the United States to acquire an empire finally got their wish as America embarked on a war with the Spanish, ostensibly to help those Cuban rebels gain their country's freedom, but ultimately to take control over Cuba, Puerto Rico, and the Philippines.[1]

For the American military establishment, the growth of an overseas empire demanded a reconsideration of its role, its size, and its proper function. The army to a great extent and the navy to a more limited extent were forced to move beyond the era of Indian fighting and prepare for a larger role overseas. The disorganization in troop transport from Tampa to Cuba, and the failure of private business to supply the army with palatable rations, revealed that the army especially was not yet ready to take on international responsibilities, absent substantial rethinking of its system for caring for the troops.[2] The acquisition of empire, therefore, provided a justification for those within the military services who had concluded near the end of the nineteenth century that a vastly expanded navy *and* army was a necessity for an America entering, in Peter Karsten's words, the "dog-eat-dog world of international commerce, imperial rivalries, conscription armies and Dreadnought navies."[3] But the inadequacy of planning to anticipate the needs of an expanding military revealed during the Spanish-American War also left the army and navy with a substantial amount of thinking to do about what a modern military required to arm, clothe, feed, and keep soldiers and sailors in action.

The events of 1898 marked the beginning of a long, slow growth in the authorized strength of America's military. In April 1898, a total of 28,747 men were serving in the Regular Army. To fill the manpower needs of the military as it prepared to move into Cuba, units of the National Guard were accepted into federal service so long as they volunteered as a body, while other new state units and volunteers for federal service were also incorporated into the armed forces. Congress also authorized an increase in Regular Army strength to 64,719. Thus, by the end of May, 1898, along with the growing Regular Army, the military was able to claim at least 124,804 volunteers in uniform for the national emergency. Although the rapid success of the soldiers in Cuba, along with the collapse of the Spanish forces in the Philippines, reduced the need for further growth, and led to the suspension of further recruiting in August, the army never again fell to pre-1898 manpower levels. Indeed, the continued fighting between units of the American army and Filipinos favoring independence for their islands led Congress in March 1899 to require the maintenance of the Regular Army at 65,000 men and to ask for the enlistment of 35,000 additional volunteers to deal with the Filipino insurgency.[4]

Despite the growth of the military at the end of the century, commanders initially paid little attention to how best to entertain the troops. Indeed, officers were not specifically trained to meet soldier welfare needs through sport, even though the two military academies had developed football programs during the 1880s, playing extensive intercollegiate schedules. Although the annual Army-Navy game was suspended from 1893 to 1899 by civilian political pressure stemming from allegations of a near-fatal duel at the Army-Navy Club after the 1893 game, the resumption of interservice play led to a long tradition of intercollegiate athletic success for both schools. Significantly, however, despite the incorporation of organized sports into West Point's program, the basic physical education program at the Point remained relatively unchanged. As late as 1905, Cadets were required only to participate in fencing, dancing, and horsemanship aside from their regular drills. Although boxing and wrestling were added to the educational agenda in 1905, formal instruction in intramural football, hockey, lacrosse, baseball, and similar team sports for the cadets remained in the future.[5]

The fact that most service academy graduates had had little experience in playing sports themselves or in organizing athletic competitions, was reflected when it came to training and entertaining America's soldiers in 1898. Although Henry Cabot Lodge argued that the "time given to athletic contests and the injuries incurred on the playing field are part of the price which the English-speaking race has paid for being world-conquerors," and Theodore Roosevelt recruited his Rough Riders from among the men of his acquaintance who had played sports in the past, neither man was ready to insist that the nation's military include sports as part of the regular training regimen.[6] Even those who were in fact quite committed to encouraging athletics among the troops of the expanding army encountered monumental difficulties in trying to implement an organized sports program. First the health problems generated by the yellow fever, malaria, and dysentery experienced by the soldiers in Cuba rapidly reduced the ability of most to participate in any sort of strenuous physical activity. And since most of the volunteers for service in 1898 never left stateside training camps, the military's failure to plan for long-term stays in those encampments led to low troop morale, and to the growth of disease due to the filthy conditions in those camps as well. Thus, although a Red Cross official visiting the camp near Tampa, Florida, where soldiers were waiting to embark for Cuba described troops lounging and smoking, but also playing handball, Theodore Roosevelt lamented that the fellows stationed in Cuba were left with nothing to do.[7]

Since the Army in 1898 was unprepared for the rapid deployment of its forces, lacking plans for moving, feeding, and training those troops, the Army was also unprepared to entertain those soldiers. Even Roosevelt, who believed in the value of sports, and the rigorous life, and who recruited among athletes for his Rough Riders, didn't anticipate that a system of organized athletics would contribute to the well-being of the troops under his command before being faced with the results of a lack of a formal program for troop entertainment in Cuba. However, in subsequent years, as representatives of the United States' Army served as occupation troops on the island, sports, particularly baseball, became an important part of their lives. As the historian Louis A. Perez, Jr., has suggested, baseball had been identified by Cuban patriots by 1898 as a game in which they could express their distinctiveness from and opposition to that Spanish culture typified by the bullfight. During the years of United States' occupation, American soldiers and Cuban civilians played many baseball games against each other, with American soldier leagues also being established on the island. In this, future military-civilian contacts through sports were prefigured.[8]

Because the 1898 army raised to fight the Spanish included a substantial number of African-American troops on the assumption that they would be more likely to be immune to the tropical diseases endemic in Cuba, the question of whether they would make good soldiers under those combat conditions inevitably arose. Since the Regular Army already included the African-American Twenty-fourth and Twenty-fifth Infantries as well as the Ninth and Tenth cavalries, who had distinguished themselves during the Indian Wars in the American West, the men of those commands were subjected to substantial scrutiny during the Spanish-American War. While serving in Cuba and later during the Philippine Insurgency, these soldiers demonstrated their ability and commitment to the American cause, fighting on San Juan Hill with Roosevelt and caring for the victims of the epidemics that decimated the Fifth Army Corps in Cuba.[9]

Because black and white soldiers were serving side by side, albeit in segregated units, they often participated in athletic competitions against each other, especially during the Philippine Insurrection, when the army's provisions for its troops had become relatively better organized.[10] This competition on the playing field between African-American and European-American soldiers inevitably revealed much about assumptions concerning race at the turn of the century.[11] Despite the preservation of the color line between black and white troops, the turn of the century Army provided competitive opportunities that might not otherwise have been available to African-American sportsmen. As the historian of black athletes, Arthur R. Ashe, Jr., has argued, "with the vested interest in the physical well-being and high morale of its soldiers, the Army provided facilities, competition, coaching and encouragement for its black enlisted men."[12] Since African-American men were being excluded from professional baseball by the 1890s, the chances for interested athletes to play the game while in the military must have been welcomed by the soldiers. Thus, the Twenty-fifth Infantry stationed in the Philippines in 1901 challenged any team, including those drawn from European-American units, to play baseball against them. Similarly, African-American men stationed in the Philippines actively participated in the track and field meets being staged for the American army's occupation troops, with the Ninth Cavalry winning a meet in 1908 by defeating teams from the European-American Third Cavalry, the Fifth Field Artillery, and the Twenty-sixth, Twenty-ninth and Thirtieth Infantries, as well as an African-American team from the Tenth Cavalry.[13]

As the army in the Philippines settled down to an occupation of the islands, it was faced with the dilemma of how best to maintain the interest and enthusiasm of the soldiers. Among other things, a formal sports program was developed for the first time by the military. Thus, even as civilian society devoted more attention to organized, modern athletic competitions, similar competitions were being conducted by the army.[14] And in so doing, the problems of race and class that had so affected the civilian population became critically important within the military. Since athletic excellence had by the turn of the century become a marker of the superiority of both a man's body *and* his character, the athletic successes of black soldiers competing against whites from other units provided a challenge to assumptions about the relative inferiority of African-Americans.[15] As would be the case when athletes from other nations competed successfully against athletes from the United States in subsequent wars, sports provided a means for reinforcing cultural hierarchy.

Although there continued to be opposition to the presence of United States' forces overseas, the Spanish-American War seemed in most minds to have concluded favorably to American interests, and the heroes of that conflict, including Theodore Roosevelt, Adm. Thomas Dewey, and Gen. Leonard Wood, were held in esteem in subsequent years as exemplars of American manhood. Yet males in American society remained the subject of continuing cultural discourse about how they should develop themselves to represent the United States and its people. Therefore, American men continued to seek out arenas in which they could develop their strength, character, and power. The sports world remained a site for demonstrating masculine superiority after 1900 as it had begun to be before the war with Spain. And within the army, sport would finally be recognized as a viable means of maintaining soldier health and morale.

In the years between the Spanish-American War and the United States' entry into the First World War, Maj. Gen. Leonard Wood became one of the first commanders to actively promote the value of athletic training as an adjunct to drill and as means of instilling the values of teamwork and cooperation in the troops. He had come from the Medical Corps and was directly interested in the physical health of the American soldier, but he also loved to participate in athletics, as demonstrated when he was stationed at the Presidio in 1892. There, he joined the San Francisco Olympic Club's football team and played left guard against a team from the University of California.[16] As an old crony of Theodore Roosevelt, General Wood was famous for his physical fitness and for the aggression with which he played games such as single stick—a game that he and the President played so roughly that Roosevelt occasionally lost the use of a hand or suffered black eyes from injuries incurred while playing.[17]

As chief of staff of the army, Wood concerned himself with the training offered to new recruits. In some respects, his vision of the training necessary to make a good soldier reflects the conventions of pre-Civil War warfare, since as late as 1914, Wood argued that troops needed to have at least twelve months' training at 150 hours per month to ensure their readiness for combat.[18] During World War I, Gen. John J. Pershing would find to his surprise that less general training was needed, although the exigencies of that conflict demanded that the doughboys receive substantial special education in trench warfare. Later, during World War II training time was drastically reduced, especially as replacements were needed for those soldiers lost in battle in the Pacific and in the fight against the Nazis in Europe.[19]

But more important to General Wood's vision than the number of hours dedicated to training was his attempt to impose common fitness standards on all of the men potentially liable to service should the United States again go to war. Among other things, this meant that the men in the various state National Guards, as well as the soldiers in the Regular Army, would be expected to meet similar physical standards. To facilitate that process, the war Department distributed a manual for the physical training of troops in 1914.

In the Introduction to the *Manual of Physical Training for Use in the United States Army,* General Wood said that he wished that the physical training of all enlisted men be conducted according to the precepts set down in the *Manual*, since there was "nothing in the education of the soldier of more vital importance than this."[20] According to the War Department, physical training was necessary not only to promote general health and bodily vigor, or muscular strength and endurance, but also to help the enlisted man become more self-reliant and to conduct himself with "smartness, activity, and precision."[21] To accomplish those goals, the soldier was to be required to participate in setting-up exercises (coming to attention, for example), to march at quick or double time, to use the dumbbell, club, or rifle to increase upper-body strength, to climb a rope, to jump, and to work with apparatus such as the pommel horse. More significantly, aside from the assigned physical fitness activities, the soldier was also expected to participate in athletics and swimming competitions. And, although the *Manual* didn't require every soldier to box and wrestle, the War Department suggested that they be encouraged to do so. Thus, for the first time, general military training included time for sports and athletic contests.

Although the writers of the *Manual* emphasized that the contests and competitions were not to resemble competitive athletics and therefore were not to be about breaking records or establishing individual prowess, they also recognized that such contests and competitions would "never fail to induce the usual rivalry for superiority attending personal contests."[22] Thus, the *Manual* suggests a disjunction between the idea that sports and athletics within the military could serve to unite soldiers together in physical fitness and the notion that sports and athletics would necessarily encourage the kind of interpersonal competitiveness also thought to be useful in combat. The War Department's *Manual,* therefore, created conflicting missions for those who would have to implement the sports program. On the one hand, such a program might surely lead to each soldier's greater physical fitness and a willingness to commit his body when asked to do so, and the soldier might also learn to respect and admire those within his unit who exhibited greater athletic ability. On the other hand, competition and rivalry among soldier-athletes also posed the danger that it might get out of hand, resulting in the destruction of the loyalty and group cohesion needed within the military. So long as the rivalries could be kept in check, presumably through the acquiescence of the young men involved in a hierarchy based in part on athletic ability, the sports program would help train and maintain the morale of the soldiers, but if the rivalries engendered by athletic contests became too great, the ultimate goal of creating a unified fighting force would not be met.

In discussing the recommended athletics program, the *Manual*'s writers recognized the disjunction between the goal of identifying the best while ensuring the fullest possible participation by the many. According to the *Manual*, the "value of athletic training in the service is dependent upon the effect it has upon the mass, and not upon the effect it has upon the individual few."[23] But the writers also pointed out that a sports program geared exclusively to the majority of soldiers would not allow the athletically gifted to fully develop their talents. Accordingly, they recommended that an annual field day be organized at which individual skills could be displayed and the most skillful be determined.

Although the *Manual* provides specific descriptions of the bulk of the proposed physical fitness program, illustrating the descriptions with photographs of men engaged in the various exercises, it does not include any information about how to box and wrestle. Although the War Department therefore encouraged soldiers to engaged in those sports, their physical fitness instructors were not given the means to adequately coach them. As the army would shortly discover, the troops needed not only to be encouraged to play sports, they needed to have training in how to play particular sports, training that civilian instructors would have to provide during the emergency of the First World War.

Despite its failure to provide for trained physical fitness instructors, with the publication of the *Manual of Physical Training* the army began moving toward the recognition that organized sports within the military could help meet its need to quickly develop in new recruits those qualities deemed to be necessary to the good soldier. Young men within the military would attain more than the stamina developed through marching and drill. They would learn through sports to cooperate with each other, to identify with the members of their team, and to recognize their common bonds. By participating in or watching sports, they would learn how to face and overcome adversity, not only on the playing field, but later on the battlefield. And with the *Manual*'s publication, sports and athletic competitions took their place as an integral part of military life.

The journey to the inclusion of sports as a part of military training in 1914 had been a long one. The crisis of masculinity that gripped elite white men throughout the Western world at the end of the nineteenth century was not easily overcome. But as a style of masculinity emphasizing aggressiveness and physicality was reclaimed, and as the idea that a young man's character could only be fully developed through athletic contact with other men was embraced, the search for a place where men could act out their physical aggressions was intensified. Because the business of sports had organized and modernized along with so many other enterprises at the end of the century, the playing fields were available to which men could point as the place where they could be most fully in touch with themselves. And as they grew stronger by playing sports, or learned how to honor that strength in others, many American men in particular concluded that their masculinity could also be saved by leading their country into the modern imperial world.

Yet that first attempt in 1898 to create an Army for overseas service revealed many deficiencies in the system devised for asserting the interests of the United States on the world stage. Not the least of this was the failure by the army to provide adequately for the health and entertainment of the soldiers going off to war. After the immediate crisis of 1898 was concluded, Gen. Leonard Wood and others in command rediscovered what those civilians enamored of sports had believed all along—that athletic competition builds the man. Acting on their belief that participation in sports would help prepare any man for competition not only on the ballfield or in the boardroom, but on the battlefield as well, military commanders began looking to athletics as a crucial part of preparation for war.

2

WORLD WAR I AND MILITARY ATHLETICS AT HOME AND IN THE FACE OF BATTLE

When President Woodrow Wilson asked the U.S. Congress for a declaration of war against the Central Powers on April 2, 1917, he spoke for a nation whose army and navy were only beginning preparations for joining the European conflict. The president had notably proposed to Congress as late as January, 1917, a "peace without victory" plan, offering to serve as a mediator in negotiating a settlement. And even though the United States broke formal diplomatic relations with Germany in February, a decision whether to ask for a draft of able-bodied personnel had not yet been made.[1]

With the war declaration, units of the Regular Army and National Guard which had lately been stationed along the Mexican Border were, however, rapidly reconstituted as the First Division and sent to France in response to urgent French requests for reinforcement, while planning went forward to bring the army up from its authorized strength pursuant to the National Defense Act of 1916 of some two hundred thousand men, which it reached on April 1, 1917, to the more than three million six hundred thousand men who would be in uniform on November 11, 1918.[2] Although those units which had served in local conflicts in Haiti and Mexico were presumably trained and ready to fight, at the time the United States became involved in Europe intense debate still persisted about the amount of time needed to raise and train a mass army. Furthermore, the infrastructure available to feed and house a mass army to represent America's interests in the world war did not exist, either in America or in Europe. Yet even more important in some minds was how the troops' social and emotional needs were going to be provided for as they were brought together from the cities and farms of America and concentrated in newly built staging areas.

The process of raising a mass army and navy to fight in the war allowed those who had been trying since the end of the nineteenth century to reduce and regulate prostitution and to restrict the sale of alcohol to promote their agenda as a mechanism for ensuring good order on and around military bases. They used the excuse of the wartime emergency to continue their push for prohibition. They also pointed to the growth of huge training encampments and suggested that the eradication of prostitution close to those camps was compelled not only because of the danger to the health and safety of the troops but also because of the danger to those young women who might be seduced by the possibility of payment for sexual favors. The fear that innocent young men would be transformed by military life not only by the brutality and terror of combat but by the allures of illicit women demanded no less than the strict regulation of their off-duty time.[3] Accordingly, as the young soldiers and sailors were gathered together, they were encouraged to direct their energies toward preparing for war, and toward the wholesome recreational opportunities being made available on base, rather than toward the enticing possibilities presented by being away from home and watchful family.

In order to meet President Wilson's pledge to return the young men of America "in strengthened and more virile bodies as a result of physical training . . . in minds deepened and enriched by participation in a great, heroic enterprise [and] in the enhanced spiritual values which come from a full life lived well and wholesomely," twin Commissions on Training Camp Activities were organized for the army and for the navy.[4] According to Edward Frank Allen, the chronicler of their activities, the need for the Commissions was obvious from the experience gained along the Mexican Border, where thousands of young men cut off from their accustomed relations and usual means of worship and recreation rapidly acquired a taste for alcohol and "loose women" that reduced their fighting efficiency.[5] Therefore, Allen explained in 1918 that the Commissions were established to provide for the young soldiers' welfare, both in the areas outside the training camps through the suppression of liquor and prostitution and within the camps by providing alternative forms of recreation. According to John D'Emilio and Estelle B. Freedman, this decision to suppress vice in and around training camps was made by Gen. John J. Pershing, who apparently concluded that the army's ability to fight in Europe would be compromised through exposure to sexually transmitted diseases, and represented a shift from the pattern that had been allowed to persist along the Mexican border. Therefore, Pershing emphasized treatment of affected soldiers even more than he emphasized punishment of those doughboys whose actions led to their exposure to venereal disease.[6]

To accomplish the task of promoting soldier welfare a Commission organizational structure was created. The Army's Commission was organized into five divisions: an athletic division presided over by Dr. Joseph Raycroft, professor of hygiene at Princeton University; a law enforcement division; a Department of Camp Music; a Military Entertainment Committee; and a "National Smileage Committee." The Navy instituted a similar program, with Walter Camp, the legendary Yale football coach, directing the Navy's General Commission of Athletics.[7] By drawing on the resources of the Young Men and Women's Christian Associations, as well as the National Catholic War Council, the Jewish Welfare Board, the American Library Association, the Salvation Army and the War Camp Community Service organization, the members of the Army's Commission hoped to provide a variety of activities to "keep the man in uniform healthy and clean, physically and mentally, by safeguarding him against evil influences and surrounding him with opportunity for sane, beneficial occupation for his spare time."[8] At camps in the United States huts were erected to provide space for the varied activities conducted under the Commission's auspices, where representatives of the YMCA and other organizations helped write letters for those young soldiers with limited literacy,[9] conducted Bible classes, refereed boxing matches, and organized group singing, games, and other types of distractions.[10]

According to Chairman Fosdick, the decision to include athletics as one of the services offered by the Commission on Training Camp Activities did not grow from the army's previous sports program which led to championship competitions in a variety of sports dating back to the Philippine Incursion. Rather, Fosdick argued that the value of sports to the fighting man had been demonstrated by the English and Canadian experience in Europe. He suggested that their experiences had shown that athletics helped promote and maintain military efficiency and morale.[11]

Accordingly, camp Athletic Directors were appointed to train the soldiers in athletics and mass games to ensure the participation of every young man. Reflecting the underdevelopment of athletics within the military, and the limited number of trained coaches and instructors in the services, Athletic Directors were often recruited from the civilian population, as with the thirty boxing and special instructors who were assigned to the camps to teach the young soldiers athletic skills and game rules. This athletic program was designed not only to keep the soldiers' minds off of alcohol and illicit women; the organizers of the athletic program anticipated that other benefits would accrue from this physical activity, as they believed had been the case in other armies such as the British, where organized and spontaneous sports had been played since the beginning of the war. Chairman Fosdick described in his Commission Report how the troops developed a quality of courage and aggressiveness not only from their physical training but from their experience in personal contests and games.[12]

And Edward Frank Allen was quite certain that by learning how to get bumped and not to mind it, the troops gained a quality of persistence through athletics that they might not have learned elsewhere. That quality of persistence enhanced the development of that fighting spirit that would be necessary when the army arrived in Europe.[13]

Furthermore, the Commissioners expected that this athletic training would engender a toughness among the men, elevating those "narrow-chested clerks" and "lean-visaged philosophers" described by Allen to a new vigor. As Donald J. Mrozek has pointed out in describing military athletic programs both before and during World War I, athletics were expected to provide the men with an alternative, nonsexual, bodily commitment, "meanwhile bolstering the equation of masculinity with roughness."[14] The development of harder, stronger physical bodies among soldiers would then embody the harder, stronger masculinity being promoted within the army, a style of masculinity rescued from the effeminizing and weakening effects of home and office.[15]

In short, the Commissioners appointed to oversee the provision of soldier welfare anticipated that a sports program provided substantial benefits to the doughboys for whom they were responsible. By keeping the soldiers occupied with sports and other wholesome recreational activities, they believed the soldiers would be able to avoid the dangers of alcohol and illicit sex. This reflected the experience that many of those involved in soldier welfare had had in providing alternatives to the idle young men of America's urban centers, in which they believed they had demonstrated that a physically active life reflected the physicality of Jesus Christ and his disciples. It also reflected a self-consciousness definition of masculinity drawn from a class-specific vision of Christianity. Although the Commissioners believed that the experience gained from hitting and being hit in aggressive sports would help the individual soldier when faced with combat, they also believed that physical aggression was only appropriate within a strictly regulated format. Accordingly, wherever possible, the Commissioners emphasized the roughness and ferocity of sport while also emphasizing the ways in which that roughness and ferocity built character. By doing so, they believed that they were rescuing men from the effeminizing effects of life at the beginning of the twentieth century. And, drawing on the experience gained by the British during the Great War, they anticipated that the sports program they designed would promote greater military efficiency and morale as participating soldiers learned teamwork and group loyalty through athletics.[16]

Although military planners no longer believed that years of practice were necessary to prepare an army to take the field, American officers were not yet convinced that training time could be reduced to the minimum thirteen weeks of training allocated to infantrymen during the Second World War.[17] As late as 1914, Gen. Leonard Wood argued that the soldiers of a modern army needed at least twelve months of training at 150 hours per month.[18] Hence, the program for soldier welfare would be needed for an extended length of time, both in the United States and when the troops arrived in Europe to continue their education in trench warfare techniques. In fact, because of the increasing mechanization of the armed forces, and because of the peculiar conditions along the Western Front, the doughboys spent their time mastering a number of different skills, rather than on the regular and repetitious drill to which soldiers had devoted themselves at the time of the Civil War.[19]

In further contrast to the Civil War, the army being raised to fight in Europe would be an army mostly composed of draftees. The Civil War draft had filled only 6 percent of the military's needs, while the draft for World War I would supply 67 percent of the troops. Furthermore, the soldiers brought together to fight in World War I created an army in which, as had been the case during the latter part of the nineteenth century, foreign-born white men were overrepresented. Thirteen percent of the doughboys were African-American, making that population group overrepresented as well, given that individuals of African descent comprised only 10.1 percent of the American population. Also, the percentage of illiterate soldiers within the military appears to have been higher than the percentage of illiterate men among their age cohort.[20] Thus, the armed forces could not depend on a system devised solely for literate native-born European-American men to educate and motivate the doughboys. Because of the variety of backgrounds and experiences of the newly inducted soldiers, military planners recognized a need to make special efforts to bring together this diverse group into fighting cohesion.

By placing representatives at every camp to teach young men how to play together in team sports subject to commonly understood rules, the Commissions provided a mechanism for overcoming some of the complications inherent in the diversity of American's new fighting force. Indeed, Edward Frank Allen, the chronicler of training camp activities, is quite explicit that military athletics were designed to contribute to unit cohesion, comparing the concerted effort and team enthusiasm of the interregimental and intercompany athletic competitions to those developed in the college game.[21]

Finally, by contrast to previous American wars, fewer people died from disease during World War I than died of battle wounds, despite the deleterious effects of the 1918 influenza epidemic.[22] The decision to authorize Chairman

Raymond B. Fosdick's group to organize matters crucial to social welfare may have contributed to the reduction of disease as soldiers had enhanced opportunities to play games, communicate with home, gather together for group singing, and talk about their problems and concerns with people outside of the military command structure who were dedicated to improving the personal hygiene and physical fitness levels within the training camps. By reducing the opportunities for soldiers to mix freely with the civilian population, and by encouraging the soldiers to keep busy and interact among themselves, the training camp program devised by the Commissions established a model for attending to the welfare of future American armies.

Given the substantial diversity among the soldiers and sailors of World War I, and the concomitant variation in skill and commitment levels, the army was forced to turn to novel mechanisms for bringing the men together into a fighting force. With that diversity, military planners had to create a means of communicating the progress of the war and the individual soldier's place in the grand scheme of war in language that everybody could understand. Since the Spanish-American War, the military had used sports to provide metaphorical explanation for issues which had no intrinsic relation to physical training and to connect the incidents of combat to events in civilian life.[23] For the doughboys in France during World War I, sport metaphor also served as a means of communication, keeping them informed about conditions at the front, and the fighting character of their German enemies. But the use of sport metaphor as a means of communication assumed a common language and a common interest in certain sports among the soldiers. On the one hand, by allowing sport metaphor to serve as the language of war, the army created a potential gap between those who appreciated the language of sports and those who did not, contrary to the army's presumed intention of bringing the men together in the common cause. On the other hand, by assuming that all men within the fighting forces understood and appreciated the language of sport, the military did create a semblance of a common bond among the men. Once the doughboys' understanding of the war depended on their understanding of sport metaphor, they were united in the category of *men* for whom that language was reserved. The male gender was therefore separated and distinguished from the female gender, not only because it was men who went to war, but because only men could appreciate and use the words of war. Sport metaphor therefore further separated the men of the fighting force from their female contemporaries as it refocused attention on sport as a common language among men, as even those men ordinarily uninterested in sports were placed into the category of those who could understand sporting language, as opposed to the category of those who could not—civilian women.

In February, 1918, the first issue of the newspaper *Stars and Stripes* appeared. The weekly publication was created at the direction of Gen. John J. Pershing who saw it as another means of keeping up troop morale.[24] Although Pershing wanted the newspaper to be for and by the soldier, so that no official Allied Expeditionary Force (AEF) control was maintained over its editorial contents, the newspaper's copy was controlled by the censor to the extent that unit designations were only attached where the location of those units was not of importance to the enemy. From a small beginning, by the Armistice circulation exceeded five hundred thousand copies per week. Explaining its significance and popularity, the writer Alexander Woollcott characterized *Stars and Stripes* as the "irreverent, homespun and highly unmilitary . . . contribution to the defeat of Germany and to the art of war."[25]

The newspaper began using sports metaphors almost immediately after the first troops arrived in France. With its first issues *Stars and Stripes* offered a regular sports page, on which stories about the fortunes of stateside professional and college teams and athletes were juxtaposed with stories about unit teams and requests by individual soldier-athletes wanting to get together with others for competition. A banner headline typically appeared at the top of the sports page such as that of April 5, 1918, declaring "Uncle Sam Pinch Hitting on Western Front." Similar headlines appeared on March 15, 1918, "Huns Hit .000 Against Lorraine Hurlers," April 12, 1918, "Huns May Request Waivers on Kaiser," May 10, 1918, "Kaiser Calls Bench Warmers Into Play," June 28, 1918, "Austria Groggy at End of Fourth," and on July 5, 1918, "France Makes Fourth a Double Header."

But why should *Stars and Stripes* have resorted to this metaphorical language on a sports page, especially since the language was clearly referring to the progress of the war rather than the progress of a game? In the first place, the decision to include such a headline on the sports page may have been intended to ensure that those readers interested only in sports would still be apprised of necessary information about the war, even if they in fact read nothing but the sport page. Second, those readers who had trouble decoding the lengthy discussions about the war elsewhere in the newspaper because of their lack of facility with the English language might have been able to understand at least the language of sport—particularly in an age when the metaphors came from the language of the preeminent national sport of baseball and when newspapers throughout the United States were regularly providing elaborate accounts of games.

But the use of that metaphorical language had other purposes as well. By using baseball terms *Stars and Stripes* reinforced a gender order which privileged athletic men over their brothers unadept at sports, obliging those doughboys whose primary interests lay elsewhere to learn enough about the sport so that they could engage in the community conversation about the war. By insisting that all men in the army learn about baseball if they wanted to learn about the war, the editors fixed the soldiers in a hierarchy, with those at least conversant with the game at the top, and those young men uninterested in sports at the bottom. Furthermore, the use of baseball terms tended to tie together the diverse elements of the American army into a common discourse, as immigrant soldiers from Eastern and Southern Europe where other sports dominated were forced to learn about the American national game in order to appreciate the metaphors being used.

Sports metaphors appeared in other contexts as well. An editorial cartoon in *Stars and Stripes* by "Wallgren" is an example of the way in which a sports metaphor could have visual impact. In that cartoon a doughboy is shown swinging his baseball bat at an incoming missile, which on impact is returned to the German lines. The caption explains that the cartoon illustrates that applying the skills of baseball to war represents "Business and Pleasure."[26] Through this cartoon, the reader learns that sport and war are tied together, that war is like sport, and that the pleasure derived from sport can also be achieved through battle. Thus, for the young man facing battle, a metaphor is provided to remove some of the terror by making combat seem more familiar, more like a game.

In describing his experiences in an artillery engagement for the newspaper, the former major leaguer Eddie Cicotte explained that Walter Johnson's fastball was "a floater compared to some of the things a Boche cannoneer can heave at you." Luckily for Cicotte, the Germans were "pitching strikes" right over his head, and although "Fritz made about two runs in his inning [he] couldn't get us out at all after we went to bat."[27] By explaining the artillery bombardment in terms he could understand, Cicotte also expected that those hearing the story would appreciate the significance of the fact that Fritz was, for example, pitching strikes, so that Cicotte was saved from being killed by an errant shot. Cicotte also humanized and personalized his experience by interpreting it through the language of his former life as a professional baseball player—a life experience denied to the vast majority of men caught up in the war, but a life experience presumably within the imagination of many readers.

The War itself was often referred to as a game, as despite the years of mass slaughter on the Western Front many still clung to a notion that participation in battle could be similar to participation in a game. By describing the war as a game, individual men caught up in the process of fighting the Central Powers could see themselves as part of the larger process involved in subordinating their particular interests for the good of the team, thus meeting the gender expectations that had equated team play with masculinity since the end of the nineteenth century.[28] Furthermore, the persistence of the game metaphor despite the ample evidence that the fighting of the Great War in no way resembled a game suggests the persistence of the idea that a young man's true occupation lay in playing games, games through which he—unlike his sister— would discover the important lessons of life and be prepared for the future. During 1918 *Stars and Stripes* often described the conflict as a game, noting, for example, on July 12, 1918, that it would be hard to take any "youngsters away from Uncle Sam while the present hot game is on in France," and on August 2, 1918, that "the only real game left today is that of beating the Hun."[29] And as Cpt. Robert J. Whitfield wrote his mother from the Central Officers Training School at Camp Pike, Arkansas, "Certainly hope I can 'get across' to see the finish [of the war] and have a little hand in the game."[30]

By contrast to World War II, when efforts were made to ensure the continuation of major league baseball for the duration, during World War I many asked whether baseball should complete its 1918 season or release its players to the war effort. This question got tied up with an argument over whether those professionals who kept playing were fulfilling their masculine obligations.[31] Although many pacifists argued otherwise at great personal expense, as mobilization became a reality and Americans began fighting and dying in Europe, men were expected to obey the cultural message that in order to be men they must embrace the military life. If they were reluctant to become warriors, the message went, then maybe they weren't men at all. The men who played baseball professionally were therefore placed in an untenable position. Despite the manifest demonstration of their manliness every day at the baseball park, that manliness was now being questioned, since it didn't appear to match the hypermasculinity necessary for success at the battlefront. Given the cultural assumption that the best athletes would necessarily be the best warriors, the presence of so many good athletes on the baseball field rather than the battlefield engendered a community debate about the value of sports in times of national crisis.

During the 1918 spring training season, baseball magnates avoided criticism of their failure to suspend play until the war's completion by encouraging professional teams to play in exhibition games, with each other and with service teams, with some of the money raised going to soldier charities. This idea was supported by the *Stars and Stripes*, which reported in March, 1918, that the troops at Camp Sheridan had asked the YMCA to bring the Cincinnati Reds and other major league teams to the camp for spring training games against army teams. That spring the New York Giants played the army aviators training at Waco, Texas, in an exhibition for the Red Cross, while the Yankees played a team from the 124th Infantry before the formal professional season began.[32]

During the summer, baseball owners also tried to deflect criticism by engaging in a campaign to provide the troops with athletic equipment. Ban Johnson and other American League owners agreed to provide five thousand dollars worth of bats, balls, mitts, gloves, chest protectors, and masks to those playing baseball while serving in the army in Europe.[33]

Baseball owners also loaned their players to the military to provide instruction in the particulars of the game. For example, three Chicago Cub players spent part of their 1917 season coaching at the Great Lakes Naval Training Station.[34] Finally, the owners tried to make baseball look like a training ground for future soldiers, requiring American League players to learn close-order drill taught by regular army sergeants.[35]

After reporting extensively on baseball's spring training, *Stars and Stripes* continued during April, May, and June, 1918, to provide the doughboys in France with information about the progress of their favorite teams. This apparent acceptance that sports should continue as normal in the United States while the AEF took care of business in Europe applied to sports other than professional baseball as well. *Stars and Stripes* took the editorial position in April, 1918, that Princeton University was right in choosing to continue intercollegiate competition despite the war because American troops who followed college sports wanted to know that the outcome of the Harvard-Yale game was determined through the "old time, blood-and-iron variety of football, played by regulars, not by 'informal' teams, whose members aren't to be awarded their letters."[36] Later, *Stars and Stripes* reported that although Indiana University voted to suspend Big-Ten play, the other conference schools had decided to continue their fall football schedule because they had "decided that athletics are essential to put men in shape for real warfare."[37]

But the circumstances governing American involvement in the war changed profoundly between March and July, 1918. In March, most soldiers were still engaged in training and drill, but by Memorial Day, 1918 the war got hotter and the stakes got higher, as, for the first time, American units from the Second Division joined French troops in defending the line at Chateau Thierry.[38] For the first time as well, army sporting events in Europe were interrupted by the war. For example, an American athletic meet that Memorial

Day was broken up by the arrival of an allied aviator who needed his plane serviced that he might return to the battle. With his arrival, according to *Stars and Stripes,* "the manly art of self development resolved itself into filling gas and oil tanks."[39] Once doughboys were being put at physical risk in the trenches, the editors of *Stars and Stripes* seemed to have found it increasingly difficult to explain why some young men's athletic skills exempted them from participating in the war effort. Indeed, as early as April 12, 1918, Quartermaster Sergeant Stuart Carroll argued that despite the efforts of the citizens of Cascade, Iowa, to raise enough volunteers to keep the White Sox's Red Faber from being drafted, Faber should have joined the military as Carroll had always assumed that a man like Faber "would rather be in the big show than engaged in 'making the pennant safer for Chi.' "[40]

Even if athletics helped to train men for war, and even if the survival of professional baseball provided entertainment and distraction for those on the home front and for those doughboys who liked to keep up with their teams while serving in Europe, by the summer of 1918, despite the efforts of Ban Johnson and other team owners to prove that baseball had the best interests of the war effort at heart, *Stars and Stripes* had begun to directly question whether professional sport should be suspended for the duration. During June and July the newspaper named the players who enlisted or were drafted, leaving the major leagues without star players such as Rabbit Maranville and Grover Cleveland Alexander, and created a proposed all-star lineup of baseball players serving in the army and navy.[41]

As the debate over whether league play should be suspended grew, *Stars and Stripes* began to question the commitment to American values and American democracy, and even to their own manhood, of players such as Ty Cobb who seemed to be choosing to wait to enlist until the end of the season, or stars such as Shoeless Joe Jackson who played baseball while working in wartime industry. Finally, the newspaper announced that it was suspending its sports page for the duration. In its own words, "Sport among the troops must go on—for that is part of the job. . . . But the glorified, the commercialized, the spectatorial sport of the past has been burnt out by gunfire."[42] By deciding to eliminate news of professional baseball from its sports page, *Stars and Stripes* revealed a new tension about how masculinity should be properly expressed. For the newspaper's writers the manliness of sport was clearly subordinate to the manly sacrifice of war. In this case, participating in sport as a means of meeting the cultural definition of masculinity was not sufficient. Only by participating in the present conflict could a man achieve true manhood.

Despite the suspension of the sports page, with its news of the progress of the major league season, *Stars and Stripes* continued to keep its readers informed of the discussions between the secretary of war and major league owners over the secretary's "Work or Fight" rule. Apparently, at one point the baseball magnates offered to send a professional team to Europe to entertain the troops once the regular season was concluded. An editorial in *Stars and Stripes* emphatically rejected that idea, stating that the AEF did not want such a team to play for it, especially as so many real players were already in khaki, demonstrating their courage and willingness to face the enemy. Indeed, in September, 1918, an all-star team made up of those players in the service, and who had established by joining the military that they were worthy of doughboy respect, were set to tour military locations.[43] And in response to the attempted hold out by the Boston Red Sox at the 1918 World Series, an Editorial in *Stars and Stripes* implied that those men "who are today throwing grenades instead of baseballs, who are wielding bayonets instead of bats, will be adjudged the men who played the game 'for the good of baseball.' "[44] In other words, by the fall of 1918, the preservation of the beauties and virtues of civilian life symbolized by sport required the abandonment of sport and the embrace of war.

Although *Stars and Stripes* represented just one source of information for the doughboy in Europe, its editors' struggle with the decision whether or not to endorse the continuation of professional sport during wartime reflects a struggle that would be played out again and again in the minds of those interested in determining how best to create a fighting spirit in the young soldier. If, on the one hand, athletics were useful in preparing young men to fight, whether physically or emotionally, then surely the very best soldiers should be drawn from the ranks of the very best athletes. But, on the other hand, the very best athletes might better serve to show the values for which the American soldiers were fighting if those athletes were allowed to continue to exhibit their sports skills outside of the army or navy. During the First World War in particular, when baseball was the preeminent professional sport, and when the need to encourage support of the war effort was rendered especially acute because of the large numbers of United States citizens sympathetic either to peace or to the cause of the Central Powers, the continued existence of major league professional baseball, despite the many calls for its suspension, served in many minds as an example of the best that could be found in American life.

Despite disagreement about whether to continue baseball at the professional level, there appears to have been a general consensus that athletics were crucial to doughboy health and morale. The athletic program being conducted at Camp Kearney, California, late in the war suggests the extent to which sports permeated the lives of soldiers in training. The emphasis of some aspects of this camp training on the ferocity and aggression inherent in certain games reflects what athletic organizers believed had been demonstrated in France about the special skills doughboys needed to be effective in combat.

With the admonishment from Raymond Fosdick, just back from an observation tour in France, that participation in baseball games helped make individual soldiers into good fighters, the young men at Camp Kearney were offered the chance to participate in that and other sports.[45] Football, boxing, tug-of-war, volleyball, and basketball were all made available, although fencing was rejected for any purposes other than training as, according to the camp newspaper published by the YMCA, *Trench and Camp,* it lacked the "rough and tumble" that the American craves.[46] By failing to endorse fencing as an organized sport at Camp Kearney, athletic organizers and the *Trench and Camp* reporter who detailed their work apparently chose to emphasize the development of a particular kind of masculinity through sport. Rather than the grace and concentration necessary to fencing, they chose to encourage the development of roughness.

Significantly, the sports played at Camp Kearney were primarily sports with American origins and structures, rather than European imports such as fencing and soccer, suggesting the desire to equate American masculine values with rougher sports. The emphasis on American sports also suggests the extent to which the army was committed to converting immigrant soldiers to the recreational and leisure time activities of the people of the United States rather than of the countries from which they came. Furthermore, since this was an American army being raised among the people of the United States, organizers apparently felt it crucial that it be distinctive from the other allied armies, even in the games it played.

Beginning a process that would be re-created during World War II, athletic contests were staged for mass appeal, as with the football game between the Thirty-second Infantry and the Sixty-fourth Field Artillery in October, 1918. The reporter for *Trench and Camp* counted the crowd attending that contest at five thousand people.[47] And the Twenty-first's tug-of-war team was sent to Los Angeles to compete in a Liberty Fair athletic carnival staged for the benefit of soldier relief.[48]

Even injured soldiers and those undergoing treatment for minor illnesses were required to participate in athletics at Camp Kearney, where a special program of sports and games were arranged to promote the "healing power of a cheerful mind."[49] Soldiers with limited athletic ability were not left out.

At Camp Travis the athletic program was specifically designed to include every man on the post so that "they may enjoy wholesome recreation and at the same time develop themselves along physical lines."[50]

Beyond the recreational value of sports, their ability to distract was exploited, as even on the ships taking the troops to Europe sports programs were conducted for the entertainment of the soldiers. As O. W. Lomady of the 320th Infantry recorded in his diary, after target practice one day he watched a boxing bout on the aft deck of his ship.[51] Second Lt. William F. Todd also used his diary to describe the boxing matches he saw on his afternoons aboard ship.[52] Although we cannot now determine the extent to which these efforts to bring the young men of America's World War I army into sport succeeded, it seems clear that the expectation was that participation in, or observation of, sport would in all cases be of benefit to the soldier.

To that end, the welfare organizations charged with serving the needs of the soldiers in Europe began a program to supply athletic equipment to the troops. Despite their involvement in the war, efforts were made to assure the doughboys that they were going to return to civilian life as they had left it. Because participation in and interest in sports and athletics provided a bridge between military and civilian life, the links between the two were emphasized by the organizations providing sporting goods to the troops. Thus, while American League owners provided baseballs, bats, and gloves to the doughboys, sporting goods manufacturers tried to take advantage of the situation by tying their products into the patriotism growing out of the war effort. For example, Alex. Taylor & Co., of New York City, placed an advertisement in *Stars and Stripes* that showed a hurdling doughboy over the caption "Athletes Make the Best Fighters." That advertisement then announced that the company had been awarded a contract to fill the sports equipment needs of the troops.[53]

But a problem soon arose with purchasing the equipment in the United States and shipping it to France. The commanders of the U-boat war against allied shipping made no distinction in what ships they sank, so that boats carrying athletic equipment might be torpedoed at any time just as if they were carrying more lethal materiel to Europe. Indeed, after the liner *Oransa*, carrying thirty thousand dollars worth of baseball equipment, was lost the YMCA contracted with French manufacturers to make fielder's gloves. The YMCA and the Knights of Columbus also ordered the manufacture in Europe of four thousand baseball bats during June, 1918. Although the reporter for the *Stars and Stripes* found the French gloves and bats acceptable, he noted complaints about the French-made baseballs which, in his words, blew "up under a Heavy Bombardment."[54]

Even where units arrived in France carrying their own athletic equipment, they often found it necessary to abandon that equipment, either on arrival, or as they neared the front. When the Eightieth Division disembarked at St. Nazaire, and arrived at their rest camp, they first participated in a field meet and then had to strip down to travel forward. As Maj. Harry P. Holt later recalled, "Our excellent assortment of football, and baseball equipment, the fruit and work of months of labor, was a great loss, although at the time we did not see the need of such activities. Later days proved that the loss of this equipment was a serious one."[55] For the men of the Eightieth Division, therefore, the best efforts of the civilian welfare agencies and of their own commanders, remained inadequate to the task of ensuring that they would have the sports equipment needed to keep them busy and active before and after combat.

Despite the difficulties in obtaining sufficient balls, bats and other sports paraphernalia, throughout the AEF an extensive athletic program was conducted under the auspices of the YMCA, the KC's and other welfare organizations. And results from the games and matches played among the troops were regularly reported in the *Stars and Stripes,* whose sports editor, B. F. Steinel, was a former boxing promoter from Milwaukee, working in France with the Red Cross. Steinel asked his readers to send in game accounts to be shared with their fellow soldiers, and he maintained a regular section on doughboy sports until the cancelation of the entire sports page during the summer of 1918.[56]

Describing the organization of the sports program, the writers for *Stars and Stripes* explained that as units arrived in Europe instructors in boxing and wrestling were assigned to each, while every company was expected to form a baseball team for intercompany play. Later articles in the soldiers' newspaper reported that stars such as Mike Donlan, and maybe even Christy Mathewson, were going to come to France to help coach baseball.[57] As with the use of metaphor to reduce a soldier's horrific wartime experiences into the safe and comforting language of play, these extensive sports programs were intended finally to create a reassuring and familiar environment even for, as *Stars and Stripes* put it, "Those athletes right within the Zone of Advance [who would be provided with] the games everyone is used to, the games everyone wants to play, with all the facilities for playing them."[58]

As sports metaphors helped soldiers understand the progress of the war, analogies made between sporting activities and military skills helped them to put what they were learning into context and prepare them for combat. During their first few weeks in Europe, most American troops were nowhere near the fighting. Rather, they were involved in further training exercises to prepare them for the tasks they would face as they approached the front. In General Pershing's view, aside from learning how to protect themselves from gas attacks and how properly to dig a trench, the doughboys needed to be perfected in "hand-to-hand fighting with the bayonet, grenade and dagger."[59] As Pershing wanted those skills emphasized, sports reporters began to describe the baseball games being played by the troops as a means to enhance their skills with the grenade in particular. Thus, a story about a game played in the Tuileries Gardens in February, 1918, claimed that pitching a baseball to the batter, or throwing a baseball across the diamond was roughly analogous to tossing a grenade at the enemy.[60] Similarly, the need to learn to use a gas mask because of the dangers to unprotected lungs from gas warfare required the soldiers to undergo extensive training so that they would be comfortable with the equipment should they encounter such warfare. To break the monotony of training and to lessen the fear of gas, mock baseball games were organized in which the players wore the masks, discovering that if they could play ball while so encumbered, they surely could make war.[61] Finally, to encourage the soldiers to become comfortable with the aggression they would need when encountering the enemy in France, the rules of boxing were modified at the training camps, to prevent stalling by shortening the time for each round. As a reporter for *Stars and Stripes* remarked, modifying the rules to encourage aggressive play was beneficial during training as that "is the kind of boxing that will aid the boxers in their real warfare."[62]

Formal baseball leagues were rapidly established as the number of American forces in Europe grew during the spring of 1918. The Paris League included twenty-two teams, including those of the Military Police stationed in Paris, the base censor's office, the disbursing office, two teams from the Aviation Headquarters, and the Motor Mechanics. Later in the summer a league in Tours featured sixteen clubs, which, as the *Stars and Stripes* pointed out, made the Tours League bigger than the American and National Leagues combined.[63] And in Great Britain, an Anglo-American League of American and Canadian armed forces teams was organized under the sponsorship of civilian individuals and organizations such as the William Cross Vacuum Oil Company, the O'Cedar Mop Company, Higginson and Company, Robert Grant, Jr., and Newton Crane, an attorney.[64]

Many soldiers remember baseball as an integral part of the wartime experience. In the words of Seaver Rice, "In France we had YMCA huts for reading and letter writing—we also had a regimental baseball team."[65] Similarly, Private Henry K. Carter of the Eighty-second Division, while off-duty, "washed my clothes and went to ballgames."[66] Sgt. Maj. Benjamin H. Heath described in a letter home that on the Fourth of July, 1918, he "went to a neighboring town and watched a ball game and then got in a scrub game myself for some innings."[67] While in France, Clarence O. Pearson played baseball, as did George McMahon, Pvt. John E. Cooney, and Charles Van Citters, while Herbert C. Smith, Jr., and Walter Frei played football.[68]

Aside from the extensive organized and casual baseball program in the AEF, elaborate and highly competitive track and field meets were also conducted. For example, a battalion meet was held on a field laid out especially for that purpose by that unit's engineers, a meet in which the short sprints were won by 1st Sgt. Charlie J. Rice, a competitor at the 1912 Stockholm Olympic Games. Often the track and field meets included not only the events which were typically part of prewar meets, but new events such as the hand grenade throw, the platoon drill, the manual of arms, and a company exhibition drill.[69]

Although Raymond Fosdick believed that running track or playing baseball helped turn a young man into a good soldier, the sports programs conducted within military units were also intended to help ensure that young men remain good men. At least Samuel Arthur Devan, a chaplain during World War I, and general director of the General Commission on Army and Navy Chaplains during World War II, believed that to be the case. In his World War I diary, Devan recorded his work in organizing athletic competitions, with baseball games regularly scheduled after Sunday services, and with a huge athletic program as part of the July 4, 1918, celebration. Describing the program, which included events lasting the entire afternoon until mess time, Devan said that it "was designed to cover the whole day and evening in order to give Satan no chance at filling idle soldiers with noxious liquors!"[70] Clearly Devan believed that keeping the soldier occupied with sport would help him avoid being occupied with other, less wholesome, leisure activities.

Despite Chaplain Devan's hopes and plans however, veterans of the First World War apparently found many ways other than sports to occupy their time. Although Paul C. Meads of the Eighty-first Division played baseball for recreation, he also played cards, as did William Rufus Mitchell, who played dice as well. These card games caused many doughboys financial problems. As James R. Clyburn pointed out, professionals often appeared to play poker and craps with the troops. According to Clyburn doughboys gambled not only while playing cards, but on the outcome of baseball, football, and basketball games, a result that surely would have distressed Chaplain Devan.

Even more distressing was the consumption of alcohol among the troops, consumption that was not always prevented by the participation in, or observation of, athletic contests. Although liquor was difficult to obtain in and around training camps in the United States, that was not the case in France. Allen T.

Johnson, for example, spent his off duty time drinking wine and beer. Of course drinking, while not an intended part of AEF culture, was an integral part of French culture. In Howard N. Norton's words, during the war he found it a "treat to go to a home for a meal. Mostly French fried potatoes, omelettes, and wine or beer."[71]

The military's sports programs was developed not only to provide wholesome recreation for the troops and to assist in their physical training. An equally important function of army athletics during World War I was to demonstrate that American sports and American sportsmen were superior to those of the allied armies. Because the United States entered the war after the combatants had sustained years of slaughter on the front, American military planners intended to avoid the mistakes which had led to that slaughter. Thus, they continued to reject the advice proffered by the British and French general staffs and sought to go their own way. But to justify the refusal to adopt European military standards entailed risk, unless it could be established that the Americans were so superior in every way that they would inevitably prevail.

Even though the United States entered the war allied with France, England, and Italy, a concern expressed through sport, as well as through diplomacy, was that the American soldiers maintain their autonomy. Since General Pershing was specifically instructed by the secretary of war to keep the forces of the United States separate and apart from the allied troops, sports provided one among many means to demonstrate that the doughboys were capable of surviving on their own, under American command.[72] This struggle to prevent the amalgamation of American troops into British and French units has been well documented, and became an integral part of the postwar discourse about the efficacy and importance of the participation by the United States in the Great War to the final successful outcome of the struggle.[73] By conducting a sports program that emphasized American skill in American sports, the army emphasized the separate status of the doughboys and illustrated that they were competent men ready to fight under their own leadership without the help of their allies.

Stars and Stripes demonstrated the impulse to show that Americans would prevail in athletics as they were doing on the battlefield. Although the soldiers of the U.S. Army were, of course, trying to defeat the Germans on the battlefield, sports competitions often involved a demonstration of American prowess to the citizens and soldiers of allied nations. As the doughboys came late to the conflict, it may have seemed crucial to the American authorities to establish the superiority of American males not only in war but in peaceful activities, both to gain the respect of the allies, and to reassure the troops that they had nothing to fear from combat, so long as they continued to succeed in other endeavors. The editors of *Stars and Stripes* tried to show how allied and civilian soldiers learned to appreciate the fighting spirit and excellence of the American troops by watching AEF athletes competing against one another. For example, *Stars and Stripes* reported during the summer of 1918 that a Frenchwoman who accompanied her husband, a major in the French army, to a series of boxing and wrestling matches, remarked after seeing the exhibition that "if the Americans called beating one another up a pleasure, what wouldn't they do to the Boche."[74]

To ensure that the allies got the message that this one Frenchwoman received, doughboys and their commanders regularly invited French and British officers and men to American athletic events. The May 10, 1918, base-section two boxing matches were attended by officers from both the French and American armies, as well as "scores of beautiful French women, whose stunning evening gowns gave resemblance to a night at the opera in the States."[75] The big Memorial Day track and field meet held in base-section two was also watched by two French generals, the mayor, and the local department prefect. The opportunity to show off American athletic skills to the French also allowed the Americans to ridicule the French lack of understanding of their sports. Thus, baseball games in the Bois de Boulogne were regularly interrupted as the French spectators were injured by foul tips because they did not understand they should not stand directly behind the catcher. To the *Stars and Stripes* reporter describing these events, this failure to avoid injury by learning the intricacies and etiquette of baseball, made the French look ridiculous.[76]

In Great Britain as well, efforts were made to encourage civilian spectators to come out and watch American athletics. Games in the London Anglo-American Baseball League were well attended, with a game between the London AEF team and the Taplow Canadians at Swansea drawing fifteen thousand people, whose admission fees went to the British POW fund. Unfortunately for the Americans the two-time champion Canadian team won by a score of 10-3. The reporting on that particular game again demonstrates the way in which the language of war and the language of sport became conflated, sharing metaphor as a means of explanation. According to the *Stars and Stripes*, the result of the game, "demonstrates the value of an effective barrage of preparation. The Eskimo neighbors bombed their way to seven runs in the first push, then were held until the seventh when they got another, making the final two in the ninth. The Yanks bayoneted their three in the fourth, fifth, and seventh innings."[77] Although this metaphorical language may have helped explain the tactical language of warfare to the troops, the doughboys must have found it curious that all this athletic mayhem was directed not against their ostensible enemy, but against their allied "Eskimo neighbors" to the North. But, of course, the Canadians had been at war since 1914, so that they needed to be assured that their new allies, the Americans, were ready to fight and die in the trenches beside them and that, indeed, the arrival of the Americans meant the end of the Central Powers.

Despite the occasional lack of American athletic success, the soldiers apparently wanted to know that AEF athletes succeeded more often than not. Thus, the reporting on the loss to the Taplow Canadians in baseball was contrasted with a victory by the U.S. Naval Air Men over the Canadian Foresters. And in France, the army conducted track and field trials to pick the best team to face the French on July 4, 1918.[78]

Discussions about sport were also used during the war to distinguish the American character from that of the enemy Germans. As Q.M. Sgt. Stuart Carroll explained in *Stars and Stripes*, "Sportively speaking the Huns aren't good sports at all. They try to spike the opposing runner, their pitchers are trained only in the use of the bean ball, and they even admit that the Umpire is on their side."[79] For the doughboys who entered the war assured that their side was the side of democracy and purity against an enemy guilty of "raping" Belgium, the assertion that the Germans couldn't even play fair in baseball must have had special resonance—even though the Germans probably didn't play baseball at all.

As sport was used to demonstrate national values and to demonstrate the superiority of American men as they succeeded on the field of battle and on the playing field against the men of other nations, within the U.S. military a discourse concerning racial and ethnic stereotypes also occurred. In the AEF Native American, African-American, and European-American sportsmen had joined together in the effort to defeat the Central Powers. At their separate training camps, and during their leisure time they engaged in sports. When they played each other, their relative skill in sports served as another method of ordering the participating men within the military's hierarchy. But the athletic skills of African-American soldiers in particular provided a special challenge to racial stereotypes as they proved themselves to be capable of success in a realm presumed to be indicative of fighting ability. The young men whose race was deemed to render them incapable of exhibiting the discipline, endurance, and courage necessary for combat seemed to disprove that as they exhibited discipline, endurance, and courage on the athletic field. The rationale for excluding African-American soldiers from combat alongside European-American troops seemed to break down when they demonstrated themselves to be fully capable of competing equally in sports. Thus, as they fought and as they played, the doughboys were faced with challenges to the manifest racial, ethnic, and class differences among themselves, and forced to decide the extent to which athletic talent should be a marker for those differences.

But, according to *Stars and Stripes*, the physical differences between the soldiers were becoming less important as the war progressed. The newspaper explained that every soldier was coming to resemble every other doughboy, as "An American scientist discovered, not many years ago, that out of the melting pot that is the United States there is developing a peculiarly American cranium—that is the bone under our hair."[80] This notion about the development of a distinctive "American" cranium, rejecting as it did the scientific racism of the time that would have assumed distinctive differences in the skulls of members of different races, reflects again the need to emphasize the unity and cohesiveness of the Army against attempts to separate and divide the troops.

Another aspect of this rhetoric involved an assertion in the media that the U.S. Army was an army open to all, with every soldier sharing common values and aspirations. Even when acknowledging racial differences, *Stars and Stripes* continued to tout the purposes common to all members of the AEF. As one writer in *Stars and Stripes* put it when announcing that a member of the Sioux nation had been named a captain in the AEF, "The cycle of the races has been completed. Every color, shade and complexion on the face of the Earth now is represented on the Western front in the fight for Democracy."[81] The irony that a Native American would serve as an officer in the American army less than one generation after that Army completed the conquest of his people seems to have escaped the writer.

Yet despite this rhetoric of inclusion and denial of difference, nativism and systemic racial prejudice worked to prevent the military's promise of equal treatment.[82] Contact between white and black troops was strictly controlled during the First World War, as military authorities strove to keep the black soldiers from standing side by side with white soldiers on the battlefield. For example, *Stars and Stripes* announced that Binga Dismond, who in 1916 set a world record in the 440-yard dash, would serve in the army as a first lieutenant in the Illinois *colored* infantry (emphasis mine).[83] And wherever possible, athletic contests maintained similar segregation. Thus, for the Memorial Day, 1918, athletic program planned at base section two, a special seven inning baseball game was scheduled between the "colored boys from two different camps, any one of which would have been fast enough for the old Cuban Giants in their palmiest days."[84]

The separation of white and black athletes may have had especial importance in maintaining the color line and a belief in white superiority. Arthur R. Ashe, Jr.'s, study of the black athlete has shown that when representatives of the African-American units stationed in the Philippines at the turn of the century began competing against white troops, white commanders became quite anxious about the superiority of those soldiers. This athletic superiority became a matter of pride for the black units before and during the War. As George A. Burton, of Company G, the Twenty-fifth Infantry, recalled, in interregimental athletics "We were the tops."[85]

By keeping white and black soldiers in separate units apart during the First World War, and by strictly limiting the number of competitions between African-American and European-American athletes, the overall focus of the military effort—that of beating the Central Powers—was maintained and racial conflict was minimized. And the fiction that the American army was open and inclusive remained unchallenged. The rhetoric that suggested that all members of the AEF were equal in their desire to make the world safe for democracy and shared common values, hopes, and aspirations remained unchallenged. And the possibility that competition between white and black regiments might yield results that would belie the idea that those European-American "narrow-chested clerks" whose masculinity had been in crisis since before the turn of the century could achieve competence in sport through military training was avoided.[86] Finally, the matter of determining whether the masculine athleticism of European-American, Native American, or African-American soldiers was superior was deferred to another day.

In creating the military's sports program for the mass army raised to fight in World War I, the army's Commission on Training Camp Activities initially focused on providing that program as part of an overall package designed to protect and preserve the mental and physical fitness of the young soldiers. Thus, Chairman Raymond Fosdick and the Commission's chronicler, Edward Frank Allen, described a system in which the men's minds would be filled with matters other than alcohol and women. But an army also requires its soldiers to find a means to overcome fear. During World War I a model was developed using athletics for just that purpose. The military's sports program was designed to alleviate anxiety by providing the young soldiers with distractions. But the sports program also helped the doughboys deal with their fear by analogizing the challenges they would face in battle to the challenges they faced on the playing field. Thus, war became a "game" described in the familiar language of civilian life.

Moreover, the sports program provided training specifically in those qualities in which many of the young men brought into the army were presumed to be deficient. Wherever possible the aggressiveness of sport was emphasized, as many soldiers learned to take a punch for the first time in their lives and learned that throwing a baseball could be just like throwing a grenade. America's young soldiers also were encouraged to discover through team sports the military value of team play; the individualism of civilian life had to be subsumed within the structure and hierarchy of military life if the army was to function effectively, just as each individual athlete had to place his talents in the service of the team.

In 1917, American troops became involved in a war in which they were allied with soldiers who had been fighting and dying for years. The entry of the United States into the Great War did not necessarily mean that America's doughboys were going to be accepted as equal partners on the battlefield. Even before they entered combat, the soldier-athletes of the United States sought to establish their strength and masculinity by engaging allied soldier-athletes in sports. As they did so, they helped General Pershing and other AEF officers resist the demands of the British and French that American troops be integrated into their combat units. Thus, the military's sports program served yet another purpose—persuading the Europeans that the soldiers of the United States were fit and ready to fight.

During World War I American soldiers encountered numerous new challenges. Immigrants and native-born men of European and African descent, men from the city and from the country, men with sophisticated educations and virtually illiterate men were gathered together and sent to war. Although they all wore the same uniform, they came from vastly different backgrounds. But the assumption was that, as men, they were all interested in and could be made adept at sports. Even if they were indifferent to athletics, the military ensured that they could not long remain so, as an understanding of sports was defined as necessary to the American soldier. Through sports, the doughboys would learn how to be men. And if fulfilling their masculine obligations might require the doughboys to kill the enemy, their hesitations about adopting that style of masculinity could be overcome by enveloping the act of killing in the rhetoric of sport and game.

3

PLAYING IN THE POST-WAR WORLD AND PLANNING FOR THE FUTURE OF MILITARY SPORT

The Armistice that put an end to the fighting of World War I left the American government without any clear plan about how best to demobilize the army and return its soldiers to the United States.[1] In addition, the Army had no clear idea about how best to provide for the troops scheduled to remain in Europe as occupation forces. But the Army did recognize that they would need to be entertained, in part by continuing the program of sports and athletics established during the war. But the military also initiated changes in its postwar sports program in response to new needs. Armed forces athletics would serve new purposes and be conducted in new ways. Physical fitness and morale would be promoted through athletics, but so would the diplomatic needs of the United States. And after demobilization problems associated with the World War I sports program would be addressed so that improved methods for providing athletic opportunities to the troops would be in place should the need arise in the future.

When the guns finally went quiet on the Western Front on November 11, 1918, many of the soldiers who had left the United States and gone to Europe to participate in the Great War and had served either behind the lines or in battle discovered that they would not be returning home immediately. Even though they were technically no longer at war, they found that their commanders intended that they continue to maintain the same high level of physical fitness while waiting to be demobilized which they had established during training. This continued training was designed to help the doughboys avoid laziness and boredom in the absence of battle. To further prevent the disintegration of troop morale because of the lack of activity they were also encouraged to play sports or to watch others playing, to attend educational classes, and to solve mock combat problems. Furthermore, soldier-athletes in the military of the United States were asked to participate in competitions against the soldier-athletes of other nations, in exhibitions designed to demonstrate the superiority of American sports and sportsmen.

Before American disengagement from Europe, many doughboys also became involved, either as participants or as observers, in a great athletic festival staged in Paris and designed to demonstrate that the soldiers of the victorious allied armies could unite for peaceful purposes as well as for war. These 1919 Inter-Allied Games directly preceded the 1920 Antwerp Olympics, and on the surface they appear to have many similarities to those grand international sports meetings reestablished by the Baron de Courbetin less than thirty years before. But the Inter-Allied Games also displayed striking dissimilarities in organization and purpose connecting them more to the diplomatic struggle being waged at the Paris Peace Conference for the future of Europe than to other international athletic competitions.

Most of the troops who had gone to Europe to fight in the Great War were demobilized by the end of 1920.[2] Back in the United States, Douglas MacArthur, wartime commander of the Forty-second (Rainbow) Division, took over as Superintendent at West Point and created a program of intramural athletics for the cadets based on his understanding of how best to train future officers. And during the subsequent decade, officers in the American army determined to study the ways in which sports had been provided to the soldiers and sailors during the First World War and to apply their experiences to planning for future engagements overseas. A series of lectures and meetings at the Army War College during the 1920s led to significant changes in the way opportunities for recreation were made available to those in the military. As American planners began to raise the mass army that would ultimately fight the Second World War, the design of the sports program through which soldiers and sailors were trained and entertained reflected new thinking, not only about the practical purposes of such a sports program, but the philosophical purposes behind the creation of an American masculine ideal through sport.

Although the Armistice of November 11, 1918, effectively ended American involvement in combat on the Western Front, those troops who had been sent to Europe to participate in the war were not sent home all at once. Soldiers were needed to occupy the Rhineland in anticipation of an eventual peace treaty, and soldiers were needed to begin the long process of restoring the French and Belgian countryside to its prewar condition. Furthermore, regiments dispatched to Russia to deal with the consequences of the 1917 Revolution remained in Archangel and Siberia until 1920. The presence of large numbers of troops from the United States in Europe after November, 1918, required Army authorities to plan for their entertainment and amusement. As they waited for demobilization and for the final treaty of peace to be negotiated, the doughboys had time to kill, and the army and the representatives of the Young Men's Christian Association handling soldier welfare matters for the Army, instituted a series of athletic competitions to fill the soldiers' days.

The sports program devised by the YMCA and other civilian agencies at the behest of the military ultimately met the doughboys' need to be distracted and entertained while waiting to go home. But like the athletic activities that had occurred during the war, these postwar competitions also helped reinforce the dominating position held by America's soldiers in a Europe devastated by war. They served to drive home the message that participation in American sports taught values required in a rapidly changing world in which the United States had seized a major role. Finally, the military's sports program provided further evidence of the superiority of American men, whose success on the battlefield was reflected in their athletic successes.

David M. Kennedy has described how the Army chose to deal with post-Armistice idleness by requiring its troops to solve sham training problems, to participate in education classes, and to take advantage of the sports competitions being held down to the company level.[3] But for the Americans, sport served not only to prevent boredom, but to ensure virtue as well. Before the war many had commonly assumed that sporting activities helped keep young men both physically fit and morally clean.[4] But the military's plans for the actual practice of athletics among the doughboys remaining in Europe was much less about that romanticized vision of sport as a uniquely clean and pure endeavor (although some Division newspapers, such as the *Amaroc News,* reflected that ideal as late as 1919). Rather, the Army turned to sports as a practical device to keep the young, bored doughboys from drinking and making friendly overtures to the women of France.[5]

Furthermore, as President Woodrow Wilson struggled to achieve his goal of a new world order, the YMCA and the army discovered that athletic success could demonstrate American power and further American prestige, providing additional confirmation that the American point of view must be respected at the peace table as well. The means used by the YMCA and army authorities to promote athletic competitions show how the earlier vision of virtuous competition gave way to the reality of national diplomatic needs in the postwar period.

Although the place that idealized sport had held as a repository of virtue was never completely superseded, beyond the use of athletics as a means of instilling character came the recognition that sports for the army could have a functional purpose. Therefore, the military began to make plans to supply the soldiers with as many athletic opportunities as possible. To facilitate the staging of athletic events, a building program was undertaken that would leave the citizens of Coblenz, Germany, and other Rhineland cities with first-class athletic facilities. According to Jack Gann, writing in the Third Division's newspaper the *Amaroc News,* the Occupation army's sports program was designed to get everyone involved, whether as player or spectator, so that those not previously interested in sports would become interested, while those previously interested in only one sport would be able to learn to appreciate other athletic endeavors. Although the army's purposes in conducting this sports program appear to have been primarily instrumental, as Gann reminded his readers, unlike civilian professional sports army sports were clean and demonstrated that success could be achieved without sacrificing honesty.[6]

During that first winter in Germany, the army athletic program included regimental basketball, boxing, and wrestling. Enough people associated with the Ninth Infantry Regiment were interested in either playing or watching the matches and games that a new mess hall was constructed to handle the crowds.[7] Later in 1919, athletic festivals were staged in the Third Army area in a newly built stadium, with adjacent stables. A similar stadium was built in the Andernach area, featuring hot showers, a press box, and special boxes for the ladies.[8] At both Heddesdorf and Montabaur, baseball fields were laid out and stadia constructed so that doughboys could watch the action in comfort. And for those soldiers forced to remain in Germany during the next winter, the Young Men's Christian Association ordered five hundred pairs of ice skates and promised to have outdoor hockey rinks built for the doughboys' use. Reflecting the high-level interest in the competitions stated in the new stadia General Pershing paid a visit to the First versus Second Division baseball game at Montabaur.[9]

Successful teams and individual athletes were entertained by the YMCA. For example, the track team from the Eightieth Division's Second Battalion was treated to a special supper because they, according to the Division's newspaper, *The Whizz-Bang,* "true to the tradition of the battalion, brought it home in first place."[10] Another soldier newspaper, *The Cootie,* reported that boxing and wrestling were "by the far the most popular sports and entertainments during the winter months" for the doughboys and that basketball games in the regimental league were drawing large crowds."[11]

The men of the Eighty-first Division also had a unit newspaper. Covering the entire front page of *The Wildcat* is an enormous picture of an enraged cat, captioned "Breaking Through." At the top of the page, on the right side of the newspaper's name is an illustration of a wildcat pitching what looks like a baseball, while on the left is a wildcat holding a baseball bat in his paw. Even those doughboys with limited reading skills received a message from *The*

Wildcat's first page about the importance of sports to masculinity and wartime success, assuming they understood the presumed significance of baseball to American male culture at all (which assumption belies the fact that large numbers of American soldiers were recent immigrants to the United States, having grown up in countries where other sports, such as soccer, were commonly played).[12] Inside, a report from the 318th Machine Gun company advises that they are "very busy these days returning equipment, playing baseball, and talking of going home."[13]

According to the *Whizz-Bang,* any team or individual's athletic successes were a reflection of the tradition of accomplishment already established on the battlefield. In fact, for the Eightieth Division, the best description of their fighting ability was contained in the "Official Batting Average of the AEF 1918 Season," which was reprinted in *Whizz-Bang* from the *Stars and Stripes.* In contrast to the batting averages compiled at the end of every baseball season, however, this AEF batting average was determined not through a ratio of hits to outs, but through the number of officers and men captured, the number of artillery pieces seized, and the kilometers advanced toward the enemy. Rather than present those statistics straightforwardly, therefore, the editors of *Stars and Stripes* and of *Whizz-Bang* decided to provide an interpretation of the statistics that they believed would be more meaningful to their readers. Those *Whizz-Bang* readers were no doubt proud to learn that the Eightieth Division ranked second among divisions in the National Army in kilometers advanced and first in the number of machine guns taken. They also must surely have concluded that the fact that the Eightieth ranked sixth in kilometers advanced among the entire AEF established their fighting prowess.[14]

On the other hand, we cannot assume that all young men in the Eightieth Division, or all readers of *Whizz-Bang,* either understood the significance of baseball batting averages, or accepted that baseball batting averages could reasonably be modified to show how the division fared while in combat. As with the use of metaphorical language derived from sport in *Stars and Stripes,* the development of a method drawn from baseball to distinguish the experiences of army divisions in World War I carried with it assumptions about what the doughboys knew, or should know, about sports. These batting averages were developed for the precise reason that all soldiers were presumed to be as vitally concerned with sports as they were with other "manly" endeavors. And if doughboys were not interested in sports, but were anxious to learn how their Division did in the war, they would soon learn from reading the *Whizz-Bang* that sport *should* be important to them if they wanted to understand their place in the world. Thus, a hegemonic ideal of masculinity was reinforced by tying together the language of sport and war, marginalizing those men uninterested in or alienated from athletics.

Aside from their own interunit competitions in sports like baseball, basketball, and boxing, the Americans also continued the pattern they had established during the war of encouraging soldiers in other armies to play those sports common in the United States but not in Europe. And as they had during the war, American soldier-athletes participated in track and field meets against athletes from the allied armies. But in the postwar world, representatives of the United States military and of the YMCA were even more anxious to establish the dominance of American men and the way of life which had created this superiority by demonstrating their prowess in athletics. To that end they organized sports festivals to which they invited representatives of other armies, and built large athletic complexes both in France and in occupied Germany. Despite a consensus that victory on the playing field was a predictor of victory in other endeavors, the army and the civilian agencies working with the army to organize sports were unable to reach agreement on how best to ensure American athletic domination. They were unsure whether it would be best to identify and train elite athletes or emphasize the athletic abilities of regular soldiers—especially as Americans began to compete against allied athletes.

The American attempt to acquaint allied troops with American games began as soon after the Armistice as circumstances permitted. The French were introduced to basketball in April, 1919, as the game was set to become a part of the French army's athletic program. Basketball also was included in an athletic meet held by the British Rhine Army in July 15, 1919.[15] Meanwhile 2d Lt. Eric Ojerholm was dispatched for the Cologne bridgehead in June, 1919, armed with baseballs, bats, and gloves, to teach the British how to play the American game. And the French were treated to a demonstration of America's national game by baseball teams from the Second Division stationed at Wiesbaden.[16] As Clark Griffith, owner of the Washington Senators put it, "America has a direct and very personal interest in the dissemination of baseball love by the doughboys."[17] Griffith seemed to have anticipated that the spread of baseball throughout the globe would lead to a larger pool of talented players from which to draw, but what other reasons might there have been for the Americans' interest in sharing basketball and baseball?

Although the common foot soldier may merely have wanted to show how much fun baseball and basketball were, other factors must also have led to this eagerness to see the French and British playing like the Americans, especially in those cases where it appeared that the athletic representatives of the allied armies might successfully challenge the doughboys. The fact that during one three-day period American athletes broke eight French track and field records meant little when soldier boxers were struggling to survive in the ring with French boxers—especially since boxing seemed to be a uniquely manly sport.[18] Indeed, at one point it appeared that the only way an American boxer was going to be able to stay with the French champion, Farney, was if he were paid. Accordingly, in an example of a case where romanticism about sport gave way to practicality, Leckie of the U.S. Army accepted the twenty-five franc per round incentive offered by Earl Brannon of the YMCA and pocketed two hundred fifty francs at the end of a bout held in June 1919.[19]

However, Leckie's success, as well as the successes of American athletes at other times during 1919, were not believed to be sufficient to establish finally the superiority of the United States and its men, to show the Europeans (whether in the victorious allied armies or among the occupied populations) the "snap and go" that, according to the Second Division's *The Indian,* the doughboys had exhibited at the front.[20] This was especially true as American soldier-athletes met defeat at the hands of the sportsmen from the allied armies.

Early in 1919 an editorial in *Amaroc News* explained that the secret of the "wonderful fighting and staying qualities of the American Army" was due to the fact that every soldier was an athlete, a situation said to be unlike that in the European armies who maintained a distinct group of professional athletes capable of making records.[21] But despite the fact that every American soldier was athletic, their physical abilities were still not sufficiently developed to ensure certain success against the soldier-athletes of other nations. Accordingly, by midsummer the *Amaroc News* reported that the Army proposed to open a permanent sports training facility along the Rhine to provide for those soldiers who were going to compete on an elite level, thus adopting the European system of separating the best athletes from their peers.

Even with that new training facility, apparently built after accepting that to be competitive American athletes had to train more regularly, Inter-Army matches held in October, 1919, revealed that the British were still in better shape than the Americans.[22] Fortunately, the readers were offered an explanation for the Americans' lack of athletic success—not only were the British competitors "professional" athletes, but the Americans were outnumbered and unable to devote full time to training because they could not be released from military duties! Therefore, Pat Brannon of the YMCA asked that fifty athletes be placed on special duty so that "in a short time Americans will clean up on the best men that the British and French have."[23] As the *Amaroc News* commented, in order for their athletes to achieve success, American athletic officers were going to have to work harder to ensure that each organization enter competitors

in at least 70 percent of the events of an upcoming sports show which would
feature competition between American units as well as competition with the
British and French.[24] The struggle to ensure that American athletes beat their
ostensible European allies reflected more than the mere desire to win on the
playing field. In 1919, as in 1917 and 1918, the strength of any country seemed
to depend for proof on the strength of its sportsmen.[25]

Although the emphasis on competition with the athletes from the allies
sometimes led to a deemphasis of sports for fun, W.H.W of the Sixty-sixth
Field Artillery still demanded that he and his buddies be allowed to organize
their own entertainment, with baseball games between different batteries, rather
than just between regimental teams. And the men of the Eighty-first Division
also tried to get in as many company baseball games as possible while waiting
to return to the United States. Those games were planned by the soldiers in
the division and described in their newspaper.[26] Thus, despite the regularization
of postwar military competitions, at least some soldiers wanted to continue the
pattern established during the war of spontaneous and unorganized sporting
activities.

When American units of the Second Division and the Third Army engaged
in athletic contests with each other, the *Amaroc News* said they were displaying
the same old spirit "that made the 2nd Division so unpopular with the Germans
and so popular with the American people." According to the editorial, that
spirit was characterized by the support of the team and a refusal to quit.[27] The
eagerness to distinguish the American spirit as revealed through sport from
that of the allied French and British, extended even more to the spirit of the
Germans who, in the words of one writer for the Second Division's newspaper
The Indian, "had never learned to play."[28] According to *The Indian,* the Germans
believed only in the utility of sport as it might enhance military preparation.
Therefore, they could never understand why American soldiers played baseball,
a game leading to nothing in particular, to be played simply because the participants enjoyed it. Of course, the pleasure many soldiers received from playing
baseball was but one reason for playing the game, as it and other sports were
endorsed by military leaders precisely because they believed that participation
in sports was so important in soldier training.

Although Americans competed against each other and against the British
and French in a variety of sports, by the end of World War I the sport that
had come to be seen as the truest test of masculine excellence was boxing.
Despite opposition earlier in the century from some who did not wish to see
respectable young men from good families engaging in physical brawls, during
the war the Young Men's Christian Association and the Knights of Columbus

both provided instruction in the "manly art." Workers from both organizations also served as boxing promoters and referees for the fights which they arranged, promoting fights not only between American soldiers, but between soldiers representing the British and French armies. Thus, Pvt. John E. Cooney and his buddies boxed against the French on their national holiday.[29]

During the postwar period a debate occurred over the value of American participation to the ultimate outcome of the Great War. After the Armistice most people in the United States and in its armies and navies were convinced that the allies would have been defeated absent American intervention. Meanwhile the English and French maintained that American help, though useful, did not materially increase the possibility of allied success. As the debate intensified, arguments about which nation had the strongest, most courageous, and most masculine men, suggested that the contribution of the United States to allied victory could best be determined by measuring the athletic ability of America's soldiers against that of the cobelligerents. Since the truest test of manhood off of the battlefield was believed to be in the boxing ring, the YMCA's boxing matches assumed great importance.

The importance placed on the outcome of interallied boxing matches is reflected in the problems faced by fight organizers in determining the rules to be followed by the participants. As Pat Brannon of the YMCA discovered in October, 1919, when he tried to arrange a fight program, the British would not participate if they had to box by American rules. Nor did Americans want to box by British rules. Why? In Brannon's words, fighting by the British rules would be "too much of a ladies' affair to suit Americans. Their rules are much more complicated than ours and there are many more possibilities for fouls. From what I have seen of the British fighting, a blow struck hard enough to hurt a boxer is generally called a foul."[30] Because of the impasse over the rules, the boxing tournament between the British and the Americans that Brannon had proposed—a tournament to be held for the entertainment of the Germans as well as the soldiers of the occupying armies—was canceled.

Brannon's explanation for the difference between the two countries' rules provides an example of how success in sports could be connected to diplomacy and masculinity. First of all, Brannon says that the British rules are complicated. As the army had been concerned earlier in the year that American soldiers were unable to devote time to training because of their commitment to their military duties, the rejection of complicated British rules has great resonance. Since boxers from the U.S. Army would presumably fight best if they could fight "naturally" and with little training, using the British rules which demanded higher skill levels would put them at a competitive disadvantage. This is especially important in light of earlier concerns about the extensive training and the higher level of professionalism among British military athletes.

In dealing with the British desire to box by their own set of rules, Brannon was faced with a situation not dissimilar to the one that faced President Woodrow Wilson at the peace table. Brannon found that the British wanted to beat Americans in sport, just as Wilson found that the British wanted to assert their own interests at the peace talks. But Brannon also discovered that the British wanted to ensure that any sports confrontation be on their own terms. The historian Jeffrey Richards has argued that the British emphasis on the concept of "fair play" and adherence to a specific set of rules served the British particularly well as their "ideology and religion were subsumed into Imperialism" in the late nineteenth and early twentieth centuries.[31] In Richards's view, Imperial Britain used to their advantage the notion, derived from modernizing nineteenth-century sport, that so long as they seemed to play fair, any result could be justified. Ideologues for the Empire then contrasted the British adherence to their own rules to the national character of their opponents who had no regard for fair play. Hence for the British to agree to play by the American rules would have meant rejecting basic national values. Thus, as Wilson discovered, having a common enemy in the Germans did not necessarily create similarity of purpose between the French, the British, the Italians, and the Americans.[32]

But even more important is Brannon's suggestion that the British rules rendered boxing a "ladies' affair." As the Americans were anxious to establish the validity of their claim to having won the war despite their late entrance into the conflict, and as many Americans believed by 1919 that participation in war established a young man's claim to manhood, no doughboy could consent to having his masculinity reduced by participating in a ladylike sport.[33] For Pat Brannon of the YMCA a debate over the rules became a discussion of how best to establish the gender dominance of American males over their British allies. In the post–World War I discourse, this equation of gender dominance with national might effectively subverted the possibility of an alternative vision of masculinity not tied to national and international needs.

The establishment and preservation of a gender hierarchy demanded not only that masculine males be distinguished from effeminate males and that the gender superiority of American men be established, it demanded as well that women be placed firmly at the bottom. The *Amaroc News* often reported about attempts by American women to perform athletically, such as when the war worker Mildred Morris swam the Rhine, "just to show the Yanks down at Andernach that masculinity didn't rate to grab off all the palms for athletic supremacy."[34] As Susan Cahn has shown, because swimming was viewed as consistent with femininity, female swimmers were often accepted even as other sportswomen were subject to ridicule.[35] But when a group of "Y girls" proposed to organize a baseball team, their efforts were taken as comic relief, as the men they were to play were asked to wear skirts and play left-handed by the male promoters of the event. Yet despite the mockery which they received, the *Amaroc News* reporter had to concede in the end that the women of the YMCA did demonstrate some real baseball ability, despite their "powder puffs and vanity cases."[36] There should have been no surprise by 1919 that at least a few women had some baseball ability as women had been playing the game collegiately since just after the Civil War, yet maintenance of gender norms required each generation to forget the athletic achievements of the previous generation's women.[37]

In any event, commanders continued to find it difficult to get all soldiers involved in sports. To meet that challenge, the army determined by January, 1919, that a championship competition should be conducted to determine the best teams in a variety of sports. According to the plan circulated by the AEF, those teams were not to be composed of All-stars, but rather of the best representative team from each army. Thus, Headquarters would have one team, as would the First, Second, and Third Armies and the District of Paris, while the Services of Supply would have two teams in the competition. The winners from the AEF championship would, according to the army, go on to represent the U.S. military in international competition.[38]

But enlisted men of limited athletic ability were also expected to participate in an "All-Point Company Championship," in which they would score points in a pentathlon composed of runs of 100 and 880 yards, a broad jump, a shell put, and a pull up. The shell put was derived from the standard shot put, but "owing to the impossibility of securing sufficient numbers of regulation 12-pound shot, dummy Stokes Mortar shells, weighing about 12 pounds, have been substituted."[39] This company championship scheme was specifically designed to get every man involved, as even those men sick and in hospital were to be counted as present and competing for the purpose of determining the company champion. Indeed, in the words of the *Training Bulletin* that explained the competition, "The fighting efficiency of a company depends upon its training and the number of physically fit men it takes into the firing line. The same principles apply to these contests."[40] By determining victory through points earned, and counting every man in a company as having participated whether or not he was physically able to do so and gain points for his team, the army created a system where soldiers uninterested in athletics would be subjected to pressure from their peers to play anyway. The system also ensured that nonparticipants could be held responsible for their company's failure. In other words, through the "All-Point Company Championship" the army was trying to accomplish what less direct means of persuasion had been unable to do and force all soldiers to be sportsmen.

Although through this scheme the army tried to ensure that all soldiers waiting to return to the United States would become involved in athletic competition, many doughboys remained uninvolved in sports.[41] In fact, among those World War I veterans who responded to a Military History Institute survey, not one specifically mentioned having been involved with a company championship such as that envisaged in *Training Bulletin No. 2*. Apparently despite the efforts by the AEF and the YMCA, the fact that doughboys had to be coerced into the All-Point Company Championships through threats that they would be counted as if they were there even if they were sick and unable to perform belies the notion that the American men in the World War I army "naturally" or "instinctively" wanted to engage in sports. Rather, for many of these young men, failure to engage in athletics meant merely that they didn't want to engage in athletics, not that they were any less manly. And this reluctance to participate may also suggest the frustration among the athletically unskilled soldiers with a system that demanded that they play while providing them with no reward for playing, while valorizing the successes of those among them with excellent skills. Thus, despite the many strenuous efforts to link sports success to superior masculinity, many doughboys, for many reasons, were able to reject that connection, at least at it applied to themselves.

After the Armistice, aside from the large number of unit competitions being conducted either spontaneously among American troops waiting to return home, or being conducted on an organized basis by representatives of the social welfare agencies charged with keeping the troops occupied, planning moved forward for a proposed "Military Olympics" involving athletes from the victorious armies. The original suggestion for this athletic competition had actually come before the war ended, in an October 15, 1918 memorandum from Elwood S. Brown, director of the Department of Athletics for the Young Men's Christian Association in Paris, to Colonel Bruce Palmer of the AEF.[42] Brown envisaged the proposed Military Olympics as an opportunity for cementing on the field of sport those "friendly ties between the men of the Allied Armies that have sprung up on the common field of battle."[43] Brown's stated purpose in suggesting a "Military Olympics" reflects the persistence of the notion that athletic competition could reflect high values and aspirations and that social cohesion could be promoted through sports. But as the planning for the games went forward,

Brown's lofty notion, which Donald Mrozek identifies with the culture of the Victorian rather than the Modern Age,[44] came into conflict with the new rhetoric that identified national success with success on the playing field.

For many reasons, the idea of a huge athletic festival appealed to the American authorities, and by April, 1919, the work by the committee charged with the responsibility of organizing what became known as the Inter-Allied Games was well underway. One of the first matters the committee had to determine was what sports to include. Recognizing that many, if not all, sporting activities can have military applications, the committee asked whether physical challenges unique to the circumstances and technologies of the Great War should be recognized as official sports. Having determined that indeed a grenade toss competition (using the French F-1 field grenade and allowing throwing techniques derived from either baseball as the Americans preferred or from the method taught to the French troops) should be added to the usual running, jumping, and throwing events, the Committee then decided not to add a bayonet competition, as they feared there would be no satisfactory method of judging who won and who lost while ensuring the safety of all competitors.

The Americans' overall decision to sponsor and support a series of postwar athletic events among their own troops remaining in Europe, culminating in a meeting of sportsmen drawn from the ranks of the recently victorious armies, illustrates the way in which sport had come by 1919 to serve as a reflection of national and international values and aspirations. Richard Mandell has argued that "performance-oriented, disciplined, democratic, theatrically presented sport suits well the spiritual and mythic needs of a rapidly industrializing society" and the Inter-Allied Games illustrate how the officers and men recently caught up in a disciplined, performance-oriented, and industrialized war sought to have their need for spiritual meaning satisfied through nonlethal competition.[46] The games also demonstrate, once again, that the language of sport and war share metaphor, that sport and war serve to define the parameters of masculinity, and that national success at sport provides the same kind of satisfaction as national success on the battlefield.

The Games were similar to, but different in a number of important ways, from the Olympic Games which had been reestablished in 1896. By contrast to the Olympics, in which only amateurs were allowed to compete, the Inter-Allied Games were open to any athlete who had worn the uniform of one of the victorious allies at any time during the Great War, even if that athlete had been or was presently a professional. The organizing committee also chose to include athletes from nations which were created from the ruins of the defeated Austro-Hungarian Empire, even if during the Great War their nations had been subsumed under the aegis of one of the defeated powers. The decision to allow amateurs to compete with professionals would be repeated in athletic competitions during the Second World War, with special rules allowing athletes to retain their amateur status even if, as soldiers, they were technically competing for pay. Perhaps the decision to allow professionals to compete in the Inter-Allied Games reflects the inclusion in Army competitions of professional athletes such as William Wambsganss, who recalled for the Military History Institute that his occupation before being inducted into the army was professional baseball, and who was placed on his base baseball team immediately after induction.[47] Including professionals also allowed for a breadth of competition as the Inter-Allied Games included matches among professional golfers who had served in the armies of Great Britain, France, and the United States.

But while allowing professionals to compete with amateurs, the Committee chose not to include on the program any sport which depended on subjective criteria in determining the winner. Russell Weigley has identified an "American Way of War" in which military success means a complete and unambiguous victory over the enemy.[48] This definition of wartime success as requiring the total collapse of the enemy left the Armistice of November 11, 1918, as an unsatisfactory conclusion to the epic struggle that preceded it in many American minds. In order to avoid unsatisfactorily ambiguous results at the Inter-Allied Games and to ensure that no final result would be left open to interpretation or accusations of bias on the part of the judges, the organizers decided to leave diving, gymnastics and race walking (which while allowing for measurable results also allowed for disputes about the walkers' techniques) off of the official program.[49] The decision to leave off the program subjectively judged sports connects the organizers' emphasis on rules and clearly established victories to the impetus behind the Olympics and other modern sporting activities—the desire to establish records derived from objective achievement, but also shows how the Inter-Allied Games were unique in rejecting the notion that judges and officials could overcome their national biases and reach fair decisions through adherence to higher ideals. As Modris Ecksteins has argued, World War I may be an expression of the modernist impulses also reflected in art and dance. If so, the sporting epilogue to the Great War, while beginning with the rhetoric of the previous century also seems to reflect the impulses and desires of the modern age.[50]

Finally, because the organizers wanted to encourage participation by as many athletes and nations as possible (so long as they had fought on the right side), they decided to encourage national sports committees to ask that sports in which athletes from their nations especially excelled be included. Thus, both types of wrestling, Greco-Roman, in which the Americans had little tradition, and "Catch-as-Catch-Can," the style to which Americans were accustomed were offered. Likewise, the organizers included all three types of football: soccer, American intercollegiate, and rugby (although there was ultimately no competition in American-rules football as there were no entries other than that from the championship army team). And riding competitions were conducted not only in the familiar forms of show-jumping and three-day eventing, but in the form favored by the athletes of Hedjaz (a newly recognized nation carved out of the late Ottoman Empire, which ultimately became part of present-day Saudi Arabia), who provided a demonstration of camel racing. The decision to include equestrian events reflected the lingering belief that cavalry still had a place in the age of mechanized warfare even though some national teams were unable to provide their own mounts without turning to privately owned stock (reflecting the sacrifice of much of the horseflesh of Europe during the war).[51]

Although the organizers of the Inter-Allied Games wanted to provide every nation with opportunities to excel in some type of athletic competition, they in no way wanted the United States to fail. Even though the American YMCA and the AEF representatives on the Games committee never explicitly stated their desire to show the superiority of American masculinity, the troops watching preparations for the games implicitly understood that underlying all of the reasons for having an athletic competition lay the desire to show American soldiers and sailors in the best light. After all, as one writer for *Stars and Stripes* pointed out, America must keep its place "on the top of the international athletic heap."[52] Therefore, money was collected in the United States to pay passage for the return to Europe of those especially talented doughboy athletes who had been demobilized and gone home.[53] And, a special army training bulletin detailed the options open to officers and enlisted men who had earned a place on the United States team for the Inter-Allied Games if their units were being returned to the United States. Those athletes were entitled to request that they be allowed to detach from their outfit and stay in Europe until after the games. If they chose to stay in France, they would be assembled at the Athletic Training Camp near Colombes Stadium for the duration of competition.[54]

David M. Kennedy has suggested that World War I was in part about a reaffirmation and reassertion of masculinity, after the so-called crisis of masculinity that engulfed Western culture at the end of the nineteenth century, and indeed, according to Kennedy, many American feminists opposed the United States' participation in the European conflict precisely because they feared that that participation would valorize masculine aggressions.[55] And in explaining the hold the military had on the American imagination at the beginning of the twentieth century as a place where manliness and masculinity were not in crisis, Donald J. Mrozek has argued that military service during the First World War was particularly appreciated as a refuge, a strong, though temporary, male preserve to which men might escape from obligations toward women.[56]

In many ways the Inter-Allied Games were also about the reaffirmation of masculinity and about establishing yet another masculine preserve. Therefore, despite the fact that American women served in the Navy as "Yeomanettes" and other women served in a civilian capacity as telephone operators and ambulance drivers, no provision was made for them to compete in the games.[57] Women with the YMCA and the Red Cross were, however, invited to the athlete's village to serve as hostesses or to dance with the assembled athletes although the official record of the games explains that in the absence of sufficient numbers of women the soldiers felt free to take on the costumes of women.[58] Women war workers were also encouraged to attend the competitions to cheer on their favorites. Thus, even those women who had served their nation in war were returned to their prewar roles of helper and spectator, separate and apart from the manly business of sport.

Clearly, the organizers of the games believed that American interests would be served in a number of ways by the successful presentation of a grand "Military Olympics." For one thing, the essential superiority of the American way of life would be demonstrated, as, in the words of the *Amaroc News*'s Jack Gann, "the Balance of the world will gain in the newly acquired realization that Americans can play just as hard as they fight or work."[59] And the games themselves would serve crucial diplomatic and strategic purposes as President Woodrow Wilson and the other allied leaders negotiated the final treaty of peace with the Central Powers. After World War I the face of Europe was changed through the break-up of the Austro-Hungarian and Ottoman Empires and the recognition of new nations in central Europe and the Balkans. The recognition of these newly independent countries was one of Wilson's goals and the Committee organizing the Inter-Allied Games helped promote that goal by extending invitations to teams from Romania and Czechoslovakia.

The symbolic effect of their participation cannot have been unintentional. For example, editors of the games's official memoir noted that the participating Czech soccer team had been subjected to a ten-year boycott by the Austrians, who had prevented the team from playing in international competition.[60] Similarly, the participation of a team from Serbia, chosen by the "Comite Serbi-Croate-Slavine," reflected the role that Serbs had played in precipitating the war. Curiously, however, that team competed not as a team from the new Yugoslavia, but as a team from Serbia, reflecting the state of confusion prevailing in Eastern Europe and the Balkans as peace negotiators tried to draw effective new boundaries. And the organizing committee's decision to invite participating nations to propose competitions in their national games, along with the decision to award no overall recognition to the nation accumulating the most victories, but rather to award a trophy or prize to the winning nation in each type of sport, ensured that each nation might have its moment of affirmation.[61] This emphasis on the guarantee of national rather than individual success at sport is again in contrast to the rhetoric of the Olympic Games, whose representatives continued unsuccessfully to present the games as an opportunity for individual achievement in the succeeding decades.[62] As Thomas J. Knock has suggested in his recent study of Woodrow Wilson's diplomacy during the war and postwar years, the President desired to establish a community of nations in the postwar world—a community of nations not unlike that invited to the Inter-Allied Games—and hence the Committee's decision to promote the games as a gathering of nations rather than a gathering of individual sportsmen seems to have paralleled the president's thinking.[63]

But the decision to sponsor the Inter-Allied Games served yet other American purposes as well. President Wilson was anxious to establish America's preeminent status at the peace talks, and to promote the idea that because of American entry into the war the allies were able to prevail.[64] One way to establish the strength and power of the American army, aside from its active presence on the battlefields of the Western Front at the end of the conflict, was through a demonstration of its organizational and engineering ability after the war. Accordingly, army engineers and troops took over building the new stadium designed for the games, which would be named after General Pershing. The army also offered to feed and house all participants in the games at American expense, establishing the status of the United States as a surviving world economic power by providing for those teams whose countries were too poor to provide for themselves. As the official history of the games explained, "The visitors gasped at the magnitude of the entertainment arrangements. Free ice cream and other dainties were things that been unknown for a long time in some of their war-ravaged countries."[65]

Furthermore, as European- and African-Americans worked to finish the facility within which the track and field, equestrian, baseball, basketball, boxing, and wrestling competitions of the Inter-Allied Games would be held, the AEF hoped to demonstrate as well the way in which the United States had resolved conflicts within its own interracial society. This demonstration, as black Pioneer troops labored under the direction of white engineers to build roads around Pershing Stadium as well as the Stadium itself, obviously was fraught with hypocrisy, especially as the place of African-American soldiers within integrated American units had been consistently denied during the war. Yet the games' official account endeavors to make it clear that a multiracial contingent of American soldiers was working to ensure that the competition would begin on time in a finished facility. And although neither army units during the war nor the athlete's village was integrated, African-American athletes were accepted on the American team, including Solomon Butler of Dubuque College, who placed first in the running broad jump.[66] Since many of the new nations of Europe were going to be created by bringing together members of traditionally hostile ethnic groups, the army perhaps wanted to show how racial and ethnic tensions could be overcome within a society by pointing out how white and black troops were able to cooperate in preparing a venue for the Games.

Although the organizing committee and the chroniclers of the Inter-Allied Games may have wanted to suggest that Butler's success proved the harmonious state of race relations in the United States, the nation's black newspapers were well aware of the contradictions between military rhetoric and reality. That Sol Butler jumped farther in Paris than the European-American winner of the national championship broad jump, and that Butler defeated the future Olympic champion Charlie Paddock in the 90-meter race at the Tuileries Games, was, according to the *Pittsburgh Courier* and the *Chicago Defender,* reflective not only of his individual athletic superiority but of the absurdity of the restrictions placed on African-Americans both within the military and in civilian life.[67] Indeed, James Heyman and Robert Hayden of the 815th Pioneers who finished second and third respectively in the 220-meter run at the Inter-Allied Games later returned to France rather than stay in the United States where they did not feel welcome.[68]

Ultimately, the strength, virtue, and manliness of all of the allies was to be confirmed through athletic competition. Germany had been given the 1916 Olympics Games, which were not held because of the war. Neither Germany, nor Austria, would be allowed to participate in the Inter-Allied Games. This was appropriate according to the *Stars and Stripes*, "as the Allied nations have always been the leading promoters of organized sports and have taken the principal role in the revival of the Olympic Games. . . . The absence of the Central Powers will not be an important loss, for the reason that Germany, Austria, and Turkey have never been real devotees of sport."[69]

In any event, the Inter-Allied Games proved to be a rousing success. The citizens of France as well as many of the soldiers remaining in Europe filled the ninety thousand seat Pershing Stadium to overflowing on more than one occasion. Although the Americans swept the majority of the track and field medals, the French war hero Jean Vermeulen, running with an arm damaged in the fighting, won the cross-country run and the modified Marathon. The pre- and postwar Italian Olympic champions continued their dominance in fencing. Czechoslovakia's soccer team defeated that of France. Australians and New Zealanders did very well in rowing and swimming. Belgians and Serbs excelled in Greco-Roman wrestling. And Chaplain Fred C. Thompson, U.S. Army, established the no doubt still-standing world's record in the hand grenade throw with a toss of 74.929 meters. Indeed, the success of the games is reflected in the 1927 and 1938 guides to battlefields and monuments of the world war published by the War Department to allow Americans to revisit the scenes of the Great War, which include information about the sites of the Inter-Allied competition.[70]

When he became Superintendent of West Point after World War I, Gen. Douglas MacArthur brought with him certain strong beliefs about the value of athletics to the man in battle. In order to ensure that future officers were imbued with a sense of the importance of sports, MacArthur established an intramural training program in the sports of baseball, football, basketball, soccer, lacrosse, track, tennis, golf, and hockey. He argued that athletic competition "brings out the qualities of leadership, quickness of decision, promptness of action, mental and muscular coordination, aggressive, and courage" necessary for the soldier, and demanded that Academy cadets meet rigorous standards in sports themselves that they might later be effective leaders of men.[71]

After the First World War, other army officers made a concerted effort to analyze where the institution had succeeded and where it had failed in its mission to bring a massive number of soldiers into battle along an extensive European front. Through its schools system, the army also asked its best and brightest young officers to begin making plans for how the military of the United States could best be utilized should it be called on again to engage in warfare overseas. This process involved not only questioning such matters as how a division should be organized and equipped, or how airpower should be brought into support of ground troops, but how the welfare needs of each individual soldier should be met.

In a 1929 lecture at the Army War College, Brigadier Gen. Edward L. King described the organization of the army's G-3 Division and what the Army had developed to ensure that the problems of soldier welfare, especially those involving sports, encountered in France in 1918 would not be repeated. He described a system in which an entire section of the Division's Training Branch was given over to the control of education and schools. Moreover, according to King, that section was responsible for all general athletic questions pertaining to the army, including the preparation of War Department policies relative to the conduct of army athletics, maintaining the liaison with the National Amateur Athletic Federation, the American Olympic Committee, and other organizations interested in the promotion of amateur athletics, and finally, controlling the army's Athletic Fund.[72] In other words, King described a system in which the army maintained total control over all aspects of a soldier's athletic life.

How did the army come to seize that control from the social welfare organizations which had conducted Army athletics during the Great War? And what advantages and disadvantages to the military, and to the individual soldier athletes, came with the new system? Finally, what lessons were learned during the First World War that persuaded the army that it should govern its own system of sports and athletics?

Certainly, the Young Men's Christian Association and other welfare organizations such as the Knights of Columbus and the Jewish Welfare Board were able during 1917 and 1918 to provide opportunities for many soldiers and sailors to participate in a variety of sporting activities, whether as part of their training in the United States or as part of their leisure-time activities while in Europe. However, there was considerable competition among the different welfare agencies to show how efficient and accommodating each could be in providing the best equipment, referees, and coaching to the troops. This competition led to confusion and frustration for many soldiers who observed that equipment was often not available when they needed it most. As the *Amaroc News* sardonically commented in May 1919, with regard to the arrival in Europe of boxes of baseballs, eighteen months before, when the YMCA ordered all of those baseballs, the Yanks and "Heinies" were fraternizing in a big war game, and now that the balls had arrived, the doughboys were going home.[73]

Soldier complaints regarding the availability of athletic equipment and playing opportunities might not have led to the changes described by Gen. Ernest L. King absent a 1922 lecture at the Army War College by Raymond B. Fosdick, the civilian who had served as overall coordinator of social welfare matters for the military during the Great War. Although Fosdick had earlier described in glowing terms the planning which created a system of sports, games, hostess houses, and facilities for writing home to loved ones at every American training facility, by 1922 he apparently had concluded that the need to provide diversions for soldiers and sailors could better be met through the military itself.

Although Fosdick continued to believe that saloons and disorderly houses outside military bases harmed morale, if not private morals, and continued to argue that an alternative must be provided if saloons and disorderly houses were to be shut down, by 1922 he had determined that the preventive system provided during World War I was sufficiently flawed that another system must be put in place. In explaining his reasons why an organization such as the YMCA should not be put in charge of recreation in the future, Fosdick first explained the problems which had occurred in 1917–1918, when representatives of the Knights of Columbus and the Jewish Welfare Board also tried to provide welfare services to the troops. According to Fosdick, this led to an unnecessary and inefficient duplication of effort in some areas while in the Second Army area the soldiers were provided with not a single baseball.[74] Although the lack of adequate equipment and professional organization did not keep soldiers from playing games on their own, and many observers argued that the fact that American soldiers were able to play games despite their lack of equipment showed how tough and well-prepared they were to fend for themselves in battle if need be, Fosdick argued for a system that ensured that the troops would not need to improvise a game with sticks and socks, rather than bats and baseballs.[75]

Despite Fosdick's suggestion that some nonsectarian group might be able to organize welfare programs for the military (with religious matters handled by the chaplains), he ultimately argued that such a group would need a lot of military supervision to be sure that every soldier received the recreation he needed. Accordingly, Fosdick concluded the army should organize its own athletics and recreation program for the soldiers in the future. He called for a well-equipped library on every post, a "Hostess House" where soldiers could "meet their women folks under rational circumstances," group singing, educational programs, and a system of organized athletics.[76] Significantly, despite the YMCA's active involvement in the Inter-Allied Games, and in promoting championship boxing along the occupied Rhine, Fosdick rejected the notion of athletic specialization in favor of games of mass participation. As Fosdick said, he believed that "you can get better psychological results when you get the crowd playing than you do when you get the crowd watching a team play."[77]

Fosdick's determination that the military should take over the responsibility of providing welfare services to the troops surely was influenced by his study of matters on the Western Front, and the problems associated with civilian control over those services. But he must also have been anxious to avoid a repeat of the 1919 incident in Newport, Rhode Island, in which civilian Christian ministers who had served as advisers to the sailors congregating in Newport as part of the World War I buildup were accused in a naval investigation of homosexual misconduct. Although the ministers argued that their service at the naval hospital and at the YMCA in Newport was an expression of their Christian brotherhood and desire to provide charity to those young men in need of help, the navy insinuated that they were motivated by homosexual desires, and that no "normal" man would wish to work at a hospital or YMCA unless he was interested in sexual relations with the men to whom he providing services. Despite the navy's efforts, with the support of the ministerial community of Newport the accused clergymen were able to persuade a jury hearing the charges that they were innocent of sexual misconduct. Rather, they were able to convince themselves and the jury that the intimacy of their relations with the young sailors was not perverted because they engaged in no specific sexual acts.[78]

Raymond B. Fosdick must have understood that the Newport inquiry, involving as it did allegations of misconduct between YMCA war workers and sailors, did not lessen the danger of similar allegations against YMCA workers serving soldiers. Therefore, his anxiety that the military take over these social welfare duties must have been even greater than publicly acknowledged. And the army must have welcomed his suggestions as they provided another means of ensuring the masculinity of their soldiers. No longer would they be exposed to the brotherly ministrations of civilian Christian ministers, but would instead receive their religious instruction and their entertainment from uniformed men, whose sexuality was under the military's control and reflected the twentieth century's new emphasis on self-conscious heterosexuality as a marker of masculinity.[79] Similarly, soldiers' sporting lives would be organized and promoted by their fellow soldiers, men whose masculinity was presumably guaranteed by their manifest athletic ability.

Thus, Gen. Ernest L. King's 1929 description of the duties of the G-3 Training Branch seems to reflect many of Fosdick's suggestions, although when King spoke the army had apparently already deviated from Fosdick's recommendations in a number of ways. The army adopted the notion of athletics and education, although the idea of group singing rapidly fell out of favor. And significantly, the army chose to continue its liaison with the American Olympic Committee and the NAAF to ensure that elite athletes as well as those with little physical coordination or interest in athletic activities would be provided for within the military. Indeed, during the Second World War, a large program of service baseball and boxing was developed to showcase the professional talents of men such as Joe Dimaggio and Joe Louis.

At the end of the First World War, the American military undertook an elaborate program to ensure that the troops waiting to be demobilized would stay under control. Athletics was a part of that program. For the doughboys, sports were a means of maintaining physical fitness, high morale, company cohesion, and entertainment. But sports, when played between soldier-athletes from the victorious armies, also helped develop a hierarchy distinguishing not only the more physically adept individual from the less athletic, but a hierarchy distinguishing between stronger and weaker nations. The possession of athletic ability thus stood for more than physical coordination, it represented an entire complex of desirable characteristics, the sum of which marked masculinity and in turn reflected national virility. Although other means of establishing masculinity had existed before the war, and would continue to exist thereafter, within the military athletics seemed to have proven their value during the war, and would be developed further in the postwar world as a method of creating the masculine soldier for future conflicts.

4

Building Strong Men and New Facilities for Another War

Many of us find it hard to imagine the time between the first and second world wars, when America had only a small military establishment requiring minimal financial support. Even as the country lost the postwar economic confidence that had inspired the boom of the 1920s and slipped into Depression, few ascribed the boom or the subsequent bust to the cost of maintaining the army and navy. And even fewer suggested that the country could spend its way out of the Depression by creating a larger more aggressive military to reinforce the overseas diplomatic and economic policies of the United States, or to serve as a place for the employment of the young men with limited prospects abandoned by the economic collapse. Instead, during the 1920s and 1930s the American military establishment was faced with the challenge of justifying its existence and providing employment for the officers and men who remained in the service after World War I, or who enlisted in the service during the two decades. Officers commanded the Reserve Officer Training Corps programs at colleges and universities and during the Depression they worked with the Civilian Conservation Corps. And both officers and men maintained national outposts and served the United States' interest from the Philippines to the Caribbean.

During the 1920s regular conferences among the nation's military officers provided a forum for discussing the lessons of the previous war, and planning for future engagements. At the same time, young men interested in military careers attended the military academies or studied skills necessary for those in uniform through the Reserve Officer Training Programs at many universities. Years later, many officers with long careers were interviewed about the applicability of what they learned during the interwar period to their army experiences. In retrospect, the men indicated that their participation in sports and athletics were a critically important component of their lives. Indeed, the interviews show that these men were convinced that success in sports led to success in the military.

Describing their experiences, they emphasized that aspect of their education having to do with athletics. In explaining how the lessons learned through sports helped each individual command troops, those interviewed connected physical domination to social dominance. Thus, the officers seem to have believed that the most athletically adept men within the military necessarily were the men best prepared to lead other men when war came. In other words, in the memories of those interviewed, the systematic creation of a hierarchy based on physical coordination and strength presaged the recreation of that hierarchy elsewhere within the military.

Despite the apparent economic successes of the 1920s, the end of that decade saw the United States slip into the Great Depression. Whereas previously a man's worth might be defined by his ability to support a wife and children, men unable to find work during the Depression often found their masculinity challenged as they were unable to meet their families' needs for food, clothing, and shelter. This was particularly true where they were forced to rely on their wives' or daughters' income to keep their families off of the relief programs that were being established both at the local and federal levels. The strategies the newly poor relied on to retain their dignity in the end led to a strength and self-reliance that the military drew on during the Second World War. But during the Depression, many observers wondered whether men would ever be able to recover the masculinity that had been lost with their jobs.[1]

As the young men who would lead others into battle were studying military skills at the end of the 1930s, and as men and women in Asia and Europe again faced war, the United States began a military building program. Built initially by employees of the social welfare agencies developed by the Roosevelt administration to create a new system of roads, bridges, armories, rifle ranges, and airports, this infrastructure proved critical to America's own war effort after Pearl Harbor. Then, with the institution of the first peacetime draft in American history at the end of 1940, bases were expanded to train the draftees and the units of the National Guard that were being called into national service as it became ever more likely that the United States would be drawn into war. Having determined that in the future the army should provide its own sports and recreation program, the men planning for this expanding military ordered the construction of athletic facilities on bases alongside the construction of barracks, runways, storage depots, and command posts. The development of the fields, stadia, and gymnasiums, and of the sports programs that would use the new facilities provides an opportunity to see how the lessons of the First World War were being applied to preparations for another armed conflict. That story also demonstrates the extent to which those in the military hierarchy remained convinced that a good soldier must be an athletic soldier, and that masculinity required an interest in sport that should be assiduously cultivated by any means necessary.

One of the first things a visitor notices when entering the Gen. Omar Bradley Museum at the Military History Institute at Carlisle Barracks in Pennsylvania, is the prominence given to Bradley's pre–World War I sports career at the Military Academy. Football and baseball game balls are on display along with photographs of the General and his fellow classmates participating in athletics while at West Point. And preserved in the memories of those who care about West Point football are the words of General Bradley's contemporary at the Point; Gen. Dwight D. Eisenhower said that he would prefer his entire staff to be composed of ex-footballers as they were the men who he could be sure would fill the leadership roles demanded of them in the army.[2] During the years between the first and second world wars, future officers were trained at the Military Academy and at other institutions for their military careers. In reflecting on their training, they have consistently connected their career success to sports.

Gen. Douglas MacArthur's belief that athletics should be an important part of every young officer's military education was apparently an influence on many of these men during the interwar period. While superintendent at West Point, MacArthur reorganized the academy's educational system, making sports and athletics a critical part of that process. Cadets received instruction in baseball, football, basketball, soccer, lacrosse, track, tennis, golf, and hockey, while an elaborate system of intramurals was also established. MacArthur explained his reasons for placing sports at the center of Academy education in 1922, saying, "Nothing more quickly than competitive athletics brings out the qualities of leadership, quickness of decision, promptness of action, mental and muscle coordination, aggressiveness, and courage. And nothing so readily and so firmly establishes that indefinable spirit of group interests and pride which we know as morale."[3]

Whether future officers played or coached while studying for their military careers, in retrospect many seem to believe that their participation in sports was valuable in their professional lives. It was they who were the beneficiaries of the postwar decision that the army create its own sports program, which required that they be prepared to serve as athletic models to their men. But where did that leave men who were less athletically adept? In the obviously hierarchical world of the military, athletic ability, and particularly athletic ability in rigorous and dangerous sports, created a parallel hierarchy. Even those young men who were not interested in sports, but who wished to serve their country in the military, were locked into a system that rewarded those who believed in a connection between sports and war and were consequently judged by their ability to meet the demands of that system. A hierarchy of gender based on athleticism demanded no less.

Many retired officers who were young men before World War II and who continued in the service for many years after that war have recently been debriefed. Aside from specific recollections about their experiences in combat, and their understanding of strategy, tactics, and the changing nature of warfare, the men also discuss important influences on their early career and whether they participated in sports, either during their officer training, or after they had received their commissions.[4]

For the young men who received their commission during the interwar years, organized physical activity seems to have had great personal importance. Indeed, according to Lt. Gen. Hobart Raymond Gay, he chose to remain in the service after World War I precisely because he became a member of the army's very successful polo team.[5] The sports which the young officers played also apparently served them well within the military as they were influenced by more senior officers whose athleticism provided them with a model. For example, Charlie Gerhardt served as an inspiration for Gen. James H. Polk's early professional life, because according to General Polk, Gerhardt "was a tremendous athlete and tremendous man who excelled in all things." Charlie Gerhardt also influenced the career of Gen. Robert W. Porter, Jr., due to his skills as a polo player.[6]

While serving in a cavalry regiment during the 1930s, General Polk competed in a variety of equestrian sports, racing horses, playing polo, and jumping in shows. In his view, this personal interest in horses and horsemanship helped him and his fellow officers maintain good relations with the civilian community as they invited the townspeople of El Paso, Texas, to post horse shows and polo tournaments. The idea that military-civilian relations could be enhanced as the military provided the civilians with sports entertainment of course was not new since the Army encouraged soldier baseball teams to compete with professional teams during the 1918 spring training season. These military-civilian contacts through sport were repeated elsewhere in the years before World War II and continued during the war as civilians were exposed to military sports both on base and off. Thus, Polk's experience in El Paso reflected the use of sports by the military to forge bonds between the state and civilian society.

By contrast to General Polk, who primarily discussed his athletic life after being commissioned, Gen. Robert W. Porter, Jr., found that the sports he played before attending West Point helped shape his life. According to Porter, he used sports to overcome his small size (as a high school football center he weighed only 110 pounds). During one high school football game he was struggling to control a larger player on the opposing team until they fought with each other. Porter's father afterwards commented that it was a great "little fistfight." Later, while playing scratch baseball, General Porter missed the pitched ball, but swung so hard he hit the much larger catcher in the head with the bat. Although he feared that the catcher would want to fight with him, Porter discovered that the catcher instead respected him for how hard he could hit.[7]

From these encounters and from the approval he received for fighting back and hitting hard, Porter learned that aggressive response and physical strength were the attributes he should cultivate in order to be accepted in his cultural milieu. This valorization of aggressiveness, even where occurring outside the rules of the game, as happened during the football game in which Porter engaged in fisticuffs, as well as his father's approval of his violent response to his inability to control the larger man otherwise, reinforced the message that a man's worth might be measured by his ability to subdue another. It also implied that a man unable to establish his place through aggression would be less worthy of approval.

In Porter's view, the West Point intramural program established by General MacArthur served himself and his fellow officers very well, "because as quickly as the officers went to their regiments, they had to coach, referee and deal with problems of athletics and sports in their outfits. . . . If he [the young lieutenant] was nothing but a bookworm, he would have trouble getting through to some of these people [the enlisted men in the regiment]."[8] For General Porter, then, a young officer's main duty was to establish control over his regiment, with sports as the means of gaining that control. From the time of World War I military sports had been justified as a means of creating group unity among the diverse members of a unit. As General Porter suggests, that unity could only be achieved if everyone understood that the officers demanded that unity through sport. A young officer unfamiliar with sports, or uninterested in athletics, or lacking in athletic ability, must surely have learned that a successful military career demanded that he embrace sports nevertheless.

Even if that young officer tried to avoid participating in sports, or tried to find ways to occupy his time other than by attending athletic events, his commander might demand his presence. Lt. Gen. Stanley R. Larsen found that an officer's absence from an athletic event could lead to censure by his commander. General Larsen, who graduated from the Military Academy in 1939, was assigned to a post in Hawaii later that year, where he served as a track coach. Although Larsen enjoyed athletics, his enjoyment was tempered by an element of coercion that demanded he devote his social life and leisure time to the support of the post sports program. In Larsen's words, "We were required to support all evening athletic events, such as boxing. The Regimental Adjutant knew when we weren't there. We were expected to attend daylight games as well."[9]

Carl Ulsaker, who spent the summer of 1937 preparing for entry into West Point, would apparently have agreed with General Porter's assessment of the need to use sports as a means of communicating with enlisted men and noncommissioned officers. He worked at the Camp Bullis mess that summer with a mess sergeant who had been playing service football for about ten years. Ulsaker found that he was able to establish rapport with that mess sergeant because he shared an interest in sports. According to Ulsaker, the football played at the Point was the most important of all sports because of its resemblance to war. As Ulsaker said, football "embodied the use of strategy, tactics, and tough, concerted action to achieve its objectives. It employed various formations, required intensive training to prepare for its ultimate commitment to action, and it provided a means for developing leadership and teamwork."[10]

Maj. Gen. Earnest L. "Iron Mike" Massad, who received his commission from the Reserve Officer Training Program at the University of Oklahoma, where he was a football All-American in the late 1920s, also believed that playing football had a profound effect on his later ability as a commander. But by contrast to some of his fellow officers who valued the games they played for the social skills they taught, or for the mental skills they required, General Massad argued that his own athletic experiences were most important because they made him physically fit. At the end of his career, he concluded that it would be impossible to be "an effective leader if you were weak and didn't have the energy to participate in all military activities."[11]

Massad's emphasis on the physical fitness benefits to be obtained from athletics, particularly football, reflects his belief that the conditioning required to play sports inevitably led to a strong body. But Massad's own experience as a football player, and the culture within the military which valorized the more violent sports, resulted in a conflict between the desire to condition soldier-athletes and the possibility that those soldier-athletes might suffer disabling injuries while playing their games. Indeed, as Michael Messner has shown, the bodies of most retired athletes, especially football players, are so broken and battered from sport that those men in fact have more physical disabilities than men who never participated in violent contact sports. Although the men of Massad's generation, and men like General Eisenhower whose knee was ruined playing football at the Military Academy, wished to overlook the danger of injury in violent sports like football and boxing, during the wartime emergency the army did take steps to keep the soldiers fit to fight. Thus, during World War II contact football was deemphasized for most recruits, both because of the cost of the equipment, and because of the attendant dangers to the bodies of the soldiers who would be required to "give up" their bodies in other ways.[12]

In his retirement, Gen. Andrew J. Goodpaster also emphasized the value of physical fitness. To Goodpaster, who didn't discuss any sports he might have played before attending the Military Academy, or any sports he might have played while at West Point, the key to a West Point education, aside from the academic, moral, and military preparation it provided was in its demand for physical development. As he put it, the physical testing and physical demands put on a young cadet left that cadet, "as a young officer, physically fit and able to do the things that he would have to do."[13]

General Goodpaster also provides an insight into the state of physical fitness among the new recruits he encountered after graduating in 1939. He was first stationed at Camp Claiborne, headquarters for the 390th Engineer Regiment, which was at that time an African-American unit. Goodpaster recalled that the soldiers under his command were "wretched physical specimens, hungry, weak, [with] poor teeth [who] needed to be built up."[14] Since the country was just coming out of the Great Depression in 1939, and since the effects of the Depression were even more profound in the rural areas from which the men of the 390th Engineer Regiment were drawn, Goodpaster's assessment of their physical condition allows us to see how years of poverty and neglect can destroy the fitness of any man. Therefore, even aside from the other benefits to be derived from physical training through sports described by Polk, Porter, Ulsaker, Massad, and Goodpaster, it was critical that the young men entering the military in the late 1930s and early 1940s be fed enough to have the energy to work their bodies.

During the interwar years there were, however, at least a few occasions when questions were raised about the value of sports for training the soldier. According to Massad, in 1935 he was ordered to create artillery football, baseball, basketball, and equestrian teams to compete with teams from the cavalry. After beginning football practice with every man on his post who weighed more than 175 pounds, Massad was called to headquarters by his battalion commanding officer, who asked him, as Massad recalled, "How in the hell am I going to train these people to fight a war and you've got them out on a football field?"[15] As Massad discovered, sometimes, and in some cases, despite the almost universal belief among military officers that sports provided an excellent forum for developing the mental and physical skills and attitudes necessary for war, sports could not serve as a total replacement for other types of military training. As the United States prepared for another total war, and the time reserved for training soldiers for combat decreased, the conflict between giving soldiers the specific skills they needed to meet the enemy and providing soldiers with athletic instruction and opportunities to play games was resolved in favor of the former goal. After all, manhood did not need to be established on the playing field when there would shortly exist ample opportunities for proving it in battle—opportunities available even to the uncoordinated and nonathletic soldier.

While some young officers were playing sports between the two world wars, Gen. James Alward Van Fleet, like Massad, was coaching football. Although Van Fleet, who is remembered in West Point's 1915 yearbook for the sixty minutes he played in the army's 20–0 football victory over Navy, certainly played the game, he believed that his experiences as a coach, both at the University of Florida, where he commanded ROTC and coached the football team, and as commander of the all-army enlisted men's football team in its game for the 1927 President's Cup against a team of Marines, were even more valuable when he was asked to command men in war. As coach, Van Fleet said he learned how to create morale and the desire to win in his players. Since football had, in Van Fleet's estimation, all the elements of war, he concluded that the opportunity to combine his familiarity with the game with the knowledge of how to handle men gained from coaching served him well in his career, as it would serve any young officer.[16]

Gen. James Alward Van Fleet's suggestion that athletics were valuable to the young officer not only for what they did personally for him in learning how to handle himself physically, but for what a knowledge of athletics could do for the officer called on to coach his men appears to have resonance for other officers. Since the coach has been commonly recognized as a leader, with the best coaches being deemed to have the best leadership abilities, it comes as no surprise that officers believed they could translate those leadership qualities onto the battlefield. Certainly, General Massad and General Porter believed that the ability to coach was useful for the army officer. But again equating coaching athletics to leading men in battle leaves out those men whose ability to lead may be manifested in other ways. It also valorizes a hierarchical style of relationships among men that may not have translated well into the fluid situations faced by soldiers in the hedgerows of Normandy, for example, where cooperation among men whose units were mixed, and whose command structures were destroyed, was critical.[17]

The American army of the 1920s and 1930s was quite small. Because the terms of the First World War's recruitment and draft legislation allowed most soldiers to be discharged on the war's conclusion, the size of the AEF decreased even more rapidly after the First World War than did the Union armies raised for the Civil War. After the post-Armistice discharge of 2,608,218 enlisted men and 128,436 officers, fewer than 150,000 men remained in the army on January 1, 1920, with that force further depleted to 118,750 men by 1927. Furthermore, at the time of the 1927 reduction in force authorized by an economy-minded Congress, more than one thousand Regular Army officers were also ordered to be discharged.[18]

Despite the hope of most Americans that future wars could be avoided, by the end of the 1930s Congress and President Franklin Delano Roosevelt began to recognize that German and Japanese expansion might need to be met with force. Accordingly, from 1936 through 1938, Congress authorized a slow growth of the military to a strength of 165,000, while the President asked for additional appropriations to accelerate the naval building program that he, as a former Assistant Navy Secretary, had been promoting since 1934 when the Japanese withdrew from joint U.S., British, and Japanese talks about the limitation of their respective navies.[19] The Congress also provided for an expansion of facilities thanks to Depression-era works projects.

Although the Depression did not lead to the expansion of the military as a means to support the vast number of young unemployed men, some young officers, like Gen. George C. Marshall and Maj. Gen. Ernest L. Massad, were sent to command Civilian Conservation Corps (CCC) camps after being commissioned.[20] For these officers, the chance to govern a CCC camp provided a command opportunity that might otherwise have been unavailable within the small peacetime army. And in many communities Works Projects Administration (WPA) workers were employed creating the infrastructure that would later be ready when the military expanded.[21] These WPA workers built armories, roads, and bridges that would prove critical to the nation's ability to move men and materiel around efficiently with mobilization, while other WPA workers provided sports and recreation assistance at military bases.[22]

Thus, by 1940, at least some of the work necessary to future mobilization had already been done, either through planning within the Regular Army or through civilian projects that facilitated the military's expansion. Meanwhile the army continued to grow from its earlier low levels, with Congressional authorization during 1939 allowing an increase to 210,000 men.[23] As the "phony war" of late 1939 and early 1940 gave way to the German invasion of Belgium, the Netherlands, and France, Congress became even more willing to authorize the army's growth, finally ordering the call-up of the National Guard on August 27, 1940, and passing the Burke-Wadsworth act providing for selective service on September 16.[24]

For military planners, Congressional authorization for the first peacetime draft in U.S. history provided new challenges. As Russell Weigley explains in his *History of the United States Army,* although plans had been formulated since the last war for the rapid mobilization of troops, no one had envisioned the need for the vast system of camps within the United States to feed, house, and train the new soldiers.[25] By contrast to the First World War, where limited stateside training was followed by more intensive training overseas, during the period before Pearl Harbor, and even after, the majority of military training was conducted on American soil.

To accommodate the troops, old bases were expanded and new ones were built, and as those bases developed, facilities for an elaborate sports and recreation program were constructed. Five representative military bases demonstrate how these sports sports programs developed. Scott Field in Illinois, Bowman Field in Kentucky, Fort Sam Houston in Texas, Louisiana's Camp Claiborne, and Borinquen Field in Puerto Rico, were all the site of new construction and population growth during 1940 and 1941. This expansion put stresses on the surrounding communities that the respective sports programs at each base were in part designed to alleviate.

As each of the facilities described here expanded, the men and women on the bases and in the towns and cities around the bases were forced to consider their relationship with the growing military. Since everyone wanted to maintain the fiction that the United States was not necessarily preparing for armed confrontation with fascism, an effort was undertaken to make life on the bases as much like civilian life as possible within the constraints of military discipline. The athletic program developed on each base therefore helped to reinforce the similarities between the two worlds, adjacent to, but necessarily apart from one another.

Scott Field, Illinois, was the location for an army radio school and ultimately also served as an important location for flight training. Beginning on February 11, 1941, a base newspaper, the *Scott Field Broadcaster,* devoted itself to describing the changes occurring as the growing army demanded an expansion of the Field's facilities. What the discussion of sports at Scott Field during the following months reveals was the military's struggle to develop through sport an adequate level of physical fitness in all soldiers while providing high-level competition for the most athletically talented. The *Scott Field Broadcaster*'s sports reporters also found themselves faced with the challenge of encouraging sports participation among their fellow soldiers, while at the same time justifying the value of some of the nontraditional sports chosen by Scott Field athletes. Thus they found themselves explaining how the sport of fencing was a masculine sport, the practitioners of which should not be condemned for lacking the manhood to play violent contact sports.

From the very first issue, news about the sports played both on and off the base was an important part of the *Scott Field Broadcaster*. In that issue, writers reported that Scott Field had representatives in eleven of the sixteen finals of the Illinois State Golden Gloves boxing tournament. Although this athletic success directly involved only eleven men on the base, another article in the February 11 issue explained that they had been chosen after an extensive base tournament, involving many more men. Even for those men who did not put on gloves and get into the boxing ring, however, the reporting on the tournament provided an opportunity to place the experience of boxing within the context of the soldiers' larger purpose at Scott Field.

Just as in the First World War, soldiers preparing for the possibility of America's involvement in another war learned about war through the metaphor of sport. Since the men at Scott Field were training for flight, the newspaper used air war metaphors. Thus, that February 11, 1941 article explained how "Scott Field found itself with a bombing squadron of first-flight performance in the persons of a team of highly potent punchers as a result of the post's annual boxing championship tournament."[26]

In the following months, representatives of Scott Field competed not only in state boxing tournaments, but in the Illinois Amateur Athletic Union (AAU) state basketball finals, playing against other independent basketball teams. In the spring, a post track and field meet was held to select an athletics team to compete off of the post against other army teams and against civilian track athletes. During the summer, over one hundred candidates participated in tryouts for the Scott Field baseball team that was scheduled to participate in the local community baseball league.[27] According to Pvt. J. Edgar Kirk, in his column "Sport Pen," Scott Field's AAU basketball championship team gave all men on the post the sense that they were part of a team, but Kirk also noted that the emphasis during the summer of 1941 would be on softball rather than baseball, as it was a game that more men could play.[28]

As Pvt. Kirk's column suggests, despite the success of some post teams, the problem remained of how best to involve everyone in sport, not only because post commanders believed that sport increased physical fitness, but because they assumed that sport also encouraged team spirit. To encourage participation in athletics, particularly after it was discovered that only 15 percent of the soldiers on base were involved in any sporting activities whatsoever, a number of steps were taken at Scott Field during the summer before Pearl Harbor. Clearly, if the military was going to develop morale around athletics, and if manhood was going to be defined by success in sports, more than 15 percent of its troops were going to have to be themselves part of the project of sports.

First of all, the program of athletics was expanded to meet the varied skills and interests of the trainees. Interbarracks volleyball and table tennis tournaments were conducted, and more than three hundred men began working out for the chance to compete on the post track and field team.[29] Furthermore, four new physical training instructors were brought down from Chanute Field to work with the various squadrons and direct athletic activities for novices and beginners as not all young men entering the service had previous sports experience.[30] Yet despite the arrival of the new physical training instructors, in August, Gen. Rush B. Lincoln found on inspection that 85 percent of the Air Corps Technical students at Scott Field were still getting no exercise, neither through sports nor through calisthenics and drill.[31]

In light of this evident disinterest in athletics, other strategies were developed to encourage soldier interest in sport. New facilities were completed, including a football field, twelve hard-court tennis courts, two baseball and eleven softball diamonds, and a fifty-by-fifty-feet swimming pool, along with the bowling alleys built by the post utilities office as a morale section project.[32] To generate maximum participation that autumn bribes and prizes were offered to the members of the winning post softball and baseball teams, as well as the winners of the officers' tennis tournament, with Liggett and Myers providing free cartons of Chesterfield cigarettes to the officers and free packs of Chesterfields to the enlisted men. Apparently all of this effort generated some enthusiasm among the men, who, if they did not participate, did, in the words of Pvt. J. Edgar Kirk, appear to "root for their favorites as long and loudly as if it were the deciding game in an important series."[33]

As Scott Field grew in size, and as more and more men came to Scott Field for their training, the military's sports program served as a mechanism for relieving civilian concerns about the soldiers in their midst. In fact, the people of the St. Louis area were not alone in their anxiety about the strains being placed upon their communities by the presence of so many unattached young men with money to spend and women to meet. Indeed, as the military grew and expanded, Gen. George C. Marshall felt it necessary to invite over two hundred public relations and morale officers to Washington to discuss how best to ensure good military-civilian relations.[34]

One way to alleviate the fear of the new recruits among the local population adopted at Scott Field and at other posts was to invite the men and women of the surrounding communities to watch athletic competitions being conducted on base. Thus, on the one hand, the people of southwestern Illinois were welcomed as spectators for the post track and field meet held in July, 1941. Unlike World War I athletic competitions, this track and field meet offered no special "military" events like grenade throwing, perhaps reflecting the government and military's need to continue to play down the possibility of war in the face of isolationist opposition.[35] On the other hand, civilians were occasionally specifically banned from attending base athletic contests. Thus, outsiders were not permitted at the Joe Louis versus Tony Zale boxing exhibition held on October 11, 1941.[36] That bout was preceded by matches between Scott Field and Jefferson Barracks boxers. Perhaps civilians were not invited because Joe Louis, then at the height of his fame, would have drawn so many fans. Or perhaps civilians were not invited because in this case at least the exhibition's sponsors wanted to create something special for the men in uniform.

Another means of enhancing civilian-military relations resorted to by the commander at Scott Field was to encourage his soldiers to attend community athletic events. Soldiers used the pool at the Turner's Club of Belleville and area golf courses for their recreation as well. And men from Scott Field were invited to the opening days for the St. Louis Browns and St. Louis Cardinals at Sportsman's Park in the City.[37] In November, 1941, just before Pearl Harbor, convoys also transported soldiers from Scott Field to St. Louis for wrestling, boxing, and hockey, while the varsity basketball team left on a fourteen-hundred-mile road trip.[38]

As the number of men on the base grew, there seems to have developed an anxiety about changing definitions of manliness, and how to determine a hierarchy based on masculinity on the post. Sports served as one means of establishing that hierarchy among the soldiers at Scott Field, with those most athletically adept being placed on the so-called varsity teams while others were left to play lower-level sports among themselves. But one individual soldier's athletic success posed special problems.

Captain Fred W. Siebert was a fencer chosen for the 1940 Olympic team that did not compete because the war led to the Games' cancelation. In 1940 he was the national epee champion as well. And Captain Siebert proposed to form a fencing team at Scott Field. Despite the apparent danger and romance of swordplay, most troops at Scott Field apparently concluded that they wanted no part of fencing because they seem to have believed that it was a "sissy" sport. Despite Captain Siebert's national success with the sword, at the end of July, 1941, Pvt. J. Edgar Kirk was still reassuring his readers that if they would only go and watch fencing, they would understand that it was not, as he put it, a sissy sport, but a sport played by men.[39]

The soldiers at Scott Field in 1941 lived on a base in flux. Not only were their numbers rapidly growing, along with the facilities to train and house them. Their relationships with the community around Scott Field and with the men in their military community were also being redefined, with sports helping to ease the transition between civilian and military life.

At Fort Sam Houston, headquarters of the Army's Second Division, a sports and recreation program similar to that at Scott Field was established by 1941. Soldiers training at the Fort were treated to athletic competitions to which they were invited as fans, and were also encouraged to participate in base athletic activities. More than two thousand men attended post boxing bouts in early April, 1941, while the best of the Fort Sam Houston boxers also competed against local civilian boxers. The boxing matches against the Boys' Perpetual Health Athletic Club involved not only the promotion of good military-civilian relations, but also verified that the men of the army possessed "superior" masculinity. As the reporter for Fort Sam Houston's *Spearhead* put it, "Fighters from the Boys' Perpetual Health Athletic Club learned this week that the Army is never down."[40] To further establish the superiority of the army men, twenty-six men from the Fort entered the Texas Amateur Athletic Federation boxing tournament in May. Meanwhile, as was the case with the Scott Field–Jefferson Barracks boxers, fighters at Fort Sam Houston prepared for all-army bouts, fights to which former boxing champion Navy Lt. Comd. Gene Tunney was invited.[41] These all-army bouts were sponsored by the American Legion under the auspices of the National Defense Recreational and Service Committee of San Antonio, a civilian group promoting good military-civilian relations. Significantly, although a civilian group sponsored the boxing matches, the soldiers were trained by their fellow soldiers within the army's own athletic system. This stands in contrast to the sports program conducted during the World War I, when civilian agencies not only organized military athletics, but provided civilian instructors.

Of course, not all soldiers were prepared to commit themselves to becoming boxers, nor even if they had was there time and coaching available to allow mass participation in that sport. Accordingly, at Fort Sam Houston, as at other posts, athletic officers created an ambitious program of mixed athletics. Since Congressional appropriations in 1941 were barely adequate to meet the armament needs of the army, whose soldiers continued to drill with mock-up weapons, the officers at Fort Sam Houston turned to the Red Cross for the funds necessary to purchase needed athletic equipment, including baseballs, softballs, footballs, basketballs, and boxing gloves.[42] Once that equipment became available post baseball and softball leagues were formed, with a six-team round-robin schedule involving a team from each regiment, along with a team from the division artillery, and two teams from the special units. Some of the best players from the post were also selected to represent Fort Sam Houston in the San Antonio City Softball League, where according to *The Spearhead,* they exhibited "exceptionally fine spirit and team-work."[43]

The culmination of the summer's sports activity at Fort Sam Houston were the finals of the post baseball tournament held at Christy Mathewson Field, named for the baseball hero of World War I. As in civilian baseball play-offs, a local dignitary was chosen to throw out the first pitch, with Brig. Gen. Fred L. Walker handling that duty at Fort Sam. Although not every soldier could play in the finals, according to *The Spearhead* the troops did come out to support their favorites.[44]

Later that year, military units at Fort Sam Houston fielded football teams to play each other and to play against local Texas junior colleges. A team from the Fifteenth Field Artillery played the Twenty-third Infantry's team, and then traveled off-base for a game against a civilian team. Local fans were invited to the post games, although they were charged admission, while members of the military got in free. Furthermore, *The Spearhead* announced that an all-star team from the Second Division was to be chosen to play for the Third Army title, with the possibility that the winner would be invited to New Orleans to play in the Sugar Bowl in January.[45]

As at so many military bases before and during World War II, new construction included not only barracks, runways, and other training facilities, but the erection of athletic arenas and fields. At Fort Sam Houston, a new athletic arena was built during the summer of 1941 to accommodate winter sports, especially basketball and boxing. That new arena was designed to have 3,750 seats for boxing and wrestling matches, with seating for 2,750 when reconfigured for basketball.

Even as the U.S. Army was unable to provide each newly inducted soldier with a real training weapon, these efforts at Sam Houston and other bases to provide athletic facilities went forward with no opposition.[46] This suggests the extent to which military planners were convinced of the benefit and value of sports to the men under their command. At Fort Sam Houston, then, a system was created to ensure maximal use of the new sports venues. According to *The Spearhead,* each regiment, battalion, and special unit had a day reserved for their use at the new arena. Significantly, the arena also provided women's rest rooms, thus suggesting that the soldiers would be sharing their space with those civilian women expected to come onto the base and, as wives or dates, watch Fort Sam Houston's athletic competitions.[47] Although few expected American women to be actively recruited into the army and navy in the future, the notion that women had a place beside their men as sports spectators had a long tradition, which was upheld in the new physical space provided for boxing and basketball at the Fort.

At Bowman Field in Louisville, Kentucky, the athletic program conducted during 1941 resembled in many respects the programs at Scott Field and at Fort Sam Houston. Intrasquad baseball and softball tournaments were conducted as a means of keeping the troops occupied, while a base team was created to represent Bowman Field in community and interarmy games. Good military-civilian relations were also encouraged through sports. As *The Bowman Bomber* reported, a trophy was donated to the winner of the Field's intrasquad baseball competition by an anonymous civilian, said to be "interested in the morale of the men stationed at Bowman Field." Furthermore, when the base softball diamond was destroyed in a road-building project, the diamonds at Louisville's Seneca Park were employed for post athletics, affording interested civilians the opportunity to watch the soldiers play. Even admission prices to University of Louisville and local Louisville high school football games were reduced to encourage the men to go out into the community and support civilian athletic activities.[48]

Despite the destruction of Bowman Field's softball diamond, construction was undertaken to create new sports facilities. One new facility was a miniature golf course built by the Fiftieth Bomb Group. Of course, a miniature golf course was not likely to provide the type of strenuous activity deemed necessary for future soldiers. For more physical recreation, a post basketball league was scheduled to begin as soon as fall maneuvers were completed. Furthermore, on the first of December, 1941, *The Bowman Bomber* announced a large-scale training program designed "to utilize fully those recreational and physical conditioning facilities contributing to morale, which will increasingly become available . . . through a selected and competent group of mass exercises and games, athletics, combative contests, aquatic sports, relays and many other items."[49]

At Bowman Field, as at other training sites, athletics served many purposes. Sports helped develop physical fitness and coordination in the troops. Sports also helped maintain morale and esprit de corps. However, by placing sports at the center of each soldier's recreational life, military planners seem to have forgotten about the needs of those men with minimal interest in sports. Rather than bring all of the men on the base into a community based on a common love of sports, this emphasis on athletics may have alienated and marginalized many soldiers who remained unable to embrace that culture.

At Louisiana's Camp Claiborne, 1941 also saw the construction of many new athletic facilities. For one regiment a bare plot of ground was converted to five softball and three baseball diamonds, as well as four tennis courts, four basketball courts, and four badminton courts. In addition, as was the case at Fort Sam Houston, the regiment received two thousand dollars from civilian sources for the purchase of athletic equipment. Each company and detachment in the regiment was expected to have two softball teams, while eight baseball teams in the regiment played to determine which players would be selected to play on the regimental team.[50]

The creators of the athletic program for the Thirty-fourth Division, training that summer at Camp Claiborne, anticipated that a broadly conceived program of sports and recreation would not only promote the general morale of the soldiers but good relations between the soldiers and the civilians in the surrounding communities as well.[51] This program clearly aimed at maximum participation, as the Division's fall football schedule provided for both tackle and touch football leagues. Furthermore, every company, battery and detachment was issued its own footballs so that every one who wanted to play would have that chance. Once the war began touch football was promoted as a less expensive alternative to the contact sport that required, even in the 1940s, elaborate pads and helmets and threatened serious injury on every down. But as early as October, 1941, the presence of seven-man touch teams at Camp Claiborne signaled the military's desire to encourage physical fitness even among those who were uninterested in engaging in full-contact football.[52] To further encourage mass participation, the sports of golf and archery were also offered, as archers from the 133rd competed in the Louisiana State Archery Tournament and golfers from the 34th's artillery units were said to be going directly from the mass athletics program to local golf courses to work on their game.[53]

In contrast to the other bases already considered, a number of African-American units were stationed at Camp Claiborne. The strict segregation that had prevailed in the army during World War I persisted, particularly in the Southern states where Jim Crow laws had not yet been successfully challenged. Although once the war began military athletic teams were occasionally integrated, at Camp Claiborne the military's segregation policy demanded the creation of a separate Negro baseball league, the champions of which were a team from the 367th Infantry. Some of the men of the 367th also participated in boxing competitions, which seemed only appropriate to *The Clarion*'s sportswriter who noted that the "colored" unit had the "example of Joe Louis, Henry Armstrong, and Ray Robinson to draw on."[54] The segregation of troops at Camp Claiborne reflects the casual racism within the military, a racism repeated at Clark Field in the Philippines, where a basketball game between the 745th Ordnance detachment and the Twenty-sixth Cavalry ended in the Ordnance detachment's defeat, as according to the sports reporter for the *Clark Field Prop Wash*, "The speed of our little brown brothers left the Ordnance flatfooted and in the dust."[55]

As the Army expanded, officers needed to establish their authority over the new draftees, and over those members of the National Guard who had been called up and placed under new command.[56] One means of doing so was by ensuring that the officers had a physically commanding presence. *The Clarion* contributed to that process by detailing the athletic experience and physical attributes of the officers it introduced in its pages. Thus, Col. A. C. Ott, Commander of the 125th Field Artillery, was described as a powerful man, being well over six feet tall, who still participated in "the most strenuous forms of sports activity: Tennis, Basketball and rowing."[57] Colonel Anderson of the 185th was also said to be "athletic in type," a tall, solidly built man fond of baseball, football and basketball.[58] If the young men being brought into the army during 1940 and 1941 were sports fans, used to recognizing heroism on the athletic field, then this valorization of the physicality of these officers might have led them to look up to the officers as they admired other sports heroes. But if a young soldier didn't care for sports, there was little in these officers' introductions that would persuade a disinterested soldier that he should follow their lead.

Not all American soldiers and sailors were stationed within the continental United States in 1940 and 1941. In Puerto Rico, the military's establishment included Borinquen Field, headquarters of an Army Air Force bomber wing. In 1941, the soldiers stationed at Borinquen participated in basketball, baseball, and softball tournaments, while playing Ping-Pong on a recreational level. Furthermore, the base champion basketball team competed against a champion team from the navy in the spring of 1941 for the General Daley Trophy.[59]

During that summer the Field's baseball leagues provided an opportunity to establish a hierarchy among the competitors, as distinctions between officers and enlisted men were maintained on the teams. When the officers of the Forty-fourth bomb squad lost to the officers of the Tenth, the *Borinquen Bomber* reported that the officers of the Forty-fourth claimed a moral victory because the Tenth had two enlisted men on their team.[60] Thus, despite efforts to establish the physical superiority of the officer corps, and prove their right to lead by virtue of their physical presence, in claiming a moral victory, the officers admitted that ordinary enlisted men were thought of as more rugged.

As at other bases, teams from Borinquen Field were chosen to represent the Field in local civilian sports competitions and to represent Borinquen in a Puerto Rico Army league. In September, 1941, the *Borinquen Bomber* announced tryouts for a baseball team to compete in the Insular Army League and the Puerto Rico Semi-Pro League. According to the newspaper, especially exceptional baseball players were needed for Borinquen Field's team to be competitive, since the Semi-Pro League served as the winter home of many of the stars of the Negro Professional League.[61]

The Borinquen Field athletic program was designed to ensure that every soldier would find some sort of sport in which he could shine. Thus a number of so-called minor sports were offered alongside the basketball, baseball, and softball competitions. Borinquen Field's twelve-hole golf course accommodated approximately sixty players daily. The minor sport of horseshoes featured an islandwide tournament. Another sport offered was fencing. By contrast to the situation that prevailed at Scott Field, the masculinity of the Borinquen Field fencing enthusiasts was apparently accepted without challenge, especially when the whole fencing team advanced from Class C to Class B in the Insular Fencing Tournament, while Lieutenant Manzo and Staff Sargeant Bradley moved up to A level competition. And the newly acquired table tennis tables allowed the Athletic Department to fulfill its plan, "in all minor sports competition, of giving all troops 'not a small group of specialized and skillful players' the benefit of the Sports Program."[62]

Finally, the Athletic Department at Borinquen Field conducted a series of boxing matches leading to the Borinquen Field Individual Boxing Tournament, held in November, 1941. As Borinquen Field was the base for a bomber wing, we should not be surprised by the metaphorical language used to describe that tournament. According to the *Borinquen Bomber*, "After a month of silence, Borinquen's skies again resounded with the thud of pent-up punching power as boxing once more captured the sports spot-light."[63] The young soldiers training at Borinquen who had never experienced combat and who may in fact have feared how they would react as their planes were caught in the spotlight and came under fire, were being told, as had been the doughboys in France during the previous war, that if they could interpret that experience as being like the experience of sport, they would have nothing to fear.

Despite the military's small size during the 1920s and early 1930s, young officers continued to receive training in how to command for a future war. As they learned how to lead men in combat, they also came to believe that leadership could and should be developed through sports. Later, the expansion of military facilities within the United States and in its territories during 1940 and 1941 posed new challenges to the relationship between the military and the civilian population. The creation of athletics programs at the growing bases helped reassure Americans that military life would not materially alter the attitudes and values of the young men who answered their nation's call to serve and limited conflicts between civilians and those in the armed services. The athletics programs at each post helped shape attitudes about the proper relation between enlisted men and their officers, and between men and women on base as well. They helped to develop and reinforce expectations about masculine behavior, stressing strength, aggressiveness, and competitiveness rather than cooperation. Furthermore, at each post, the struggle to create a large military establishment in peacetime, with inadequate funding and without the dedication of civilian production to military needs, was reflected in the way in which the sports programs were conducted. Finally, the prevailing emphasis on mass participation in sports was consistently undercut by the soldiers' needs to maintain the personal fiction that they were still free to choose to play or to watch others play even though they were caught up in the great mobilization for war.

As the United States approached the shock of Pearl Harbor and full-fledged entry into World War II, both its army and navy had begun to grow. A mechanism for filling the ranks had been put in place with the implementation of a draft, as well as the call to federal service of many National Guard units. Old bases had been expanded while new bases were being planned. Young officers had been prepared to lead their men through the challenges that lay ahead. And a system to provide soldiers and sailors with opportunities for sports and recreation had been developed that would set the standard for the coming years.

5

CREATING THE MILITARY SPORTS MACHINE: SPECIAL SERVICE OFFICERS AND WORLD WAR II

My mother says that she can remember where she was, and what she was doing when she heard the news of the Japanese attack on Pearl Harbor. On the one hand, for her, and for most Americans, the years after that attack, during which America's soldiers and sailors served on every continent in the fight against the Germans and Japanese, brought unprecedented challenges. Unlike the First World War, the new war required not only the mobilization of the civilian work force and the induction of huge numbers of men into the armed forces, but required as well years of continuing sacrifice. This war, like the Civil War, would not end quickly. And unlike previous wars, this war would be truly global, putting literally millions of Americans into countries where they could have never imagined they would be.

The face of the military, and the jobs soldiers and sailors would be asked to do, would also be quite different. This war would be fought not only on the land and ocean surface, but deep beneath the ocean, and most significantly, in the skies of Europe and Asia. And for the first time, substantial numbers of women would openly wear the nation's uniforms.

On the other hand, for the individual soldier or sailor there would be much in this wartime experience that was not dissimilar to that of previous wars. The processes of learning to work as a team and discovering unknown strength, agility, and coordination each member of the military faced were challenges met in earlier conflicts. During the Second World War as well, members of the armed forces benefited from lessons learned during the last world war about how best to develop unit pride and cohesion, avoid boredom, and recognize some common ground from which to approach the task of war.

For this war, the military provided its own athletic officers to instruct and train servicemen and women in sports. They organized competitions on many fronts, and worked to ensure maximum participation. As had occurred during and after World War I, athletic competitions during World War II often involved soldiers and sailors from allied governments. And as happened before, the relative success of athletes from the United States was believed to be a marker of the superiority of the American system. Through the efforts of the athletic officers (AOs), therefore, sports during World War II kept the troops occupied and entertained, and helped develop a common sense that the American athlete, like the American warrior, was superior above all others.

Although the government had instituted the first peacetime draft in 1940, early expectations were that those drafted would serve for a year and then be released. Furthermore, although the navy was actively involved in escorting ships on the North Atlantic before December 7, 1941, the army had attempted to avoid alarming civilians with the extent of the prewar buildup by forbidding soldiers in most cases to wear their uniforms off post.[1] And, despite the growth and expansion of army and navy bases throughout the United States in 1940 and 1941, the focus of industrial preparation for war was on manufacturing the weapons and other materiel to be shipped to Britain and the Soviet Union through the Lend-Lease program. In other words, many in the United States continued to hope that active American participation in the war against fascism could be avoided.

The Japanese attack on Pearl Harbor and the subsequent German declaration of war obviated that hope. The country had to rapidly convert its industries to the manufacture of even more ships, airplanes, guns, tanks, trucks, and military gear. Furthermore, once the United States declared war on Japan and then Germany and Italy declared war on America, the manpower needs of the services expanded quickly. Both draftees and enlistees were thereafter required to serve for the duration of the conflict absent special circumstances. And there were no further attempts to disguise the extent of America's commitment to the war.

Although initial war planning, reflected in the Victory Program of 1941, anticipated the need for 213 army divisions, in the end only 91 divisions were formed, with a peak strength devoted to the ground war of approximately six million men, with an additional two million men serving in the air and support forces. A further four million men spent time in the navy.[2] On average, and by contrast to the military that fought the First World War, the World War II military was disproportionately white, educated and well-off, with African-Americans and European-Americans with the least education and lowest socioeconomic background underrepresented. Despite the upward bias within the military as a whole, and despite the best efforts of infantry commanders to ensure that they would receive the best recruits, the Army Ground Forces

tended to get the least fit, least educated, and, according to the army classification tests, least intelligent of the men who volunteered for service or were made
available through the draft.[3] Physically, soldiers as short as five feet tall, and
weighing only 105 pounds were admitted into the service, extraordinarily low
numbers in light of the 132 pounds the average GI was expected to carry during
the North African landings of 1942. And once in the army the soldiers were
then classified either as fit for general service or as fit only for limited service.[4]

Once in the army, the soldier needed to be trained. During the first two
years of the war, most effort was directed toward whole unit training, especially
at the division level. After the last divisions were activated in August, 1943,
training continued on an individual basis, as new GIs were prepared to be
replacements for the men lost to disease, injury, or combat.[5]

Replacement training especially reflected a change in thinking about how
long it should take to create a soldier. While training for the men of the armies
of eighteenth-century Europe was expected to require years of hard work, by
1940 the army believed it could prepare a man to serve in thirteen weeks.
Although that meant in 1940 that each man received thirteen weeks of basic
training before moving on to combined training in the coordination of the various
weapons of the regiment and division, finally culminating in divisional maneuvers such as those conducted in Louisiana and North Carolina in 1941, once
the various divisions began to move to Europe and the Pacific, new soldiers
would be denied those experiences.[6] And because replacements in many cases
would not have served with their units before entering combat, the problem
of creating loyalty and cohesion among the troops continued to be acute.

As the service primarily faced with the replacement problem, the army
tried to extend the benefits of athletic competition to those units undergoing
initial training to provide them with a cohesive identity and loyalty to their
particular group of buddies. The army also employed athletic competitions as
a means of integrating large numbers of replacements into outfits already in
the field, to bring together those men recovering from combat experiences,
and those men who had not faced that mortal danger. Within the army, the
responsibility for conducting the GI sports and athletic program was assigned
to the Special Services Branch.

Almost immediately after Pearl Harbor, then-Maj. Leon T. David, FA,
who would later serve as chief of the entire Special Services operation in the
Mediterranean Theater, delivered a paper at a Morale Officers' Conference,
detailing his vision of how sports and athletics contribute to soldier morale.
As David pointed out, creating good morale demanded more than entertainments
and should not be confused with soldier morals, rather he defined morale

as "conviction, team play, resolution, tenacity, stubbornness, bravery, [and] heroism."[7] Having said that, he argued that one way to ascertain the state of morale within a command was to look at the amount and quality of athletics in which the troops were engaged.

The belief that men participating in sports and athletics can, through their participation, maintain the high level of fitness and discipline needed in good soldiers of course had a substantial history by 1941. Even before the First World War, men such as Theodore Roosevelt had concluded that athletes made good soldiers. However, what David suggested has broader meaning. The GIs preparing to fight the Germans and Japanese were expected to spend long periods of time in training camps before being sent overseas and entering combat. As with any group of people living under crowded, stressful conditions, they might become frustrated and turn their frustrations on their fellow soldiers. But what if their fellow soldiers were part of their team? And what if their team could express the frustration and stress of its members through organized athleticism?

In David's view, if they could do so, on the one hand, their morale would be improved—especially as the boredom they would surely experience along with the stress and frustration was alleviated by organized activities. On the other hand, the soldier wanting time to himself would find that desire deflected as he was encouraged to spend yet more time with his fellows. Indeed, David and his fellow Special Services officers seem to have assigned a value to activity for its own sake, assuming that the idle soldier was the most likely to get into mischief, become homesick, or brood about the future dangers he faced.

Although Special Services officers were concerned with sports, they had other responsibilities as well. Not only were they required to arrange for athletic competitions, they were also charged with promoting other distractions for the soldiers, organizing the dramatic and ridiculous soldier shows prevalent in every theater of the war as well as other types of recreation and games. To ensure proper training for Special Services officers, a Branch School was held from March 3 to November 21, 1942. Faculty minutes reflect the debate among the trainee officers as to whether they should emphasize sports, free recreation, or mass entertainment as the troops got closer to combat. Furthermore, the training faculty extensively debated whether the Special Service officer should be an athlete himself, or whether he should serve instead in an organizational capacity.[8]

In fact, as the war expanded and the American armies moved overseas, some athletes were assigned specifically as coaches and athletic directors while other athletes served as the "czars" of sports leagues developed through the Special Services program. And in some cases, Special Services officers had no athletic background whatsoever.[9] In all cases, however, the job of providing necessary equipment for sports and games remained that of the Army rather than of civilian welfare agencies as it had during the First World War.

In May, 1942, the army published a *Technical Manual* to be used by Special Services Officers explaining the branch organization and their duties. Special Services was organized into several divisions. One was an Army Institute (providing correspondence courses for the enlisted men), and another was the School for Special Service at Fort George G. Meade, Maryland attended by Maj. Leon T. David and others. Sports and athletics fell under the aegis of the Recreation Section of the Welfare and Recreation Division, which was charged with making plans and studies regarding "athletics, dramatics, soldier singing and miscellaneous recreation activities."[10] Special Services also included the Army Motion Picture Division, a facilities division, an information division and a research division. The *Manual* described the duties of the athletic officers working within the division, and explained the army's rationale for sports.

The athletic officer had many jobs. He was required to coordinate, promote, supervise, and prepare schedules for interunit athletic activities, to care for equipment, fields and facilities, and to manage the division teams when they traveled for outside competition.[11] According to the *Manual,* since the best American soldiers were primarily motivated by their intellectual conviction that they were the best men in the best army in the world fighting for the right cause, and since the best soldiers backed up that intellectual conviction with self-control developed through drill and discipline, a program of sports was crucial to creating the good soldier precisely because sports training also stressed drill and discipline.[12] As soldiers discovered through athletics the value of self-discipline and learned to improve their skills through constant drill, the army believed they would learn how to relate their athletic experience to their military experiences. Since the army was also convinced that the necessary self-control could not be established merely through boring calisthenics, which would not provide that "sense of relaxation or respite from pressure which is essential to esprit de corp," competitive athletics were encouraged.[13]

On the one hand, as Lee Kennett points out in his study of the American GI, army psychologists had determined that an extensive program of sports and athletics would help recreate the culture the soldier had left behind, further raising his morale.[14] On the other hand, those same psychologists failed to recognize that not all soldiers grew up in a culture in which sports and athletics were predominant—and that even if they did not every soldier accepted the values of that culture. Therefore, such broad-based assumptions effectively contributed to the creation of a hegemonic cultural idea within the military that posed the danger of excluding more men than it included in the common enterprise of war. Although sports were fun for large numbers of participants and observers, others were effectively alienated if they did not like sports.

On the one hand, although sports and athletics continued to be emphasized, the army recognized that as the men moved closer to the front their chances to take time for games were likely to be severely limited. Athletic officers were reminded that within individual theaters of operations athletics would not be conducted near the front. On the other hand, they were told to conduct small-unit athletic competitions during maneuvers—particularly where the civilian population could be involved. Furthermore, the *Technical Manual* reiterated that at outlying bases and foreign stations, "nothing should be spared to afford at least temporary playing fields, courts and recreation rooms."[15] And even as the men sailed to war, the athletic officers were told to conduct boxing and wrestling tournaments to "build and sustain competitive interest among troops aboard."[16]

To help the athletic officers in their job, the government purchased sports equipment and distributed it through the Special Services office. In 1943 the War Department contracted for the delivery of four million dollars worth of balls, bats, protective gear, and fishing tackle. According to the post newspaper *Bom Bay Messenger,* each service unit was to receive for every 125 men in its care, "several complete baseball and softball outfits consisting of bats, balls, mitts, gloves and masks; three footballs, two soccer balls, three volleyballs, three sets of boxing gloves, two table tennis sets and small games."[17] This spending for athletic equipment increased as the war progressed.[18]

As might be expected, the military intended sports to be for the benefit of all of the men, rather than a chosen few elite athletes. Accordingly, maximum participation was encouraged, as athletic officer's were reminded that the "development of highly specialized teams will not accomplish this objective."[19] To ensure the greatest participation, the *Manual* suggested that a wide variety of competitive games be undertaken, including basketball, boxing, volleyball, baseball, tennis, and football, although because of its excessive cost traditional American rules football was not recommended for small-unit competitions. Instead, various forms of touch football and six- and seven-man team football were developed during the war, again providing more GIs a chance to play.[20] Furthermore, athletic officers on some bases chose to favor softball over baseball because of the increased safety and decreased cost of the equipment associated with softball. Even in track and field competitions, the expense and danger involved in some sports like the pole vault, javelin, and discus led to their deemphasis.[21]

The purpose of all of this activity was not just to ensure that the men would be ready to fight when called on to do so, but to ensure that during their leisure time they would not be seduced into sexual encounters and contract diseases that might limit their combat effectiveness.[22] Again, the idea that participation in sports would help keep young men pure was not new, dating back at least to the beginning of the century and the Muscular Christianity movement. And, indeed, a man exhausted from a day of training, drill, and sports might be too exhausted to go into town and get into trouble. But even more, this idea suggested that sexuality could be sublimated through athletics, another strenuous physical activity. However, by contrast to the army of World War I, soldiers in the second war had access to new antibiotics, to freely distributed prophylactics, and in some divisions to disease-free prostitutes provided by their commanders.[23] Thus, if athletics failed to keep men's minds off of sex, available sex would be safer than in previous military conflicts.

As time passed and the army gained more experience with the Special Services' program for mass athletics, new instructions were prepared. A revised technical manual appeared in the fall of 1944 that reflected not only the need to continue to provide services for the men in the European and Pacific theaters as the war drew to a close, but also the need to prepare programs for the troops assigned to the occupation of Germany as others were transferred out for the confrontation with Japan. Since the military expected that the final battle on Japanese soil might last into 1946, with the participation of at least two and a half million men, Special Services officers needed to be prepared, not only with the technical knowledge necessary to the fulfillment of their mission, but with the materiel that would allow them to put on the programs as designed.[24]

In practice that meant a renewed emphasis on the importance of team play and competitive sport, as combat soldiers were reconditioned and refreshed before being shipped from Germany to the Pacific. It also meant that soldiers waiting to go home rather than to the Pacific because they had accumulated enough points for discharge were to be treated to exhibitions by soldier and civilian athletic stars.[25] Soldiers without enough points were in an anomalous position. On the one hand, they didn't know in advance that their services in the Japanese invasion would be rendered unnecessary by the atomic bomb. Therefore, they had to stay ready for combat. But on the other hand, many felt their own job was "finished" with the surrender of Germany and that consequently their acquiescence to military discipline was finished as well.

By contrast to the experience before German surrender, when efforts were also made to provide sports entertainment for soldiers close to the front, men waiting for discharge were assured that their enjoyment of sports would be not be interrupted by the intrusion of the war. This had occurred for example in Italy when Darrel Holland and his friends had to leave a Joe Louis boxing match to attend to the needs of pilots returning from a bombing mission.[26] But combat troops did have to stay prepared for a fight with Japan should the troops in the Pacific be unable to force the Japanese to quit. Therefore, the GIs stuck in Europe were expected to participate in sports and athletics as they had done during earlier training in the United States. Also, those few soldiers planning a return to a professional career in sports after the war were provided with special guidance and training.[27] Thus, as was the case after the First World War, the military provided opportunities for soldiers and sailors to watch or participate in sports while waiting to go home in the aftermath of World War II.

Like its predecessor, the new *Technical Manual* emphasized the need to involve all soldiers in a balanced program of sports and athletics, while also meeting their recreational needs with music and books. The *Manual* stressed three goals to be met through athletics. The first was to create an esprit de corps, as "with the exception of military accomplishments, nothing creates more pride in an outfit than success on the playing field."[28] The sports program was also expected to keep the men physically and mentally fit and provide spectator appeal to those observing the games. These three goals were not necessarily in conflict, and indeed seem to have been intended to catch up every soldier in the sporting life. According to the *Manual,* unit cohesion would be promoted as each individual man in the unit either played for the glory of his "team" or cheered on the other men of his team to victory, proving that his outfit deserved loyalty because it was the best. As Katherine McCrone suggests in her study of sports spectatorship among women, people watching sports receive a demonstration of heroic behavior to which they should aspire—and to which they presumably owe loyalty.[29] In this case, the inspiration provided by athletic heroism on the field was presumed to encourage all men to strive to achieve their own high level of physical fitness—as the military intended.

But by contrast to the earlier *Technical Manual,* the September, 1944 edition recognized that for many men athletics were an alien and unfamiliar enterprise. Previous assumptions about the level of interest and skill in sports that most men had achieved before joining the service were apparently no longer being made, perhaps because experience had demonstrated that in fact many men coming into the army had no previous athletic experience whatsoever. This time the athletic officer's job was more broad-based, as he was to be sure to make beginners welcome, introduce less well known sports and games rather than force men who did not enjoy football, baseball, basketball, or other major sports to play them, and offer special incentives to get the men involved. Even with those men who had enjoyed certain sports before and wanted to play those sports while overseas, the AO was reminded that if he failed to organize competitions properly, the "men will engage in impromptu play and boredom will quickly follow."[30]

But what might cause this boredom? Perhaps the athletically competitive soldier needed the spark of reward and recognition to feel that the sports he played were real or important like the sports he played before joining the service—a validation he would not receive through impromptu play. Thus, the affirmation of the importance of sports created through military organization kept athletics from being mundane. An athletic season featuring a regular schedule, record-keeping, publicity, and championship competition was the kind of athletic season to which the competitive soldier had become accustomed before joining the armed forces and absent that the games he played seemed boring. Besides stressing the need to involve all GIs in sports, and to provide competitions like those the soldiers had known in civilian life, the new *Technical Manual* recognized that the army now had troops stationed all over the globe, and suggested that the AOs might want to schedule ice skating, ice hockey, tobagganing, and skiing where the climate was suitable for those activities, as was already being done for the soldiers and sailors stationed in Alaska.[31]

Although sports and athletics had certainly been accepted as crucial to the formation of men's characters and physical bodies earlier in the century, the military envisioned a much more inclusive and compulsory program than that of the first war. To that end, in July, 1944, Lt. Gen. Brehon Somervell, commander of the Army Service Forces, authorized the award of trophies to the stateside installation having the highest soldier-civilian sports participation, and to the service command, company, and post champions in each sport.[32]

Recognizing that the award of trophies might not be enough incentive, the 1944 *Technical Manual* anticipated that sometimes, in some cases, soldiers would have to be coerced into sports. According to the *Manual,* no soldier should be exempted from the obligation to box in company competitions. Despite the risk of injury and the anxiety such a requirement engendered in those who didn't want to get into the ring, those who wrote the *Manual* asserted that experience had shown "that boxing contributes greatly toward building a good soldier [as it creates a] sense of confidence and self-assurance [that] carry over to bayonet and hand-to-hand fighting, the development of quick, decisive thinking and the practice of carrying on under physical stress and pressure . . . ."[33] Even though the army recognized by 1944 that not all soldiers came into the service interested in or capable of athletic achievement, and that not all soldiers wanted to play the major sports, the army still believed that boxing was so useful to the creation of military skills that all GIs should be required to pull on the boxing gloves that the military provided. In this, the *Technical Manual* revealed the tension between the ideal soldier and the real ones with which the athletic officers had to deal on a daily basis.

Although the *Technical Manuals* afforded army athletic officers an overview of their obligations and duties, no manual, and no amount of training, could adequately prepare them for the challenges they would face while in that position. However, the career of M. Sgt. Zeke Bonura, athletic officer for the soldiers stationed at Oran in Algeria during 1943 and 1944, provides a case study of the ways in which at least one AO tried to keep the men for whose athletic contests he was responsible fit and entertained. The Oran edition of *Stars and Stripes,* which began publication there on May 3, 1943, by devoting at least one page in every issue to sports (with the exception of the D-Day "Invasion" special), suggests the extent to which sports permeated the lives of the men stationed in North Africa.[34] And the enormous amount of time given to detailing the work of Master Sergeant Bonura suggests the extent to which he was able to comply with his mission to bring sports into the lives of the men of Oran.

Zeke Bonura had played first base for the Chicago White Sox and New York Giants before entering the army. But the athletics programs that he and his Navy counterpart, Lt. (jg) John L. Sullivan, the officer in charge of Navy Welfare and Recreation at the Arzew naval base, put together were by no means limited to that sport.[35] Indeed, according to the *Stars and Stripes,* every type of sport was played in North Africa during the war, with basketball, volleyball, softball, touch football, and, yes, baseball, leading the way. For those interested, track meets were also scheduled.[36] And organizing and scheduling competitions in each of those sports was Zeke Bonura.

Of course, Zeke Bonura could not rest once he had arranged for games to be played and sports leagues to be formed. He also had to ensure interesting competition. To that end he conducted a baseball school in May, 1944, for all men from the army and navy intending to play in that summer's Mediterranean Base Section Army Baseball League. Besides giving individual players instruction in the game, Bonura also called on those wishing to umpire to come out and learn more before the season began.[37]

Finally, Bonura helped organize the major athletic events of each season, designed to draw together the soldiers and sailors stationed throughout North Africa as fans to watch the best teams play in championship competition. Thus, Bonura helped arrange for a North African World Series between baseball teams from various stations including Casablanca and Oran—and he arranged for the winners to receive appropriate prizes, such as the baseballs autographed by General Eisenhower, presented to the Casablanca Yankees by Col. Leon T.

David, at that time the Special Services Chief of NATOUSA.[38] Then in March, 1944, Bonura ordered the construction of new stands in the basketball hangar to accommodate the thousands of fans expected to watch the Mediterranean Base Section Basketball Championships.[39] But perhaps M. Sgt. Zeke Bonura's greatest triumph was the successful staging of the Arab Bowl on January 1, 1944.

The Arab Bowl was one of the several mock "bowl" games staged on American bases during the war, from the Poi Bowl in Hawaii, to the Lily Bowl in Bermuda, to the January 1, 1945 Spaghetti and Mustard Bowls in Florence, Italy and Dijon, France respectively, to the proposed Christmas Day, 1944, Champagne Bowl, scheduled to be held in Northern France, but fated to be canceled due to the German breakthrough in the Ardennes.[40] These games, typically involving teams of Navy and Army All-Stars, or championship aggregations from the individual services, provided an opportunity for the men and women serving overseas to recall the way of life for which they were ostensibly fighting. Thus, the organizers tried to duplicate as closely as possible the atmosphere of the traditional New Year's day bowl games, providing in the case of the Spaghetti Bowl, for example, floats, bands, and hot dogs for the spectators. Also like the bowl games back in the United States, the competitions tended to draw huge numbers of fans to the games, with a crowd of at least twenty-five thousand attending the January 1, 1945 Poi Bowl.[41]

To ensure the Arab Bowl's close resemblance to other New Year's Day games, M. Sgt. Zeke Bonura arranged for the game to be played, for the necessary publicity to create interest in the game, for the bands that would play before and during the game, for cheerleaders, and, in the case of North Africa's Arab Bowl, for the presence of bowl queens. The Arab Bowl queens were drawn from the ranks of the Women's Army Corps (WACs) stationed in the area, and from the Red Cross, as was the case with Ann Goplerud, a Red Cross worker in Casablanca who traveled to Oran with the Casa Rabchasers for the game.[42] Of course, no one believed that the game could completely capture the atmosphere of the games being played back in the United States, especially since the Arab Bowl featured members of the Women's Army Corps competing in camel races beforehand, but Bonura did want the men and women of North Africa to feel that they were engaged in an important and necessary demonstration of American life. To that end, the Fighting Irish of Notre Dame were invited to participate, although the Rev. James J. Cavanaugh, the faculty chair at the university, had to report that the team would be unable to do so.[43]

Lest no one doubt it, *Stars and Stripes* stressed again and again the importance of the game to the GIs in North Africa, noting on December 31, 1943 that the Arab Bowl was being "hailed far and wide by sports enthusiasts as the biggest sports extravanganza projected thus far in the current war by members of America's Armed Forces overseas."[44]

But how did the individual soldiers and sailors who attended, or chose not to attend the game, feel about it? Apparently, the members of the 601st Ordnance Battalion thought the New Year's day festivities were an important part of their wartime experience. While undergoing training at Camp McCoy, Wisconsin, they had read that Coach Harry Stuhldreher of the University of Wisconsin believed that there was a direct parallel between football and warfare, and that the "stamina, teamwork, and coordination football men are getting on the gridiron will help make them better soldiers."[45] Knowing that, they apparently enthusiastically supported the Arab Bowl, making a point of preserving the program from the game and donating it as part of their unit memoirs to the Military History Institute. And having apparently enjoyed the game, members of the 601st Ordnance Battalion dedicated themselves to being even better football players in the future, and achieved that goal, as a team from the battalion was chosen to represent the army at the Mustard Bowl the next year.[46]

The extent to which M. Sgt. Zeke Bonura did his work in ensuring that the soldiers of North Africa remained fit and committed to their mission is reflected in the Legion of Merit he received for the success of the region's baseball program and the accomplishment of the Arab Bowl festivities.[47] And the importance his superiors placed on the successful sports program at Oran is also reflected in the award he received.

During and after the First World War, the army's sports programs included competitions between soldiers representing the United States and competitors from other of the allied armies. A similar program of competition between American soldiers and sailors and allied troops was instituted in World War II. Where troops trained together, as was the case with Navy and RAF pilots in Florida, and where they fought side by side, ample opportunities existed for friendly games. Of course, as was the case three decades earlier, American sports enthusiasts anticipated competitions in their own national games such as baseball and basketball, while the British in particular wanted to play soccer instead of football games in the American style. As had been the case before, where sports reflected different styles of play or different methods of achieving success, those differences were believed to reflect differences in national values. This would be the case with boxing and wrestling.

During the Second World War there was constant friction between the British and American commanders in those areas where their armies fought side by side. By the time the Rhine River was finally crossed, this friction had resulted in many incidents in which American soldiers expressed their disdain for the British leaders and for the troops under their command, while the British also questioned the ability of American soldiers to fight when they were required to do so.[48] The conflict between British tommies and American GIs was played out in many arenas, not the least of which was that of athletics, as each struggled to prove their nation's superiority.

Where the British and Americans were not directly involved in combat, they often found time for athletic competitions against each other. This was the case in Bermuda, where the men stationed at Fort Bell challenged other American soldiers on the island, as well as forces of the British Empire, to prove that the Bell men were not the "best fistmen on the Islands."[49] The news that army boxers had triumphed over the men of the Royal Navy was the lead story in the July, 1943, *B.B.C. News.*[50] And in North Africa, the British, French, and American soldiers and sailors stationed in the region kept up a constant round of competitions against each other, in boxing and track especially.[51] Since Marcel Cerdan, the future world champion, was stationed at Oran as a member of the French Navy, many representatives of the U.S. Army and Navy came forward to challenge him, and those matches were heavily promoted in the *Stars and Stripes* as an opportunity to demonstrate American manhood—despite Cerdan's continued success in the ring. As one writer for the *Stars and Stripes* put it, explaining why S. Sgt. Jim Toney had been placed on special duty to train for his match, Toney's commander "realizes that the hopes of thousands of American servicemen will be riding on him when he enters the ring Sunday afternoon."[52] That a soldier like Toney was taken away from his other duties to prepare for the boxing showdown with Cerdan suggests the importance the military authorities were placing on the outcome of the match. Even as Toney and others failed to defeat Cerdan, no one questioned whether national pride should be invested in the fortunes of a number of boxers. Indeed, despite the needs of the military to keep as many men as possible in readiness for service duties, time, money, and prestige continued to be committed to demonstrating the superiority of America's men under arms not on the battlefield, but in the arena.

The North African contests were followed by a series of Inter-Allied competitions held in stadia from Oran to Rome, where the former Mussolini Stadium, renamed Il Foro D'Italia, played host to an Inter-Allied track and field meet promoted by Col. Leon T. David, Allied Sports Commission Chairman, assisted by officers from the British and the French Armies.[53] For the athletes participating in that meet, the opportunity to compete, plus the opportunity to travel from their home bases to that famous city must have been quite attractive. And for the citizens of Rome, having recently welcomed their American and British liberators, the meet must have provided entertainment and relief from the generally quite wretched conditions of wartime Italy. But the meet was intended to provide not just entertainment and respite from the war, it was also about demonstrating American prowess to liberated and allied alike, as soldiers and sailors from the United States demonstrated their excellence on the floor of the stadium.

Because World War II was fought and serviced all over the globe, American athletes found themselves competing in their respective sports in many unlikely locations. And in so doing, they showcased the special ability of soldiers from the United States to make and break records on the track and in the field. Both *Yank,* and local post newspapers, provided a constant update on the exploits of the best athletes. They included Lt. Earle Meadows, the 1936 Olympic pole vault champion, who as a Special Services officer stationed at the Fourteenth Air Force headquarters set a Chinese pole-vault record of fourteen feet even, M. Sgt. Vince King, who set India's high jump record at a meet in Calcutta, and Private Nevius of the Coast Artillery who broke Bermuda's high jump record at the 1943 Bermuda Athletic Association (BAA) track and field championships.[54] Each of these provided their international audiences during the war an object lesson of the superiority of the American man when faced with a challenge, as had the successful athletes of the United States during and after the First World War.

Although Special Services officers were provided soccer balls to introduce the men in their outfits to the game, whether Americans could or should play soccer remained an issue throughout the war—particularly as it was believed to be a sport of the British. Some soccer promoters in the United States such as Erno Schwarz, player-manager of the New York Americans soccer club, maintained a correspondence with over a hundred GI soccer players, and hoped that Americans serving in Britain would be converted to the game. Similarly, men who had played soccer in the past organized games on their own when the opportunity presented itself, as was the case with Sgt. Manuel Centanio, who put together four GI teams while serving in Egypt to play in a six-team league that included two teams of Chinese players.[55] Soccer was also used as a means of promoting friendship between the Western allies and the Soviets, with the Red Army's soccer team, made up of soldiers who had seen action on the Eastern Front, touring British bases in the months before the Normandy invasion.[56] But for most Americans in the service soccer remained a slightly alien game, useful only when they needed to establish their preeminence over the British, as was the case at Pensacola. According to *Gosport,* Pensacola's sailors learned soccer so they would be rugged enough to take on the British flyers stationed there for training.[57]

Those British pilots stationed at Pensacola seem to have been involved in every aspect of the local sports program. Men of the Royal Air Force (RAF) and Royal Navy competed in the base swimming meet, and managed to win several events. They also formed a softball league, and announced plans to enter an all-star squad of their best players in the station's Wildcat League. Finally, two teams from the British flight detachment played a demonstration cricket match one Sunday afternoon to promote the sale of war bonds. Thus, the commitment to demonstrating the superiority of national sport and national sportsmen worked both ways. Even as American soldiers were demonstrating their national games in London, the British were showing Floridians how cricket should be played—and, according to *Gosport,* printing up "mimeographed sheets explaining the origin, object, penalties and other pointers" about the game.[58]

As might be expected, the belief that a nation's most popular sport reflected that nation's culture and character led many Americans to distinguish between their sports and the national sports of their enemies, particularly the Japanese. Since World War II was a war not only against fascism, but was a war in which special bitterness was directed against the Japanese as the aggressors who had drawn the United States into the war, and since the Japanese were racially unlike the majority of Americans, it became very important to demonstrate American superiority not just on the battlefield but in the games Americans played.[59] The question therefore became whether soldiers and sailors from the United States could benefit in any way from learning Japanese sports, particularly judo, or as it was more commonly characterized during the war, "jujitsu."

To answer that question, military experts asked whether judo was superior to boxing or wrestling and whether it might help the soldier or sailor in combat when faced with a Japanese enemy presumably skilled in the sport. On some bases, such as Fort Chaffee and Hammer Field, and on some Naval Air Stations, judo classes were held for soldiers interested in the sport. As Cpl. Frank Incantalupi argued, jujitsu was superior to boxing when it came to killing an opponent.[60] But most experts agreed that boxing and wrestling were superior to the Japanese sport as both a defensive and offensive weapon. After all, the army was full of boxers who had no fear of hitting and being hit and who were perfectly willing to bend the rules in order to win. This was a point that was drive home even in movies like *Stage Door Canteen* in which the heroine Jean read a letter from her marine brother in which he said that a "good round-house right" was far superior to any Japanese jujitsu.[61] But for the average GI or sailor about to go into combat against their Asian enemies, the most encouraging news must have been that in *Yank,* which asked, "If the Japanese are supposed to be so skilled at Judo, how do you account for the fact that an American Judo team won 20 of 29 matches while touring Japan in 1935? Or the fact that the Japs hired an American, Ray H. Moore, now a Seabee CPO to coach their 1932 Olympic team?"[62] Having read that, the sailor or GI must have been reassured that regardless of his own skill at the so-called Japanese sport, there were Americans capable of defeating the enemy even in his national sport, and, he hoped, in battle.

And, of course, America's own national game taught its players some skills crucial to their future military success. At least that was said to be the case with baseball. As the Armored Forces newspaper *Armodier* pointed out, "American men have always been better at grenade-throwing than the youth of other nation's because of their ball-tossing background."[63] Since the Yankee soldier was presumed to have spent the better part of his childhood playing baseball, he was presumed to have an advantage when it came to throwing a grenade at the enemy, and where he didn't, special instructions were made available, both in the sport, and in the military skill, to ensure that he would when he needed them.[64]

Although the American military had a great deal of work to do in building up forces and materiel to fight after the Pearl Harbor attack, ideas about how to provide for soldier and sailor entertainment were well developed by 1941. Special Services officers were trained to lead military sports and athletics programs and equipment was purchased to facilitate that process. Throughout the world, soldiers and sailors fought and played, thanks to their athletic officers. And the old belief that superiority in sports reflected cultural and national excellence had a rebirth during World War II.

6

STRONG MEN, STRONG BODIES, OFF TO WAR, 1941–1945

By the beginning of 1942, the U.S. military was well on the way to providing for the welfare of the millions of soldiers and sailors ready to enlist or be drafted for the duration of the war. Sports and athletics were to be an important part of that welfare effort. Rather than rely on civilian agencies, as had been done during World War I, this time athletic officers drawn from the services would be in charge. The military trained those officers, bought needed equipment, and sent them wherever service men and women congregated to do their job. The question then becomes, what difference did this program of sports and athletics mean to the individual in uniform?

According to Lee Kinnett, one of the hallmarks of the GI attitude during World War II was the soldiers' conviction that despite being a part of the military they were civilians at heart. They distinguished themselves ideologically from their enemies, believing that unlike the soldiers of Germany or Japan, they did not belong to the state. To that end, they tried as much as possible to maintain civilian ways in their daily lives, arguing that there were only a limited number of hours each day that belonged to the army. Because of this attitude, officers had to find their own styles of leadership, and to find unique ways to reinforce their authority in noncombat situations.

Furthermore, they had to counter the desire of the men under their command to be left alone when not in training. Indeed, the notion that American soldiers were civilians first and part of the military second was crucial to the rhetoric of the war, as citizen-soldiers from the United States encountered German and Japanese men who they believed had no life outside of the military and had given up their individual autonomy in the service of the state.[1]

Because many soldiers of the United States believed that as representatives of American democracy they had no obligation to maintain rank or distinction, they often struggled against the distinctions the armed forces created between enlisted men and officers. Yet the military remained committed to hierarchical leadership. Therefore, the army's sports program was designed in part to distinguish between officer and enlisted man and to maintain those distinctions even at the considerable expense involved in building separate athletic facilities, as was also the case with facilities separating European-American from African-American soldiers and sailors.[2] Quite often this meant the creation of separate enlisted men's and officer's leagues, or the restriction of play between teams of officers and enlisted men to championship games.[3] Similarly, as Harry Pruzan of the Tenth Mountain Division found, while the Division was training at Camp Hale horses for off-duty recreation were given to the officers, but not the enlisted men.[4]

The creation of different competitions for enlisted men and officers also occurred with navy sports, as the programs conducted at stateside Naval Air Stations included separate tournaments in sports such as tennis for the enlisted men and for the officers.[5] In other cases, enlisted men were welcomed to participate in tournaments only toward the end of the war. Thus, for example, as the *Armodier* reported in September, 1944, an upcoming golf tournament was to include for the first time enlisted men. Meanwhile, at the Pensacola Naval Air Station, the local golf course was opened to enlisted men on a limited basis. Similarly, a bowling tournament held at Cochran Field was opened not only to officers and enlisted men, but also to officers' wives (and not to the wives of enlisted men?) as well as civilian base personnel. But the competition for the officers' wives was scheduled on a different day and at a different time than the competition for the other players. And during 1944, the Lawrenceville, Illinois and Vincennes, Indiana country clubs were opened to NCOs, with enlisted men ultimately being allowed to participate in tournaments against local golfers.[6]

Distinctions between officers and enlisted men were also maintained when it came time to determine ticket prices for base and off-base athletic events. Thus, officers' tickets for a football game between the Navy and the University of Alabama cost $2.50 while enlisted men had only to pay 55¢.[7] Of course, on the one hand, officers did make more money than the men, so differences in ticket prices may have been intended only to allow even the least-paid to attend the event. On the other hand, if the difference in the price of the tickets also meant a difference in the location and quality of the seating, enlisted men were being asked to sit where their presumably inferior status could be confirmed.

Even where the men played together on the same team, their place in the hierarchy was often reinforced by placing limits on the numbers of officers and enlisted men that could make up a team. At Camp Chaffee, for example, the team chosen to represent the camp at the Eighth Service Command's golf tournament was made up of four enlisted men and only one officer.[8] This reflected the War Department regulation that "All football, baseball, basketball, and soccer teams organized in the army will normally be composed of enlisted men. No more than one officer will be permitted on any such team at any time in any game."[9] At Pensacola, a rule for navy athletics seems to have paralleled that for the army, since teams competing for the Commandant's Cup were allowed to have only two officers, with but one allowed to compete at any one time.[10]

Both services accomplished a number of things by restricting the number of officers allowed to play on an enlisted man's team. In the first place, if sports were intended to create group loyalty among the enlisted men in individual organizations, whether they played on a team, or watched the team play, keeping officers from dominating such teams helped promote that group loyalty. Furthermore, since officers were expected to maintain a distance, and to exercise control over the enlisted men, the presence of officers on enlisted men's teams, and in their tournaments, threatened to reduce the effectiveness of the officers' command.

At Cochran Field, the organizers of the base tennis tournament contrived a novel way to ensure the participation of enlisted men. According to the announced rules, although officers would be eligible to play in singles matches, at least one member of every doubles team would have to be an enlisted man. As it turned out, the doubles' title would be won by Lt. Col. Allen D. Smith and Pvt. Dan Roberts, the highest and lowest ranking pair of players in the tournament, although Roberts did happen to be a former Canadian tennis champion despite his lowly military rank.[11]

But perhaps the most compelling example of the self-consciousness with which enlisted men and officers interacted through sports is in the story repeated in *Bom Bay* about an incident from the Aberdeen Proving Grounds. According to this "Laff of the Week," an officers' basketball game was interrupted toward the end of a period by the referee's whistle. What was so funny about that? The referee was an enlisted man who was reported as saying, "One more trick like that and I'll throw you out of the game—SIR!"[12] With that "Laff" and with the similar "Laff" reported in the *Armodier* describing a boxing match as the only place where a private could beat up a sergeant and get away with it,[13] GIs were provided with the satisfaction of knowing that they might prevail over those imposing military discipline. But they were also reminded that that could only happen within the confines of an athletic competition. In other words, the enlisted men were allowed under such limited circumstances to express their resentment of authority.

Since most GIs believed themselves to be civilians at heart, they seem to have enjoyed their opportunities to get off of their posts and bases and interact with the local people. But although they were subject to military discipline, in most cases they were far from their own homes and family structures. Consequently, they faced unusual difficulties when visiting in adjacent towns and cities. This was particularly true in the South, where those people living near to the base were not anxious to have their traditional ways of life disrupted by "Yankee" soldiers and sailors. And, of course, this was even more true when African-American soldiers and sailors from the North brought what many Southern whites believed to be their uppity ways into their communities.[14] Finally, there were concerns about the sexual dangers posed by the presence of so many new, unattached young men on the streets where local girls might meet them.

As they had during the First World War, sports became one way of providing contact between the military and civilian populations in a safe, controlled way. To that end, military teams played civilian teams both on base and off. Individual servicemen joined local leagues and played on local teams. And civilians accepted invitations onto bases to see games between military teams. That commanders and the troops in their command were not unaware of the value of such contacts is illustrated not only by the enormous breadth of military-civilian athletic contacts, but by specific examples of the reasoning behind such contacts. When the sportswriter for *Armodier* noted with approval the presence of several soldiers in the bowling leagues of Fort Smith, Arkansas, he pointed out that the "bowling lanes not only furnish good exercise but are also an excellent place for the service man to meet his civilian neighbor."[15]

Some sports programs at places like Fort Chaffee, George Field, Hammer Field, and the Pensacola Naval Air Station were designed specifically to let the serviceman meet his neighbor. One especially important component of such programs was to get the post teams out into the community, especially after gasoline and tire rationing began to have an effect on the ability of civilians to travel.[16] To that end, army basketball, baseball, softball, and football teams often arranged to play in local gymnasiums or on local fields.[17] And in the case of the Seventh Army Air Force's baseball team, the team traveled from Oahu to Hilo on the big island of Hawaii to play a game said to have drawn most of the civilian population of that island.[18]

Although many of those competitions involved soldier or sailor teams, military teams also met civilian teams from surrounding communities on their home fields and played in local bowling and softball leagues.[19] These games sometimes served as community fund-raisers as with the Father's Day double-header held at Fort Smith involving competitions between the 259th FA Mustangs and the Paris Miners and the 174th IR Buffaloes and the Fayetteville Merchants, which was promoted by the Chamber of Commerce.[20] In other cases, such contests helped raise money for soldier and sailor relief funds.[21]

In many cases, community leaders invited soldiers and sailors to watch athletic contests off base. Such invitations often provided for reduced cost admission for the men and women in uniform. Similarly, local institutions such as the YMCA allowed servicemen into their clubs at certain times for free. Finally, interested civilians occasionally provided uniforms to the military teams. This was the case with a gift of uniforms by Cliff Case, owner of the Trenton, New Jersey Packers of the Interstate League who also arranged for free admission to Packer games for servicemen. Similarly, the Buffalo Bisons of the American Association sent uniforms to the 174th IR Buffaloes.[22] Civilians also donated golf clubs to the participants in the National Armed Services Open held at San Angelo, Texas in November, 1943.[23] Since it was not unknown during the war for those who did not have loved ones in the service to "adopt" individual soldiers and sailors to whom they would write for the duration, and since the GIs wanted to feel as connected to the civilian community as possible, these sports related contacts between military and nonmilitary people provided another mechanism to maintain a sense of joint responsibility in the face of war. Furthermore, by contributing to the success of the military's sports program, civilians were able to express their patriotism and support for the soldiers and sailors in their communities.

Local people were also invited onto posts and bases to watch contests involving civilians as well as military men and women. At Camp Chaffee a crowd of more than two thousand five hundred soldiers and civilians watched a boxing tournament in June, 1943. The following month the boys who had played American Legion baseball in Fort Smith, Arkansas were invited to Chaffee to eat army food and fire machine guns on the range. And sailors from the Pensacola Naval Air Station traveled to Fort Barrancas to box army fighters and fighters from the Pensacola YMCA in front of a large and enthusiastic crowd. In these cases, the civilian guests were being exposed to military life in a controlled way in order to alleviate the tensions Camp Chaffee and the Naval Air Station may have been generating in the local communities. By associating military life with civilian athletic pursuits, the message was driven home that the men in uniform were just like the townsfolk.[24]

The breadth and depth of the sports programs conducted by the army and navy within the United States is reflected both in the amount of space dedicated in post and unit newspapers to reporting on the contests, and also in the extent to which servicemen participated in the country's sporting life even while in uniform. Soldiers and sailors boxed in state and national Amateur Athletic Union (AAU) and Golden Gloves tournaments.[25] Swimmers from both services appeared in national AAU swim meets.[26] Army and navy golfers competed in local professional and amateur tournaments, while army basketball players were voted to all-state teams.[27] And the softball team from Hammer Field won the American Amateur Softball Association national title in September, 1943, in a game played before five thousand in Detroit.[28]

Soldier and sailor teams not only met college teams in basketball, but in football as well.[29] Most spectacularly, base football teams regularly played against top collegiate teams in games having national significance, such as the Great Lakes Naval Training Station's victory over Notre Dame at Soldier Field in Chicago, or the Randolph Field team's appearance in the Cotton Bowl.[30] In fact, the Randolph Field team attained the number one national ranking in October, 1944, edging out the football team from Purdue University.[31]

Nonetheless, all of these competitions were not without cost in terms of time lost to training by the military athletes and in terms of civilian doubts about the use of precious fuel transporting the athletes from one competition to another.[32] Indeed, the Hammer Field Raiders' softball team came very close to missing the national championships because their trip from California to Detroit lacked official sanction until the last minute.[33] Similarly, the Pensacola Naval Air Training Station dropped its football team for the fall of 1943 because in the words of Lt. Comdr. George Clark, base athletic officer, "While football is an excellent conditioner and one of the best competitive sports in any physical training program, it takes too many hours away from aviation training."[34] And as the preparations for the Normandy invasion heated up, off-base competitions at places like Drew Field and MacDill were canceled altogether for the troops to devote their entire attention to training.[35]

Perhaps reflecting nonsports related military-civilian tensions, soldiers argued sometimes that they were being treated unfairly in contests with civilian teams. As Pvt. Owen Smith suggested in his "Down the Middle" column for the *Bomb Bay Messenger,* "It has become an axiom that a soldier has to win all the way in order to get an even break from a civilian official."[36] Similarly, the sportswriter for the *Cochran Communique* expressed surprise that the base Medics' softball team, which won two games in the Macon League, received a favorable review in local newspapers.[37]

Both members of the military and civilians argued over the value of sports to the soldier and sailor training for war. Certainly, many accepted without question the need for soldiers and sailors to play sports for what they could do in preparing for combat. As the *Bom Bay* suggested in October, 1942, flyers should train for combat just as if they were training for a football or basketball game—or build up their bodies boxing in preparation for the "big tussle with Herr Hitler."[38] Thus, the analogy between sport and war went both ways— soldiers and sailors were enjoined to train for athletics as if they were training for war, and to train for war using the techniques of sport.

Yet there continued to be those who believed that sports were of no help in preparing for war. This debate became even more intense when large numbers of professional or high-performance amateur athletes began to join the service. Although early in the war President Franklin D. Roosevelt guaranteed the major professional baseball leagues the right to continue operations, as a means of keeping up civilian morale, the place of apparently healthy athletes on civilian teams was regularly questioned by those in or near combat.[39]

This conflict came to a head in a widely heard radio debate between base- ball executive Larry MacPhail and Stanley Frank of the *New York Post.* According to Frank, baseball men were hypocritical in arguing for the continuation of the national game because of its importance to the men overseas. He also argued that those who believed previous athletic training, especially in college football, was crucial to military success were wrong, as such training had been shown to be of no help in combat.[40] Although some GIs supported Frank, including the "Two College Men" who pointed out in a letter to *Yank* that servicemen only talked about baseball when they wanted to condemn those playing civilian sports and not fighting the war, other *Yank* readers apparently rejected Frank's opinions.[41]

A close analysis of the post and base newspapers published from 1941 through 1945 reveals the enormous attention paid to civilian sports. Those newspapers carried regular updates on the fortunes of professional teams, as well as the fortunes of professional players who were now in the army or navy, as did *Yank,* the soldiers' newspaper, and *Stars and Stripes,* which during World War I had canceled its sports page as the doughboys were drawn into combat during the summer of 1918. For example, *Yank's* story about the battle for Tunisia described how the First Division adopted the Brooklyn Dodgers as "their" team and how they continued to follow the team during the Sicilian campaign. *Yank* also carried a story about "A B-24 outfit in the VII Bomb Group in Burma- India known as 'Cronin's Kids' because they all wear Red Sox baseball caps." Again, in wearing a part of the uniform of their favorite civilian team, the B-24 crew demonstrated that they still believed themselves to be civilians even in the midst of war. And *The Bomb Bay* carried a report from Sergeant Barney Ross, former world boxing champion, explaining that during the fight for

Guadalcanal the Marines loved to listen to sports results on the radio and place bets on the outcomes of various contests. Apparently, even after the fighting the men on Guadalcanal still liked to listen to sports on the radio. As Pfc. Karl M. Dreir wrote in October, 1944, "The betting on the Series was booming here too and the games came over the radio."[42]

Although there was a debate about the relative value of sports during the wartime, a consensus seems to have been reached that sports did have a place in the lives of those preparing for, and participating in, combat. But we should not forget that for many men sports remained tangential to their daily lives, and many men remained uninterested in sports despite the substantial effort made to involve them. Anecdotal evidence from a survey of World War II veterans reinforces this, as does the fact that many of the soldiers contributing questionnaires to the Military History Institute remembered engaging in other types of recreational activities but not sports. Thus, although Eldon Wakefield, who served with the 360th Engineers in England, France, and Germany, had played football before joining the service, he recalls playing or watching no sports while in the Army but does remember going to the pubs and dancing while in England. And Howard Riley while with the Army Air Force visited local tourist attractions, but never attended any athletic events. Similarly, Thomas Gannon and Thomas Alexander with the Ninety-first Bomb Group remembered sightseeing and going to movies and dances while off-duty—not playing or watching sports.[43]

One of the curious things about the reporting on professional or high-performance amateur sports stars is how it echoed the reporting of the First World War. Here the metaphorical tie between sports and war was most explicit, as in the *Bomb Bay Messenger*'s story about the 135 American League players in the service. As the newspaper put it, "The Japs have been running wild on the bases in the Asiatic League but now they are up against big league pitching by the Army, Navy, and Marines."[44] Similarly, the Golden Gloves boxer, Sgt. Lafayette Pool, was said to have left the Germans "slap happy from the mauling he gave them before a lucky shot struck his tank."[45] And the former Chicago White Sox player Ralph Hodgin was said to be hoping that he would be "as effective in his Army striking as he was at the plate for the Chisox."[46] With the announcement in *Brief* that with the conclusion of the war in Europe, the "Big League War" against the Japanese home islands was commencing in the Pacific, the ties between the language of big time sport and war became clear.[47]

As had many of those officers trained between the wars, former football and baseball players finding themselves in the service often described their experiences in the metaphor of sports, or explained military operations as they might explain sports plays. Thus, Lt. Col. Louis A. Hammock, a 1929 football All-American and AAU heavyweight wrestling champion, described the interaction of infantry and armor in battle as a "team" operation. He explained in the *Armored News* that when training tankers he emphasized that before battle the tanks and the infantry they were supporting needed to work out plays for their team so that they would enter the proper formations when under fire.[48] Similarly Cpl. Eddie Waitkus, who might have been playing first base for the Cubs in 1944 had he not been drafted, described for the readers of the Seventh Air Force's *Brief* how an amphibious invasion was like baseball. According to Waitkus, such an invasion was "like stealing home in baseball. If it worked, swell. If it didn't, you looked idiotic."[49] Pvt. David C. Dennis said he put his minor league baseball experience to good use the day he heard his buddy yell "slide" and did so, thus getting out of the way of a strafing Nazi airplane.[50] John Downs of the 100th Bomb Group remembered that his flak suit was shaped "a little like a baseball umpire's chest pad."[51] And 1st Lt. Walter Scholl, Jr., ascribed his survival in aerial combat against a German ace to his use of tactics learned while playing football for Cornell.[52]

Indeed, wartime saw a continued affirmation of the value of football experience in particular to soldiers, sailors, and flyers. American sports were said not only to create a "fighting spirit" but to teach specific skills useful in combat. Ball games, of course, taught young men how to throw a grenade, but even more significantly ball games, especially football, were believed to teach young men how to persevere in the face of exhaustion, pain, and fear. According to Lawrence Myers of the Ninety-eighth Bomb Group, football may even have directly contributed to his organization's health. As he described it, one time in Italy "we all had yellow jaundice and the treatment was a three inch needle in the buttox. Played touch football that afternoon and the two teams were the only ones not hobbling."[53] In other words, it should come as no surprise that Claire Chennault trained his Flying Tigers like a college football team, providing them special quarters and food while requiring them to play football every day in preparation for their missions. Nor should it come as a surprise that even the "benchwarmers" such as the men in the Quartermaster Corps justified themselves as integral parts of the football team of war. As a Seventh AAF poet put it, "It's all team work like a football game and even the guy in the center of the line who holds fast/He does his share without carryin' the ball."[54]

Just as in World War I, boxing was described as a sport that prepared men for combat by teaching them how to hit and be hit. As the *Bomb Bay Messenger* pointed out, "boxing is a sport which rapidly develops the average soldier into a hard, physically fit, aggressive, determined soldier."[55] In suggesting that Fort Chaffee should challenge Fort Robinson "to a real walloping fist-fest," the editorial writer for *Armodier* argued that "brother, you can't find a sport more suiting to a soldier than the give-and-take game. It develops individual reliance with a well rounded developed body."[56] As this editorial implies, boxing was viewed as a means of increasing loyalty and enthusiasm among the men stationed at a particular training camp. Boxing success, even down to the squadron level, was said to be the key to developing such loyalty in the *George Field News,* which directly asked the men of individual squadrons to come down to the boxing ring and demonstrate their unit cohesion.[57] This attitude is reflected in the novel *From Here to Eternity,* in which Captain Holmes says that, "Our fighting season is the best morale builder that we have off here away from home."[58]

Further reflecting the emphasis on the value of athletics to the soldier—and to the American enlisted man in particular—were the frequent references to the phrase that Gen. Douglas MacArthur had had carved over the door to the gymnasium at West Point. In the general's words, "on the fields of friendly strife are sown the seed which on other fields, in other years, will bear the fruits of victory."[59] And he was taken seriously, not only in the army, but in the navy as well. Thus, the sailors at the Pensacola Naval Air Station were told that the squadron sports which they were playing would surely help them secure victory over the enemy, just as MacArthur had predicted. And the flyers at Bowman Field received that same message when they were referred to MacArthur's belief in sports. The *Bowman Bomber* also assured its readers that from throwing a baseball or kicking a football, America's young men had learned how to win—and that winning came more easily when on the offensive.

This conviction—that athletic participation was crucial to preparing men for combat—persisted throughout the Second World War even where men sustained injuries playing sports that effectively kept them out of battle. The former Cub Eddie Waitkus broke his arm in his first Army baseball game and was unable to play the sport or participate in war for quite some time thereafter. Similarly, 1st Lt. Raymond Schmitz of the 101st Airborne Division cracked some vertebrae while wrestling with another officer just days before the Normandy invasion, keeping him from participating in the Division's D-Day operations and necessitating the reorganization of his platoon's command structure on June 4, 1944. Other soldiers suffered broken jaws, hands, and legs playing football, rendering them unfit for combat.[60] That such rough play persisted, even in the face of the suggestion in the Special Services *Technical Manual* that full-contact football be avoided for the duration, and despite comments by commanders that players should be more sportsmanlike and save the rough play for the enemy, implies that sports were less about toughening and preparing men for war, and more about demonstrating appropriate masculine behavior, even at the cost of having fewer men ready for battle.[61]

Despite the overwhelming insistence that athletics and combat have much in common, and that the best athletes make the best soldiers, there was some dissent from that position during the war. This time, however, the dissent was unlike that which occurred during the First World War. On the one hand, in the case of the navy's V-5 Preflight Program, the former boxer Gene Tunney, the director of Physical Training in the Bureau of Personnel, argued that the sports program devised by the Navy for its student pilots, involving as it did emphasis on football, basketball, gymnastics, and other athletic feats, sometimes at the expense of direct flying instruction, was wasteful and inefficient. On the other hand, those in charge of Preflight envisioned the sports program as a means of directly enhancing the individual flyer's speed, eye-hand coordination, and equilibrium.[62]

In the case of professional sports, especially baseball, during World War II critics did not necessarily call to disband sports, but instead to stop equating sports with war. Even within the army the idea that sports were like war, should be analogized to war, and should be used to train men in the skills of war was not universally accepted. In the immediate wake of the Battle of the Bulge, an editorial entitled "It's Not Football," appeared in the *Armored News*. The editorial writer ascribed the surprise with which the Americans were taken at the beginning of the German offensive to the overoptimism that was hindering an allied victory. War correspondents were charged with exaggerating the successes of the "home team" and were told that they would "help if they would cease and desist from reporting battles as if they were football games, measuring victory or defeat in terms of yards or miles gained or lost."[63]

Some months later, the same newspaper carried the words of Capt. David Alexander "deploring" the number of times he had read a military dispatch or listened to an orientation pep talk referring to war as a "football game on a grand scale."[64] Unlike so many of his fellows, Captain Alexander apparently believed that war was not in fact like football, and should not be described as being similar to the game.

But these dissenting positions in the *Armored News* were curiously contradicted by other language in the newspaper. For example, a group of training center graduates were told in the very month that war correspondents were being chided for their own use of football analogies, that they were about to play their own part in the "Big Game." And in July, 1945, the newspaper carried the story of an armored division's exploits, explaining them by means of a "box score" detailing numbers of the enemy killed, divisions wiped out, awards and decorations received.[65] The similarity of this box score to the box scores of World War I divisions created by *Stars and Stripes* cannot have been unintentional. And the fact that despite the attempts to find language other than that of sport to describe war, sports analogies were still employed, provides clear evidence of the extent to which sports and war were indeed intertwined in the minds of many of the men writing for and reading the post and unit newspapers of World War II.

In other circumstances, the use of sports metaphor provided some relief from the unrelenting language of combat. *Yank,* for example, carried a photograph in April, 1944, of an Army private holding a concrete "ball" the Nazis had rolled down a hill toward advancing Americans. By captioning the photograph "Lethal Bowling" the *Yank* editors may have been suggesting that war could still be interpreted as a game—even if the game might turn deadly at any time.[66] Similarly, a story in the *Armored News* about a platoon's assault on the Siegfried Line, in which the platoon took more than one hundred prisoners in two days, described their experience as "golf," heading the story "Officer Plays Golf on Pillbox Course, Goes Around in Par."[67] Of course, as was the case during the First World War, the use of sports metaphor carried with it an assumption that the GI reader would understand and appreciate the message contained in the language. Since that assumption was made, the reader then had to make it his responsibility to familiarize himself with sports and athletics in order to make any sense of what he was reading. And having done so, he would have acquiesced in the system that placed sports, and war, in the realm of men.

The problem for the army's athletic officers and for their navy counterparts was that even as the connection was made between sports and war, and even as they tried to provide the opportunity to play sports to everyone, some men remained uninterested in or unwilling to participate. As the editorial writer for the *Bom Bay* pointed out in April, 1943, the men at Barksdale Field had comfortable barracks, recreation halls and Hangar Nine for athletic workouts, yet they remained dissatisfied with their situation. He suggested that they take advantage of the athletic facility to build their bodies.[68] Yet many of the GIs at Barksdale Field and elsewhere remained unpersuaded that they should do any more physical exercise than they were already doing. Whether they were reluctant to admit that they were no longer civilians and therefore used their refusal to participate in sports as a means of rejecting military life, or whether they just did not care for sports, seems less important than that the army and navy wanted them to participate in sports as a part of their daily lives. Although athletic competitions in some cases helped to link the men in uniform to their former civilian selves, that link was rejected when it seemed to be forced on them by their services.

One way of ensuring that the soldiers and sailors would participate in sports was, of course, to make sure that easily accessible facilities were available. Although there was an advantage to sending the best athletes out into the community to advance good military-civilian relations, there was no advantage to sending the unwilling sportsman off base where he might find some way out of playing. Accordingly, at Barksdale Field and elsewhere new gymnasiums, pools, bowling allies and similar structures were constantly under construction.[69]

Another way to encourage the men to play was to change the rules to the make the games easier, or to offer the players rewards and prizes, as had been done before the war at Scott Field and other bases. Thus, S. Sgt. Ben Kaplan applauded the decision by softball managers at Cochran Field to limit pitchers to underhand deliveries as it gave "the game back to the average player who, being an average player, never could do much against a windmill hurler."[70] At George Field, Illinois, the handball tournament champion received a three-day pass and two tickets to the 1944 World Series, as did the best badminton player and free-throw shooter. At Camp Chaffee, the members of the championship baseball team were given gold baseballs to be worn on the front of their vests when they returned to civilian life.

Beer and cigarettes were also used as prizes. In some cases, the winners of softball games were allowed to pay less than their fair share of the cost of the post-game beer party while basketball teams were given PX beer in recognition of their success. Orville T. Murphy provides a sense of the way in which the prospect of alcohol was used as a means to persuade men to participate in sports in describing his experiences as a wartime submariner:

When I was in the U.S. Navy in World War II and stationed in the Philippines the Navy sponsored boxing tournaments. The prize for entering was usually beer, the prize for winning was even more beer. Because I had boxed a great deal in high school and had the unfortunate masculine tendency to brag about it, my shipmates were always enthusiastic that I enter the tournaments—win or lose—so that we could share the beer.

For those sailors stationed on land, there was ample opportunity to train for the boxing matches and they did—to the great disadvantage of those of us who were on a ship where there was never enough room to train. Needless to say, the matches were sometimes one-sided massacres played out before a shouting, beer thirsty mob of spectators.[71]

A large and varied athletics program constituted yet a third way to get the troops involved in sports. Special Services officers formed leagues on most posts and bases for baseball, softball, volleyball, and basketball. In many cases, they also offered coaching and competition in swimming, track, and tennis. And reflecting the Special Services officers' *Technical Manual,* they created tag or touch football leagues at most training sites.[72]

Unfortunately for those soldiers and sailors committed to their sporting activities, the exigencies of military training often intervened. To ensure that play go on nonetheless, athletic officers employed a number of different strategies. At Cochran Field they developed an intra-outfit basketball program to operate on an intramural basis to avoid the time commitments necessary for more organized sport. On the one hand, at Camp Chaffee some basketball players involved in play at a higher level actually postponed their furloughs rather than force their teams to forfeit games as the season came to a close, while other teams had to withdraw from the league altogether as their players were transferred away from the camp. And at the Naval Air Station at Pensacola, a separate league was formed for those players attached to smaller units not involved in the Commandant's Cup or Inter-Unit schedules.[73] On the other hand, even though Col. Tracy K. Dorsett sanctioned the absence from duty of the men on the George Field football team, many chose not to play, or to take their regular furloughs instead.[74] And the *Cochran Communique* took its readers to task in an editorial for refusing to come out for basketball practice, since by doing so they contributed to the possibility that "sports in this nation, which leads them all by a tremendous margin, [might] stop of their own weight."[75] In this case, the editorial writer reminded the GIs that the survival of the American way of life for which they were fighting depended not only on their commitment to the battlefield, but also to the playing field, where American values were being demonstrated for the world.

Even if the men chose not to play, they were strongly encouraged in the base newspapers to come out and cheer on their buddies. The newspapers regularly reported on the strength and enthusiasm of the crowds for boxing and basketball, just as they recorded the numbers of athletes involved. And where the teams lacked support, that was mentioned as well. As the sportswriter for the *Banana Peelings* put it, "New players or veterans, they all like a good crowd for their [softball] games, so if you've been complaining that there's nothing to do, stroll over, come 1700, and see a good ball game."[76]

Despite the Special Services Athletic Officers' best attempts, soldiers and sailors were not always able to play sports, or had to engage in athletics with inadequate facilities and materials. As might be expected, this was particularly true in forward areas, or recently conquered territories. According to *Brief*, soon after the Marianas Islands were secured, "outfits representing every branch of the service started to organize teams and build fields for basketball, baseball, softball, volleyball, and rings for boxing."[77] Perhaps reflecting the lack of other diversions on the island, Saipan soon had more than seven hundred men competing on seventy teams in ten volleyball leagues. In Alaska as well the men started building sports facilities very quickly after they arrived. As Wayne F. Dudley recalled, "After the taking of Kiska we built a volleyball court by our warehouse and had a softball field."[78] And Ernest Stolper remembered that for Thanksgiving Day, 1944, the engineers built a baseball diamond for the men of the Quartermaster Corps outside Le Havre, France.[79]

Despite the construction of new facilities, the men found that engaging in athletics in wartime often required special sacrifices. In the Marianas for example, baseball players had to slide into second base on coral and shells, while enduring quick cloudbursts, and unintended, unintentional visits to the latrines that surrounded the field while chasing fly balls. And in the Mediterranean Base Section, the Red Cross had to make a special effort to provide tennis balls for a scheduled tournament since none were available due to wartime exigencies.[80]

The extent to which athletics remained important to some men, despite the war, is reflected in the memories of some prisoners of war, who managed to play sports even while in captivity. In a letter to his parents while he was a POW in Germany, Robert L. Shawver of the Ninety-fourth Bomb Group described all of the things there were to do in his particular camp, versus the previous places he had been held. As Shawver put it in a letter home, "in the barrack, we can play cards and read; out of doors, we can play football, baseball and other popular games."[81] First Lt. Conrad Kreps, who spent nine months as a prisoner of war in Italy, recalled that he and his comrades also played ball. They managed to take available materials and make balls with which to play catch, although the Italians didn't allow them to construct bats with which to play baseball.[82] Perhaps that is just as well, since the Japanese were accused of using baseball bats supplied by the Red Cross as weapons against prisoners of war they were guarding in the Pacific.[83]

During the Second World War, sports and athletics were intended to permeate the lives of the off-duty soldier or sailor. The sports program had many functions. It had to provide a diversion for the men who were preparing for combat and keep them from considering the deadly implications of their daily activities. It had to alleviate fears among civilians that the soldiers and sailors in their midst were out of control by demonstrating that they played sports and games just as they always had done. It also had to reassure the troops that they could maintain aspects of their civilian lives, even as they put on uniforms, picked up guns, and acquiesced to military discipline.

Within the military's hierarchy, there was another hierarchy to be created and maintained. That hierarchy demanded that the strongest and most courageous men be identified and elevated. Since the age of mechanized warfare had made strength less important on the battlefield and courage often the refuge of the foolhardy, sports served as another means of locating the "best" men. And because the athlete was valorized within the hierarchy, those men who were not athletes or who were uninterested in athletics were placed at a disadvantage within the services, further reinforcing a hierarchy defined by physicality.

Finally, the military sports program of World War II was entertaining to huge numbers of men. As military life has been characterized as a life of interminable boredom relieved only by moments of terror, participating in or watching an athletic contest must have surely created moments of escape from the dreadfulness of life preparing for war.

7

WACs, WAVEs, "Sissies," and the "Negro Soldier:" Military Sports for the Marginalized

The members of the American armed forces that fought the Second World War were overwhelmingly white, male, and heterosexual. Many, if not all, had played sports as children, had been athletes in high school or college, or had, at the very least, developed a casual fan's interest in a favorite team or player. And many, if not all, enjoyed playing sports in the service as a break from the intense daytime training and nighttime boredom of military life. But for some soldiers and sailors sports were so profoundly uninteresting that they had to be bribed or ordered to play. For other soldiers and sailors sports were so completely alien that they were unable to appreciate metaphors derived from sports, even where understanding those metaphors was crucial to their continued combat survival.

During World War II the military developed a system to ensure that every man would at least have the opportunity to play, and to develope group loyalty by associating their outfit's prowess with the success of its athletes. Because for the first time the U.S. military included substantial numbers of women, their commanders also developed a sports program to meet the needs of the WACs, Navy women (WAVEs), Coast Guard Women (SPARS), and women marines who answered their country's call. That program tested the validity of previous assumptions about the values to be gained from sports participation. Meanwhile, the military's continued accommodation to racial prejudice that allowed segregation within the services, meant that for black soldiers and sailors separate programs of sports and athletics had to be created for them as well.[1] And because of the self-conscious concern with the presence of homosexuals within the military, athletics programs needed to ensure that sports played by the soldiers and sailors, whether white or black, would not reinforce so-called sissy behavior. Thus, the military's response to the needs of the various constituencies within the services illuminated instances of racial prejudice, homophobia, and gender bias that ran counter to the overall goal of developing a strong army and navy capable of defeating the nation's enemies.

During World War II, the American military began to encourage female enlistment, in order to make more men available to combat units by using women as clerks, truckdrivers and in other noncombat job classifications. Ultimately, the armed services were unable to meet their recruitment goals as women for a variety of reasons chose not to join the army or navy, but to take advantage of new opportunities in the civilian work force.[2] Many women did, however, contribute directly to the war effort, either by joining the military, by working as nonmilitary employees on and about bases throughout the United States, or by taking jobs in the defense industry. Even girls and women who stayed at home contributed to the war effort by providing reassurance that they would remain faithful, loyal, and dedicated to the return of their loved ones.

With the influx of women into the military, however, planners were faced with a dilemma like that posed by the huge numbers of men who needed to be entertained, have their morale boosted, and be kept physically active during training. Accordingly, a sports program was created for the women that in many ways resembled the men's program. Mattie E. Treadwell, the official historian of the Women's Army Corps, points out that although the army did not see the need to "harden" women for combat, "some moderate exercise or sports appeared desirable to offset sedentary work."[3]

The format for women's physical training within the Army depended on the time at which the individual woman was inducted. In the beginning, female recruits were required to engage in exercises specifically designed to increase their strength, especially in the upper body. Later, in response to requests by WAC company commanders, a more entertaining sports and recreation program was put into place for army women. Similarly, by 1944, the navy's physical training program required three hours per week of athletics for all enlisted WAVEs, with tumbling and archery replacing the football and baseball permitted to men but forbidden to women.[4]

Because of these sports programs, female athletes in all services participated in volleyball, archery, basketball, bowling, tennis, table tennis, badminton, and softball. As with the men, women competed not only within individual units, but against women serving in different units or in different arms of the military. For example, WAVEs at the Pensacola Naval Air Station played in a badminton tournament for the Joy B. Hancock trophy, and in a swim meet held at the pool reserved for enlisted sailors. Elsewhere female army recruits swam against SPARS, also meeting the Coast Guard women in badminton and softball.[5] Also like the men's program, the program for the women anticipated not only organized sports played by teams on league schedules, but also sports for the occasional or "drop in" player, as well as instruction in different sports for beginners.[6]

The program for female athletics was organized like that for the men in using sports to reinforce distinctions between officers and enlisted women. If the game required a coed team, a private could play with a seaman, as in the table tennis game at Cochran Field where Pvt. Peter Grossman teamed with Seaman Jane Carlin. Yet in other cases officers were not allowed to team with enlisted personnel. At Drew Field such distinctions went even further. There a tennis tournament was divided into three classes, one for Air-WACs, WAC officers and nurses, one for enlisted white men and officers, and one for the black men from Camp DeSoto. In this case, it was evidently less important to distinguish enlisted women from their female officers in athletic competitions than it was to distinguish African-Americans from men and women of European descent. Yet despite this emphasis on distinctions between white and black, and officer and enlisted person, those sports programs also helped remind women that they were in fact in the military and subject to military discipline since they were specifically directed by the War Department to be out of uniform in public *only* when engaging in sports.[7]

Also reflecting similarities with the men's program, military women played civilian teams to promote good military-civilian relations.[8] In light of the problems the military had in persuading women to join the service, and in light of the negative rumors among civilians concerning the female recruits, the demonstration through sports that military women were just like the girls next door served to alleviate civilian concerns about the service women's sexuality. But athletic women were caught within a double bind. During the war, the most potent rumor directed at military women was that which accused them all of being manlike lesbians. If they played sports at a high level, their athletic skill fit the stereotype that assumed that lesbians were indeed quite athletic. Despite the regular efforts to remove lesbians and gay men from service during the war, where their skills and abilities were needed, they were likely to be protected from discharge.[9] Likewise, the military needed to keep servicewomen fit and occupied, so it continued to encourage the women's sports program, even at the risk of generating further negative publicity about the sexual preferences of the women in uniform.

Despite many similiarities, the women's athletic and recreation program departed from the program of sports and athletics developed for the men in important ways. For the men sports programs seem not to have been designed to enhance their sexual desirability while for the women this was often the case.

This influenced the sports chosen for emphasis and the way the sports were presented in the media.

The women inducted into the armed services were expected to maintain a level of physical fitness commensurate with the military's understanding of what they might achieve. Although there was some disagreement about how much strength and endurance women could attain through training—or indeed about how much strength and endurance they should be expected to achieve given the expectation that after the war they would return to their homes and take up their roles of wife and mother—military planners anticipated that the female recruits would have to be able to drill and march just like other soldiers. To ensure that that level of physical fitness would be achieved, the Army and Navy trained female officers and enlisted personnel specifically to lead their sister soldiers and sailors in athletic drills and contests. When they arrived at their posts the female athletic officers, called in the navy welfare officers, struggled to generate enthusiasm for the sports and recreation program under their direction just as did their male counterparts.[10] The female athletic officers sometimes trained alongside their male counterparts, as was the experience of Sgt. Lora Taylor who worked with other army physical trainers in North Carolina and Virginia before returning to her post at Drew Field in Florida to conduct workouts for the WACs assigned to Drew.

The experience of Sergeant Taylor at Drew Field provides a case study of the struggle within the army to maintain the assumption that men were necessarily stronger and more coordinated than women, and that they needed to be so in order to meet the military's needs, even though women also needed to be strong and coordinated in order to be useful soldiers. The existence of such women provided a direct challenge to a hierarchy based on the superior strength of men.

Sergeant Taylor's introduction to the men and women of Drew Field was used as an object demonstration both of how women could achieve physical fitness, and of how that physical fitness remained in the service of men and masculine fantasies. In the post newspaper *Drew Field Echoes,* Sergeant Taylor is pictured leading a group of men in calisthenics. According to the caption, she is doing so to prove that the physical training programs for the Air-WACs and the enlisted men are interchangeable. She is also described as the manager and second-base player for the Air-WACs softball team. Thus, Sergeant Tayler is presented in words as a dynamic, important part of the war effort.

But a close analysis of the photograph tells a different story. In that picture, she is shown on her back, in a little two-piece suit, with her naked legs in the air. The clear message delivered is that although Sergeant Taylor may have a role to play in ensuring that the women of Drew Field are physically fit, she and her sisters must never forget that that physical fitness serves in part to make her more desirable to the men on the post. In other words, passively on her back, Sergeant Taylor reflects woman's traditional role of male fantasy object— and provides yet another pin-up for the barracks wall.[11]

Women interested in archery also discovered that their athletic efforts could be used to demonstrate the place women should occupy as fantasy objects for men. For example, a series of photographs of navy women at Banana River Naval Air Station practicing archery was captioned "BEAUS and Arrows." The accompanying article explained, "These three pulchritudinous photos were made for some of our enlisted Waves on their Archery Range during a session of beaus, bows, darts, hearts, arrows and sparrows."[12] Since the dictionary defines pulchritudinous as "beautiful, lovely, especially having physical beauty," it is clear that the women of Banana River were not being admired for their athletic abilities. Nor was Marcia Modale, Slc, who was identified as a possible female cupid in her *Gosport* photograph. As the writer said, Modale was busy demonstrating "some of the finer points which 'figure' in good archery technique."[13]

Most ominous was the photograph of Ella Raines which appeared in the *Cochran Communique* in September, 1944. Unlike the navy women she wasn't shown shooting her arrow. Instead, she appears standing *in front* of an archery target, identified as a GI target "for tonight (or any other time for that matter)."[14] Clearly Raines has been rendered not a threat and her sister soldiers have been reminded that their place in sports is not as active participants but as "targets" for GIs.

Since wherever women were assigned they participated in sports, particularly softball, basketball, and bowling, male sports reporters had to decide how to cover female athletic events. Almost everywhere, this resulted in a conflict between the leering tone of most discussions of women in the papers, which featured pin-ups and jokes about the girls and women with whom the soldiers had social encounters, and the attempt to provide a straightforward account of women's sports. The simple announcement that a golf club for women was being organized at Camp Chaffee and a call for women to participate in new bowling and basketball leagues at Drew Field were made without comment.[15] Similarly, the enlistment of women who had been successful athletes in civilian life was noted with approval, although the female recruit's relationship to a famous male athlete might also be a part of the story. That WAC Lt. Betty Etten played first base for the Hill Field (Utah) softball team, seemed to be especially important because it identified her with her cousin Nick who occupied the same position for the New York Yankees.[16]

Occasionally, where the individual player or team exhibited special skill, her post newspaper acknowledged that achievement just as it would for any other athlete. Thus, the WAC softball team that came to the Pensacola Naval Air Station in October, 1944, to play against the WAVES was described as "star-studded."[17] This was also the case for the George Field softball team, which was said to play the game "with a skill and speed that would do credit to a good male outfit," and for Y3c Frances Owen, when she set a base bowling mark at Pensacola.[18] A successful female athlete could be called an "ace," and Jane Garford, SK2d, of Pensacola was deemed the "Queen of Swat" for hitting so many home runs for her softball team that it became routine.[19] In each of these cases, the women's achievements were in fact recognized with the language of men's sports.

Even more striking are the times when women's achievements against men are simply accepted. Sometimes women's victories over men in bowling were acknowledged without further discussion, and without any implication that the defeated men had lost their masculinity by losing to women in that sport. Similarly, newspaper writers seemed not to think it remarkable when women competed against men in table tennis.[20]

Although both the army and the navy were committed to providing a program of sports and athletics for female recruits, participation was limited in certain important ways. WAC use of the base gymnasium at George Field was restricted to Monday nights for example, a significant frustration for the women whose winter 1944–1945 "season, athletic and social" was said to be well on the way by October, 1944. At Banana River a schedule was created showing the hours the alleys were reserved for the WAVES, for leagues, for officers, and for enlisted men. And the enlisted men's pool at the Pensacola Naval Air Station was open to WAVEs only on Tuesday, Wednesday, and Thursday so they could meet their swimming qualifications.[21] Similarly, newly built gymnasiums often provided only one set of lockers, showers, and other changing facilities, keeping men and women from using those gymnasiusms at the same time.[22]

Women were also occasionally limited in the particular events in which they might participate. For example, the Naval Air Station swim meet at Pensacola in June, 1944, although said to be open to all, provided specifically that the "only event open to Waves will be fifty yards free style stroke."[23]

Despite the apparent acceptance that military women could be competitive with men in bowling, on other occasions the success of athletically competent women against men created considerable consternation among observers. Perhaps that should not be so surprising given the connections already drawn between athletic ability and masculine status. However, the post newspapers of World War II provide further insight into the extent to which women's military service created special challenges to the maintenance of a gender hierarchy derived from the presumably greater physical strength of men.

Even before the war, of course, women were serving in the army as nurses and were expected to maintain some level of fitness. One prewar nurse, Lucille Fowler, was a successful athlete before joining the army, pitching for the Federal Bakeries softball team of Sterling, Illinois. At Scott Field, Illinois, during the summer of 1941, she was asked to pitch for the medical officers in a game against the enlisted medical personnel. According to the *Scott Field Broadcaster,* when Nurse Fowler's team won, the losing team explained away her victory, rather than admit that they had lost to a woman with superior athletic talents. Rather, they hinted "that chivalry kept them from teeing off on the nurse's efforts, but just the same they're hoping she sticks to nursing in the future."[24]

As was the case with Sergeant Taylor, so with Nurse Fowler, female athletic achievement was allowed only insofar as it posed no threat to prevailing assumptions that women should be weaker and more passive than men. Even within the military, an institution in which agression was being encouraged in all other members, women were restricted in the extent to which they could express aggression, even through sports. In order to maintain the fiction that women were inevitably less athletically gifted than men, the medical enlisted men said that they chivalrously refused to play as hard as they might otherwise have done. And Sergeant Taylor's athleticism was rendered less important than her feminine desirability in the photograph that told her story.

Despite the fact that many men were not athletes and had to be taught to play the sports and games encouraged by the military, writers for post newspapers often implied that it was only women who needed coaching in order to learn how to play sports at a high level. Instead of equating their abilities with those of unathletic men, these writers suggested that all women were like those whose efforts on the playing field were so uninspiring. And the sports-writers seemed to believe that trying to coach women would be of no use, since they would not be able to improve. As *Yank* put it, "Lt. Bill Dickey is managing a Navy nurse's softball team in Hawaii, which is just about the biggest waste of talent in this war."[25]

At Cochran Field, WAC athletes (and their WAVE counterparts) were mocked. A softball game between the WACs and WAVEs was marked by bad fielding plays. Rather than ascribe that bad fielding to the conditions, to the lack of good equipment, or to the errors that plague even the professional male athlete, the women's bad fielding was said to be typical of how women played the game. Of course, the bad fielding by women didn't mean that the spectators didn't enjoy the game, who, according to the *Cochran Communique* had a "hilarious" time.[26]

Often athletic competitions between men and women were designed specifically as spectacles, comedic interludes away from the serious business of war. In those, WACs provided entertainment for the men. Examples of these types of competitions abound in World War Two–era post newspapers. At one sports night held at Drew Field, the language used to describe the competitors ("Dey Yanked each odder's hair, hollered and made faces") made it clear that the women were there to reassure the watching men that their sporting efforts were not to be taken seriously.[27]

As had been done during World War One and during the postwar occupation of Germany, where men played women, the men donned comical clothing or affected other handicaps, ostensibly to make the game more fair, but actually to mock the women's athletic efforts. One time a game was arranged between a team of soldiers wearing gas masks and a team of unmasked WACs. As the *Drew Field Echoes* said, "Of course, the game is a gag, but it should be something to watch."[28] And if the men did not alter their strategy to make the game fair, they argued that the women had tricks to make them play less well. Thus, an apparently serious suggestion that a male ball club from Fort Gordon Johnston play a WAC team was revealed to be less than serious when the offeror also suggested that the competition would be fair—even though the women's team would inevitably be inferior—because "if their pitcher wore shorts we'd never even see the ball, so that ought to even any advantage we might have."[29] Again, as in the case of Sergeant Taylor, women's athleticism was accepted only where it could provide fodder for male fantasies. In other words, the only way women could possibly compete with men in sports would be to rely not on their athletic talent but on their "feminine" talents.

Finally, since the women were intended to replace men that would then be free to join combat units, military women interested in sports were also assigned to roles ancillary to the games themselves. During World War II, WACs worked as ticket takers and ushers at post football games. That their presence, both within the military and at sporting events, was expected to remain marginal to the main event is illustrated by the reassurance provided spectators at a Hammer Field softball game. According to the Hammer Field newspaper *Bom Bay,* the spectators didn't need to worry about them lowering the quality of play, since the WACs were present at the games only to hand out tickets and not to replace the men on the field.[30]

Military women were encouraged to cheer on the men at play. The way that the *Drew Field Echoes* described the spectacle of WAC cheerleaders reflects the sexualized nature of cheerleading, and of the place that military women held as adjuncts to the real business, not only of sport but of war as well. As the post newspaper put it, "Dressed in vari-colored sunsuits, the cheerleaders run up and down the sidelines calling the yells and conjuring up school spirit as in the days of yore."[31] And overseas, military women were chosen as bowl game queens in order both to reassure the men that their wartime lives were not that dissimilar from their civilian lives, and to reinforce stereotypes concerning the proper place of women.[32]

Although military women were often ridiculed when engaged in sports, and on other occasions subjected to more subtle reminders of their subordinate status as sexual objects for the men, in at least a few instances military women were able to turn the use of female pin-ups to their own purposes. As Robert Westbrook has shown, during World War II pin-ups of women like Betty Grable provided an ideological justification for American participation in the war, as they represented the fight for private values and private virtues that would be embraced after the war.[33] But pin-ups also reinforced the idea that only heterosexual men, who would find both sexual excitement and comfort in the women's photographs, could adequately represent the country on the battlefield.

Military women responded to the pin-up phenomenon by asking to have their own pin-ups, demanding that as heterosexual women they be allowed to fantasize over photographs of handsome, interesting men. The *Drew Field Echoes* included the "Mysterious Air-WAC's" choices for well-groomed soldiers in 1944. Similarly, the photograph of the 174th Infantry Regiment's Buffalo baseball team, from Fort Chaffee, was published "not only to give Chaffeemen a close-up view of the star-studded team of ballplayers, but also for the benefit of the *Armodier*'s gal readers who have objected to the exclusive use of feminine pin-ups of interest mainly to GIs."[34]

In order to refute the implication that they were objectified in the way women were, the men asserted that providing images of men for female soldiers and sailors was their own idea, part of the game. This explains the *Armodier* editor's decision to acknowledge that the baseball team might be attractive to females. This also shows why the Navy newspaper *Banana Peelings* provided a "Pin-Up Boy for WAVES." As the caption explained, "Just to be different and feeling sorry for the WAVES who had to elect Admiral Ernest J. King for their favorite pin-up boy, due to the scarcity of handsome males [*Banana Peelings*] offers the one and only 'Pin-Up Boy for the WAVES' Edmund 'Cess'

Poole, Y3C."[35] But since the gender order demanded that women be the objects of men's attention and not the other way around, poor "Cess" Poole appears in diapers, tattoes, middie tie and hat, smoking a cigar. His ridiculous image subverted the sexualization implicit in the idea of the pin-up, as did the photograph of Pfc. Floyd Norman who fell while ice skating at George Field, Illinois, and who appeared in the *George Field News* on his back, ice skates in the air, above a caption that it was a "pose, cheesecake for Eskimo women."[36] That Private Norman's pose was remarkably similar to that of Sergeant Taylor did not mean that he was a sexual object, but rather that the appearance of any man on his back, legs in the air, was an occasion for laughter. And as Norman and Poole were mocked, they were also being feminized, implying that to be a sexual object is to be a female.

That military women demanded pin-ups of their own suggests that they were not anaware that the pin-ups of women adorning barracks walls, airplane noses, and ships throughout the Pacific and Atlantic, were helping to maintain the traditional constructions of femininity and masculinity, in which masculinity required that females be objectified. And finally, they could not have been unaware that a request for male pin-ups deflected the common accusation lodged at the women who answered their country's call to service who were said to be unnatural, unfeminine, and lesbian.[37]

Whether they employed pin-ups or relied on a demonstration of their athleticism, military women during the war were constantly challenged to meet their service obligations and the expectations placed on them by civilian society. Since most of these women expected to return to private life with the end of the war, they had to figure out how to apply the lessons learned while serving in the armed forces in that other world. Certainly some WACs enjoyed acquiring new skills and learning new ways to apply their athleticism. As *The Bomb Bay*'s WAC reporter concluded, in the future women would be able to use the judo they had learned in the army to punish their husbands if they came home late![38]

Although the athleticism of service women was carefully limited and constrained, the military promoted and developed the men's athleticism, particularly where that athleticism demonstrated strength and aggression. Within the armed forces there was little doubt that boxing and football constituted manly sports, and that the athletes who could succeed at those games were among not only the most physically gifted, but among those who would most likely achieve success at war. This message was constantly restated in the base newspapers the troops read.[39] As the novelist James Jones put it, describing military life in Hawaii just before the Pearl Harbor attack, "in The Profession . . . sports are the nourishment of life and boxing is the most manly sport."[40]

But not every man had the physical ability to play football well, nor did every man possess the skills necessary to avoid serious injury in the boxing ring. For those who either for lack of physical talent or interest were unsuited to boxing and football, the army and navy established an extensive program of other sports and games. The problem for the men who played those noncontact and non-physically aggressive sports was to avoid the stigma of being labeled weak, passive, uncoordinated, and generally inadequate to the task of defending the nation.[41] Even more important for some men was to establish that they were not sissies, even if they played sports that some labeled as appropriate only to the sissy.

Funk and Wagnall's 1946 *New Practical Standard Dictionary* defines a sissy as "An effeminate man or boy; a milksop; a weakling, male or female."[42] During World War II, within the American military and in the civilian world, surely few men would have felt comfortable allowing themselves to be labeled effeminate. Indeed, if a man wished to serve his country he had to hide any aspects of his physical posture, language, or behavior that the military recruiter might consider effeminate. If he failed to do so, he could be rejected for military service and face the consequent opprobrium reserved during the war for those men who appeared to be physically fit yet were avoiding service.[43]

Once within the military, the recruit still needed to maintain a facade and suppress any characteristics that might be identified as effeminate if he wanted to get along. Yet sometimes the effeminate, the sissy, or both could be useful to the war effort. Men whom the Army might ordinarily have rejected because their prewar professions were used as markers by army psychiatrists to weed out potential homosexuals were welcomed into the service if their skills fit a wartime need. Thus, men who had worked in the theater, as stage designers or drag queens, found themselves working as camouflage experts. As Robert Fleischer explained in *Coming Out Under Fire*, describing his efforts to disguise his unit's position, "The guys that were in charge were astounded because they figured [it would be] a real drag with a sissy along. [But] I turned [out] to be the one that really accomplished something."[44]

Similarly, although some of the sports that were played by soldiers and sailors were often described as "sissy" sports, they were accepted as part of military life if they seemed to serve purposes like those of other athletic contests. Badminton was one such sport. Described as a "minor" sport in most post athletic programs, the army and navy provided badminton equipment and facilities at many training sites in the United States and overseas.[45] Yet despite the opportunities for playing the game, for many it remained stigmatized as being unmanly.

How the game became acceptable provides an illustration of how a sport could lose its association with the effeminate by taking on warlike characteristics. At Fort Chaffee, for example, badminton, while still characterized as a "sissy's game" achieved new respectability when Sgt. Joe Incantalupi, the base boxing and jujitsu expert, tore a muscle in his back playing badminton after "throwing GIs around all day teaching them how to kill the enemy in one blow."[46] The association of badminton with physical injury, therefore, made it seem less effeminate.

At Drew Field, the base newspaper reported that badminton skills had combat applications. Lt. William E. Warner, ranked number three in the sport in the United States in 1941, described the game as being especially good for flying personnel as it promoted agility, coordination, spirit, alertness, judgment, keen vision, and stamina.[47] Badminton like other minor sports such as handball and horseshoes was also recommended to those soldiers and sailors who gained weight on military cuisine. And when the navy issued regulations that all officers and enlisted men under forty needed to have at least four hours per week of physical training, badminton, along with volleyball and baseball became a favorite sport.[48]

Other sports were also accused of being fit only for sissies. One, table tennis, only became acceptable when its players demonstrated the amount of energy required to play the game at a high level. As the sportswriter for *The Armodier* put it, "Thought by some to be a sissy's game, the table tennis that Kurt had to produce to finally beat down Pfc. Gilbert Ferguson, 125th Engineers, would have had Dempsey panting after the first few swings and Charles Atlas out on his feet."[49] By suggesting that a table tennis champion put out more effort than the famous boxing champion, and could have defeated the legendary body builder, *The Armodier*'s writer removed any doubt that Pfc. Kurt played table tennis because he was effeminate and less manly than those exemplars of the masculine physique—especially after he sustained a black eye and a cut lip diving for a ball during the match.

Although badminton and table tennis seem to have been most commonly identified as sissy sports, other sports also occasionally received that label. As was the case with badminton, those sports became acceptable only when a link was established between the athletic skills necessary to play the game and the skills needed in combat. Fencing was one such sport. At Scott Field reporters tried to dispel the notion that it was in any way a sissy activity by encouraging men on the base to go to demonstrations by Captain Siebert (épée

National Champion) and Pvt. James Steere so they could see for themselves the aggression in fencing. And at Drew Field, Capt. Alvin L. Goodstein explained to the troops that learning to use swords would make bayoneting easy and that fencing was similar to boxing as well.[50] Since aggression was necessary in war, the fact that soldiers could learn to be aggressive and to wield a bayonet while fencing removed the sport's stigma.

Playing an apparently sissy sport was also excused in those whose athletic talents were exhibited in manly sports as well. This was the case with a physical training instructor at Drew Field, introduced to the readers of the *Drew Field Echoes* as "a sports man with sports training" who had had years of experience playing basketball, baseball, and football, but whose spare time was "taken up with such sissy games as soccer and softball."[51] Apparently, devoting time to those games did not reflect badly on the new instructor because of his experience as a football player.

But even boxing could lose its firm place at the top of the hierarchy of manly sports if the local champion failed to fit the stereotype of the boxer. At Fort Chaffee a heavyweight fighter named Sid Schwartz seemed to have caused a lot of anxiety among fight fans when he became the base champion. Schwartz was described as being "mild-mannered, cherubic [looking] anything but a fighter."[52] Furthermore, Schwartz admitted to being frightened in the ring. And even more telling, he had worked before the war as a ladies' glove maker. With Schwartz's victory, the soldiers at Fort Chaffee had their expectations about what kind of man it took to become a fighter challenged. As Robert Fleischer's colleagues discovered in the South Pacific, other soldiers and sailors also discovered during World War II, in at least some cases a hierarchy based on outward signs of masculinity or effeminacy was perhaps not a hierarchy that could best predict either sporting or military success. Thus, although homophobia and the fear of being identified as a sissy by the sports he played proved to be a means of constraining the individual soldier and sailor's behavior, the assumption that only heterosexual men could be sufficiently aggressive to succeed at war or sports proved ultimately to be false.[53]

By contrast to the First World War, African-Americans were underrepresented in the army during World War II.[54] Despite attempts by national organizations such as the National Association for the Advancement of Colored People (NAACP) to ensure that the nation's black citizens would be able to participate fully in the country's defense and reap the benefits that service has traditionally provided to military survivors, and despite nondiscrimination guarantees in the 1940 legislation providing for selective service, that would remain the case throughout the war.[55] Blacks were even less likely to serve in the navy which had restricted African-American sailors to mess duties since the beginning of the twentieth century, and in the growing Army Air Forces where the training of black men as pilots was actively resisted since that would result in having them command white enlisted men.[56] Those troops who did serve discovered that their opportunities were restricted in many ways, not least in the chances they would have to engage in sports and other types of recreation.[57]

During the war, Brig. Gen. Benjamin O. Davis, Sr., was charged with investigating the situation of the African-American soldier and reporting on problems between both the African-American soldier and his European-American counterpart and between the soldier and the communities to which he was assigned for training. General Davis concluded that black soldiers were most comfortable and most happy in the service where they were allowed to do the same kind of work as the white soldiers, especially, as he reported to his wife, where the black soldiers were allowed to compete with their white comrades.[58] Davis's conclusion was not dissimilar to the conclusion reached among the army's high command about how best to deal with local community objections to having African-American troops quartered among them. Indeed, the army made it incumbent on local commanders to exercise strong leadership, and in the words of Lt. Gen. Leslie J. McNair, commander of American ground forces, "forestall racial difficulties by firm discipline, just treatment, strenuous training, and wholesome recreation."[59]

Unfortunately, as Stanley Sandler has demonstrated in his study of African-Americans in the Army Air Force, the quality of the particular troop commander directly influenced the ability of black soldiers to tolerate the slights and insults directed toward them both in the civilian community and on the bases to which they were assigned. Where a commander was unsympathetic to the soldiers in his responsibility or was actively racist, then trouble might very well arise. This, on the one hand, was particularly true where a commander went out of his way to create racial segregation where none had theretofore existed, or to create artificial barriers to black-white cooperation. The commander of the 477th Bombardment Group, a Colonel Selway, directly contravened the 1944 War Department directive finally prohibiting segregated facilities by creating two Officers' Clubs, one for the men of the 477th, who happened all to be black, and the other for supervisory personnel, who happened all to be white. The resulting bad feelings directly affected the 477th's military efficiency and led to a collapse of morale within the unit.[60]

On the other hand, a commander who wanted to see his African-American soldiers do well generally found that they did so, particularly where they were allowed the opportunities to rest and recreate available to white soldiers. Lt. Col. Marshall S. Carter reported to his superiors that recreational opportunities were critical to the welfare of the black troops. As commander of an overseas African-American unit, he described to General Douglas what he believed to be the key to maintaining good order and discipline among his men. His troops organized a baseball team in which he said he encouraged "showmanship," saying that he would "not let them on the field unless they are completely uniformed as a baseball team. All other teams play in the usual conglomeration of soldier clothes. My team looks like a baseball outfit. It makes a fine impression on all and makes the individual soldier unconsciously proud of his team."[61] As Lieutenant Colonel Carter commented, every man in his unit, whether playing on the baseball team, or watching its efforts on the field, was out of trouble and enjoying himself. Similarly, the men of the 332nd Fighter Group serving in Italy not only established themselves as excellent escorts for the heavy bombers in their charge but also as a group from which came good athletes when the "Red Tails" basketball team won the XV Air Force championship.[62]

For the African-American soldier, then, the athletic success of his team helped to establish his own self-worth and instill pride in his organization. But for these soldiers, the army wanted to do more through sports than create unit pride and keep the troops out of trouble. As Gen. Andrew J. Goodpaster discovered when he went to Camp Claiborne, Louisiana, just before the war to take command of the 390th Engineer Regiment, the young soldiers in that regiment were in wretched physical health and condition. Because they, and many of their compatriots who had lived through the Depression in poverty even more abject than that of most European-Americans, needed so desperately to be fed, have their teeth fixed, and get built up, athletics provided one means to the restored health and vigor they would need if they were to serve their country.[63]

For most African-Americans from the South, life in the army and navy reflected their prewar experiences as the armed services were committed to maintaining a system of strict racial separation. This meant not only that the soldiers and sailors would not serve in racially mixed units, but that they would be trained and housed separately. In many cases, this meant as well that their opportunities for sports and recreation were restricted in ways similar to those that were placed on the women in the wartime military.

In some cases, local racial prejudice and the army's decision not to fight local customs made it impossible for the African-American soldiers to take advantage of recreational opportunities in nearby towns, or they found their access to such opportunities severely restricted. Thus, it was not until well after the Japanese attack on Pearl Harbor that the St. Louis Cardinals and St. Louis

Browns ended the practice of segregated seating at Sportsman's Park, despite the fact that both teams had made it a practice to accommodate the soldiers' desire to attend sporting events by inviting groups from Scott Field to opening day and other important games as early as 1940.[65]

Even on base, African-American troops were forbidden to enter white clubs, USO's, PX's, and swimming pools and playing fields, since the Army at first provided separate facilities for them. However, this led to substantial resentment among the black soldiers who found that the type of facility and amount of money allocated to purchase their athletic equipment, books, magazines, newspapers, and other recreational equipment was based on the size of their (usually) small unit, leaving them with substantially less than their white counterparts on each base.[66] Even when there was no practical way to create a separate facility for African-American sailors, as in the case of ocean beaches used for swimming, base commanders designated particular days and times for their use. At Pensacola, the navy even provided a "colored life guard" and swimming instructor, H. E. Belmear, SpA2c.[67]

Since the army and navy intended to maintain segregated units and segregated facilities on American bases wherever possible, soldier and sailor athletes often found themselves playing on segregated teams in segregated leagues. This was true for local sports, played among the less athletically talented men, whose skills prevented them from being named to the so-called varsity teams that appeared as representatives of the base or station at off-base competitions. At Pensacola, there was a "colored" softball league for the African-American sailors, as there was for the men of Malden Army Air Force base. And the men of the 367th Infantry Regiment at Camp Claiborne played basketball, softball, and volleyball, and competed individually in boxing, horseshoes, Ping-Pong, and the nonsport of checkers.[68] Because each individual base or station often had only a limited number of African-American troops, athletic officers discovered that they had trouble finding enough men to make up the teams to play a complete schedule, especially where blacks were not allowed to play white teams. To partially offset this problem, African-American boxers and softball and football teams traveled off-base to meet other black athletes.[69]

Another solution was to schedule games with teams from the traditionally black colleges, often dedicating gate receipts to the war effort or similar worthy charities. In doing so, the military inadvertently helped ensure the continuation of athletics at those colleges, many of which considered dropping their intercollegiate athletic programs during the war, but who instead played with a larger purpose, as was the case with the 1942 Tuskegee-Wilberforce game, played at Soldier Field in Chicago for the Army Emergency Relief Fund.[70] Similarly, the wartime Tuskegee Relays featured representative teams from local army camps and naval bases, while elite African-American track athletes continued to appear at the springtime Millrose Games and Penn Relays Carnival.[71]

Despite the effects of segregation, many black soldiers and sailors competed on the same athletic field as whites. At one base field day, an African-American squad was the overall winner, scoring in every event, which included boxing, tug-of-war, running an obstacle course, touch football, cross country, softball, and basketball. At another, a black swimmer led his team to triumph by taking four swimming events and the diving competition. And Pvt. Jerry Reid, who had once caddied for Bobby Jones, placed fourth in the Central Pacific Golf Championships, playing against whites on an eighteen-hole golf course for one of the first times in his life. Similarly, black teams were not always restricted to leagues of their own, as was the case with the Hammer Field basketball league, and softball leagues elsewhere.[72] In these cases, however, teams were still segregated even if the leagues were not.

Contests between teams of black and teams of white baseball players had a long history by the beginning of World War II.[73] Therefore, it should not be surprising that the appearance of black and white teams in the same Army leagues occurred. But prewar exhibition baseball games between traveling white all-stars and their black counterparts were quite different than the implied normalization of relations between African- and European-American soldiers represented by their regularly scheduled appearance on the same field of play. As with the dilemma posed by potential victories of sportsmen from other countries over athletes from the United States, the possibility that in normal competition African-Americans might achieve success over European-Americans suggested the unreasonableness of distinctions based on the supposed superiority of one race over the other. Since the value of the American way of life was to be demonstrated in part on the playing field, and since many believed that success on the battlefield was predicted, and indeed, ensured with athletic success, the right of the white population to continue its domination over the black population was endangered by the excellence of black sportsmen.

Nowhere before the war were African-Americans accepted on major league baseball teams, with only Joe Lillard playing professional football in the prewar years.[74] But despite the attempt by the army and navy to maintain segregation, when it came to determining who would represent a base or station in competition against other bases and stations, segregation gave way to the need to field the best team. Thus, the Salt Lake City base baseball team featured Tom Martin of the Homestead Grays, one of the most important of the Negro League teams. The Salt Lake base softball and basketball teams were also integrated.[75] At George Field, Illinois, an integrated football team played a team of high school and college stars at a benefit game held in Vincennes, Indiana.[76] Thus, despite the presence of segregated teams, playing in segregated leagues, the system broke down when bases needed to put their best athletes into action. A similar situation prevailed in the Pacific where the Seventh Army Air Force placed three boxers in the Hawaian 1944 AAU Tournament, the only winner of which was identified as "Lorenza Cooper, colored lightweight."[77] And, as Arthur Ashe noted in his study of the black athlete, skilled African-American players were nor barred from playing on the six great post football teams of World War II.[78]

Wherever integration of post teams occurred, the black press welcomed the development. Indeed, in a country where the University of Missouri refused to play football against a team with any African-American players until a game with Ohio State in 1943, and where the appearance of a mixed black and white football team at New York City's Polo Grounds seemed remarkable, the integration of military teams *was* an occasion for recognizing that the color bar might be collapsing.[79] The Baltimore *Afro-American* published a photograph of Camp Lee's football team with the comment that it "took the Army to bring democracy to Virginia, where mixed competition is not sanctioned, except in rare instances, but the Camp Lee football team knows no distinction."[80] Similarly, the presence of two African-American soldiers on Camp Upton's baseball team drew praise, with the black press contrasting the Camp Upton team with the continued refusal of the white professional baseball leagues to use black players. As the *Afro-American* noted with regard to the Thirty-seventh Fighting Aviation Squadron's baseball team at Grenier Field in New Hampshire, it had "no baseball color line as the picture of the camp team plainly indicates. The soldiers know that baseball talent has no color line, although the major leagues refuse to recognize this fact."[81] As Lucious Jones of the *Pittsburgh Courier* said in naming the Fort Knox Armoraiders 1942 football team an "All-American team" for being racially mixed, "That's true democracy. That's the stuff of which the Four Freedoms are made. That's what our white and colored boys are fighting for—Victory at Home as well as Victory Abroad!"[82]

On the one hand, in utilizing the talents of black athletes wherever they could help contribute to the success of base teams, the military seems to have been in the vanguard. In doing so, the armed forces seem also to have recognized that in the war against fascism and racism, at least an appearance of American racial harmony, as demonstrated on the playing field, would contribute to the successful outcome of the conflict. On the other hand, with the continued restrictions on black advancement within the regular military structure, the services remained during the war years yet another site for reinforcement of stereotypes and cultural expectations about the abilities of African-Americans. Indeed, black athletic success seems in many ways to have then, as now, failed to translate to success in other fields where blacks were not expected to do well and were indeed encouraged to fail.

Perhaps the career of the most famous of all African-American athletes in the service will help illustrate this point. Joe Louis was the reigning heavy-weight World Champion boxer in January, 1942, when he joined the army immediately after having dispatched Buddy Baer in an exhibition bout for Navy Relief. His earlier victory over the German champion Max Schmeling had made him a national hero in the white community and a beloved figure in the black community.[83] But Louis's wartime experience also reflected the continuing tensions between his place as a recognized sports hero attempting to capitalize on his celebrity for the good of the men in service, and his place as an African-American man in a European-American world.

Certainly, most people in the black community had no illusions about the implications of the Nazi message for their own survival, while they also had no illusions about the ill-feelings harbored by many white Americans toward their race. Yet Louis's entry into the army was quickly exploited as a means to encourage support of the war effort by all Americans. For example, in May, 1942, Louis was asked to speak before a huge crowd in New York at an "I Am an American Day" rally. And the *Pittsburgh Courier,* which had been conducting a "Double-V" campaign for victory against Naziism abroad and racism at home since the late 1930s offered for sale an 11-by-14-inch color drawing of Louis carrying a rifle in front of a flag with the caption, "No Fears for the Future/No Regrets for the Past."[84] Louis therefore became a symbol of Americanism for a racially mixed crowd and a special symbol for his fellow African-Americans.

Although Joe Louis joined the army in January, 1942, the question of what role he would play within the military took several months to settle. Like many other professional athletes such as Bob Feller and Hank Greenberg, Louis was faced with an enormous income tax bill early in the war while also facing a drastic reduction in his income. Whether he should be allowed to take time from his army training to fight Billy Conn and discharge that $117,000 tax liability was extensively debated in the media. The Atlanta *Daily World* pointed out that since Louis helped the Jim Crow Army and Navy, they should help him out and let him settle his tax situation. The New York *Age* argued that by letting him fight, the government would gain $117,000 to purchase rifles, rounds, and other materiel. But Westbrook Pegler of the New York *World Telegram,* said that he did not think it appropriate that Louis should be allowed to fight—or to receive a commission just for being an "entertainer." And a white Congressman suggested that letting Louis take time to prepare for the proposed title fight would make a mockery of the army and that Americans should "stop all of these theatrical performances, football games, pugilistic encounters and devote ourselves and our fighting men to the successful termination of the war."[85] In the end, the Louis-Conn fight was barred by the secretary of war, who professed himself to be "shocked" that the proceeds of the fight were to be used to pay off debts.[86]

Thereafter, Joe Louis's military career was dedicated to giving exhibitions and training boxers during tours of bases both in the United States and overseas. Yet even while on tour, Louis was a catalyst for social transformation and for debate about the respective abilities of blacks and whites. Louis demanded that a previously established segregated seating plan be abandoned at a dinner for him and his team of boxers from Fort Riley, creating an example to be followed at future banquets and dinners he attended.[87] Louis also helped Jackie Robinson and others in their quest to attend Officer Candidate School, kept Washington officials informed about base commanders' refusal to obey the order desegregating base bus systems, and promoted the integration of base theaters overseas.[88]

During the war, the question of whether Joe Louis or Jack Dempsey was the superior boxer remained a matter of dispute. The racial significance of the resolution to that question was not lost on Joe Williams of the *Birmingham Post*. In reporting on the results of a soldier poll in which Dempsey was chosen over Louis, he pointed out that the 365th Colored Infantry gave all of their votes to Louis, "showing that the boys at least know the difference between black and white."[89] And, as Fay Young of the *Chicago Defender* reminded his readers, while Jack Dempsey was a slacker during World War I, Joe Louis was a volunteer in his country's service in the present conflict.[90]

The wartime experience of African-American athletes in the services was quite varied. Despite the military's commitment to maintaining as much segregation as possible, in units, on bases, and in the command structure, that guarantee could not always be met. Nor could the guarantee that African-American athletes have opportunities similar to their European-American counterparts be met. Thus, on some bases black soldiers and sailors found that their sports and recreational oportunities were severely limited while on other bases, black athletes, particularly those with superior skills were welcomed as teammates, and as representatives of the post in off-base competitions. That such integration did occur suggests that despite their best efforts those opposing ultimate equality of opportunity for African-Americans within the service, and in civilian life, were fighting a losing battle.

Although the number of women allowed in the military was reduced to a very small percentage after the war, the demonstration that women could provide valuable service to their country while in uniform would not be forgotten. Although military women discovered that their athletic opportunities would also be restricted while in the service, sports provided them with an outlet for the tensions of the disciplined life. Sports also provided a space to express the joy of physical activity. But still, for WACs, WAVEs, SPARs, and women marines, their participation in sports conveyed a double meaning. Yes, women could be strong and powerful and athletically gifted, but that athleticism would not be allowed to interfere with the women's primary obligation to remain sexually desirable to the men in their lives. Even as the country faced the challenge of war, that message remained as strong for those women who chose to directly serve by putting on the nation's uniform as for those who did not.

Women in the military found that the sports which they were allowed to play, and the way in which their play was presented, reinforced gender stereotypes. The message prevailed that no matter how athletic, no woman could ever be as strong as the weakest male within the military organization. But that message depended on every man demonstrating again and again through sports, and other physical activities the strength and aggression deemed to be appropriate to his gender. Although the army and navy tried to prevent the induction into the service of those men who they assumed lacked the strength and aggression for war, some men who did not meet gender stereotypes did enlist or get drafted. And since not all men wanted to play football or box, the military had to create a sports program for them as well. Although that sports program consequently included sissy sports, the gender hierarchy was maintained by demonstrating that men could become physically exhausted, could acquire useful military skills, and could even get injured, playing such sports and games.

During World War II, military athletic programs helped ensure that service women would attain only enough strength and coordination to meet their service obligations, while still remaining attractive to the men around them. Men whose interests did not lie in athletic participation were encouraged to develop interest in sports nonetheless. And African-American men were welcomed as athletes, but athletes whose chances to play would remain limited and controlled by social mores. The masculinity of African-Americans would remain in doubt precisely because of their exclusion from full participation on the playing field and on the battlefield. By preventing total participation, in each of these cases the armed forces program of sports and athletics provided further evidence that women, sissies, and blacks would remain marginal to the military machine.

8

Conclusion

By the end of World War II, members of the combined forces of the United States had served on every continent, in every kind of climate and terrain, and had faced weapons of mass destruction beyond any imagined by the troops sent to Cuba less than sixty years before. Their experiences had been tempered and shaped by the expectations that they brought to the service and by the demands placed on them by their commanders and by the terrifying enemies that they had encountered. Individual men had been challenged to find strength and courage where they might have thought they had none, while those women who joined the military during the war struggled to find their own strength and courage while maintaining the femininity expected of them. To meet those challenges, these men and women were provided with a systematic program of sports and athletics designed to teach them skills they would need during wartime: how to cooperate with the members of their units; how to deal effectively with civilians, both foreign and domestic; how to gain and retain physical fitness; how to follow orders and commands; how to recognize and honor a hierarchy based on masculinity; and how to avoid the boredom and frustrations of the military life. Whether or not individual soldiers or sailors took advantage of that program, they lived among many sportsmen and women who did, reading about the exploits of talented players in camp and base newspapers, and recognizing their athletic successes as reflective of their own superiority as part of the outfit to which the particular skilled athlete belonged. That sports and athletics should have so permeated military life by the end of the Second World War should be no surprise—they had become a critical part of popular culture by the end of the previous century. But how the armed services used sports and athletics in training the soldiers and sailors of World War II does reflect the unique needs of the services, needs anticipated by civilian rhetoric about the meaning of war and the meaning of manhood, yet not fully met until the 1940s.

When the United States embarked on its first great imperial adventure in 1898, the rapid expansion of the military, followed by the speedy collapse of Spanish opposition in Cuba and the Philippines, left the army in particular in a peculiar situation. Clearly, the system created for transporting, feeding, housing, and maintaining soldier health during the Spanish-American War proved to be inadequate to the task. Despite the mobilization chaos, however, that all-volunteer force, many of whom agreed to remain in service to deal with the Filipino insurgency, seemed to be ready to embrace the challenge of overseas service. Yet even that army of volunteers was sufficiently diverse as to challenge its commanders to find a way to establish and maintain good morale and unit cohesion under the difficult circumstances generated by disease and by continued fighting in the islands. Although the sports world had undergone significant development and modernization by the end of the nineteenth century, reflected in the creation of intercollegiate rivalries and regularly scheduled play, military commanders made no plans in 1898 to include a program of sports and athletics in soldier and sailor training. Despite the widespread civilian belief that sports helped build men, instilling in them attributes of masculinity such as force, aggression, and self-confidence, the armed services had not chosen sports as a way of testing the men in uniform. Nevertheless, in the Philippines and in Cuba a system for organized athletics was begun by 1900 to alleviate the tensions among the troops and to provide them with some entertainment. Furthermore, that system provided an opportunity to work out interracial conflicts in a relatively nonviolent way. As African-American and European-American soldiers competed against each other in the Philippines they helped begin the process that would eventually lead to the integration of the military.

Meanwhile, men such as Theodore Roosevelt and Gen. Leonard Wood, who had fought in the Spanish-American War, were so convinced of the value of athletics that following the war they worked to ensure that every man would have the opportunity to test himself on the playing field. Therefore General Wood, as army chief of staff, asked the War Department to prepare a manual for physical training to be distributed not only to the Regular Army but to the various state guard units so that every soldier at least would have a base of athletic skills on which to draw in time of war.

Despite General Wood's plan to incorporate formal athletic training and sports competitions into military life, the First World War began without an organized system for ensuring that a sports program could be put into place. As a mass army was being raised to fight in France, the military was forced to turn to civilians to provide for soldier entertainment. The YMCA and other civilian welfare agencies established a presence in most outfits both in the United

States and in Europe, where they helped soldiers write letters home, served as counselors to homesick doughboys, and ran regular athletic competitions in a variety of sports. Because the American military was not immediately recognized by European commanders as a viable fighting force, and because General Pershing and his advisers wanted to maintain the independence of the army on the Western Front, they pointed to the physicality and violence of the sports being played by American troops as a sign of the ruggedness and courage they would surely display in combat. Furthermore, when American doughboys competed against athletes from allied armies on the playing field, their successes were recognized as justifying the continued freedom of the United States military to operate under its own command.

After the war, the armed services' sports program was used again to prove that it was the United States' entry into the war which had turned the tide against the Central Powers. By 1919, the character of a nation was believed in part to be reflected in the character of its sports, and therefore the demonstrations of American baseball and other sports conducted within the zone of German occupation were especially significant. The Americans used their athleticism not only to show the superiority of the style of sport played in their own country, but also to reinforce the message that battlefield success was born of the masculinity developed through sport.

In the following two decades, lessons learned from the First World War would lead to the creation of an entirely new system for providing sports to the men of the military. Almost immediately after the war, Raymond Fosdick of the YMCA, who had chaired the effort by civilian social service agencies to serve soldier and sailor welfare needs, addressed the Army War College and argued that in the future the Army itself should take over that function. Fosdick was no doubt influenced by the fear that changing definitions of masculinity had made suspect the behavior of YMCA workers during the war. As had been prefigured before World War I, postwar culture had embraced a masculinity defined by its rejection of softness, sentiment, and physical closeness among males. Indeed, men expressing their desire for physical closeness with other men had been recategorized and would in the future be assumed to be homosexual. Men's affections for each other would in the future only be allowed where they were part of athletic team "spirit" or where they reflected the love of the buddy during wartime.

As the military prepared for the future, new officers being trained at West Point were required to undergo rigorous instruction in sports and athletics. In later years, they remembered the Military Academy's intramural program as an invaluable adjunct to their other training, as it allowed them to develop skills of leadership, poise under pressure, and confidence that they could give and receive physical pain. As young officers during the Second World War they applied those lessons and encouraged as many as possible of the men under their command to play sports. To ensure that the facilities would be available for sports and athletics, the armed services added the construction of such facilities to the building program begun in 1940–1941. That program provided not only new barracks and mess halls at the expanding bases and camps, but also provided for the construction of gymnasiums, ball fields, and swimming pools.

In general, the young men who enlisted or were drafted into the armed forces following Pearl Harbor did not consider themselves to be militaristic. Instead, they believed themselves to be civilians temporarily in uniform with a tough job to do to ensure the survival of the American way of life. Sports within the military helped to maintain that fiction. Athletics were a part of civilian life—they would be a part of military life. Sports played on military reservations looked like sports being played in the surrounding communities. And by observing these similarities between military and civilian life, both those within the armed services, and those who sent their loved ones into the service, were reassured that despite the rigors and dangers of war, the men who returned would be fundamentally unchanged.

By contrast to previous conflicts, however, this time athletic competitions were strictly under the control of the military. Both the army and navy trained and assigned athletic officers to individual bases to ensure that the troops kept playing. To elicit maximum cooperation, the Athletic Officers were provided with bribes of beer and cigarettes to distribute to the winners, with free publicity for their events in post and base newspapers, and with equipment for playing sports from the Aleutian Islands to the deserts of Iran to the mountains of China to the rest areas of conquered Europe. Everywhere the troops of the United States went, their sports followed them.

Yet tensions remained within this highly organized program for sports and athletics. During the Second World War the military remained segregated and initial planning for troop entertainment reflected that segregation. But during the war the military provided an outlet for the very best African-American athletes denied them in civilian life. Because the rhetoric justifying military sports assumed that unit pride and cohesion would be best promoted through athletic success—success that was again assumed to be a predictor of battlefield success—assuring victory on the playing field became more important than maintaining the color line. Accordingly, black men played alongside white men on base football and baseball teams as they were not yet welcomed to do in civilian society.

Sports were also provided to the women who joined the military during the Second World War. These women's athleticism was, however, presumed to be designed to improve their sexual desirability to men. Accordingly, lesbian women within the armed services were placed in an extremely awkward situation. If they played sports to the best of their abilities, they would be fitting cultural assumptions about the mannishness of lesbian women. This was the opposite of the dilemma faced by those men in the service whose interest in sports was less than keen or who gravitated to sports that were assumed to be best suited to the "sissy." By rejecting sports altogether or by choosing to participate in sports that did not seem to be sufficiently aggressive and dangerous, these men seemed to be rejecting their masculinity.

War has always been viewed as a preserve of men. Modern sports as they developed were also defined as a masculine preserve. The presence of women within the military, as well as the presence of men who rejected tough, aggressive sports, seemed to suggest that perhaps athletic success was not necessarily a marker for masculinity. If the enterprise of war, a man's enterprise, could be infiltrated by people failing to meet the definition of man, or rejecting the notion of a hierarchy of men valorizing the skillful athlete, then nothing could be certain.

By the end of World War II, sports and athletics were an integral part of military life. Indeed, they were so completely accepted within the culture of the armed forces that it was almost impossible to imagine daily life without them—just as was the case in civilian life. But the sheer enormity of the sporting life carried with it costs. Indeed, rather than unite groups of soldiers and sailors in a common cause, athletics always posed the danger of separating them, alienating from their peers those individuals who failed to understand why sports should be so important. Nevertheless, the assumption that sports should be a part of the GIs life remained potent and bad luck to the soldier who didn't understand his buddy when he yelled to him "slide."

In the years after World War II, questions about men and masculinity, as well as questions about the significance of sport to the enterprise of war, continued to be posed. Because the United States' entry into the war came at the end of the Great Depression, most of the young men who had entered the service, as well as their civilian peers, were unsure about their economic future at the end of the war. Few anticipated that the enforced savings programs of wartime, as well as pent-up consumer demand, would generate enormous growth in the economy during the subsequent decades. Therefore, few were able to anticipate that men's prewar fears, that they would never be able to fulfill their masculine function and support a family, would prove unfounded for most returning veterans. As the critical and popular success of the Academy Award winning film *The Best Years of Our Lives* suggests, Americans were not convinced in 1946 that their fears that the huge numbers of men who had fought the war would not be easily reintegrated into civilian society were unnecessary.

Furthermore, the entry into the work force of women in unprecedented numbers caused many social commentators to wonder whether men and women would be able to return to their prewar places in the gender order. As Betty Friedan demonstrated in *The Feminine Mystique,* the cultural pressure on women to return to the home and to devote their energies and attentions to the care of their children and the advancement of their husbands' careers was enormous.[1] Whether they read magazines, or books, or watched situation comedies on their new television sets, women were being advised to limit their ambitions if they wanted to fulfill their destiny.[2] For men during the late 1940s and 1950s the pressure to work hard in order to enjoy the benefits of family, a home in the suburbs, and weekend leisure, was equally intense. They no longer had an excuse for economic failure, the Depression was over. Furthermore, both men and women had to confront the possibility that all of the effort that they had put forth during the Second World War to secure peace in the future was to be in vain. Even as the War ended with atomic bombs, the possibility that that technology would proliferate, and that the Soviets would soon have a bomb of their own, cast into doubt the sacrifices of the past.[3]

For the major professional sports, the years following the conclusion of World War II resulted in the unprecedented growth of football and basketball. For baseball, as well, Jackie Robinson's appearance as a Brooklyn Dodger in 1947 signaled the end of the color bar.[4] As African-American athletes took their place on the playing field, as television began to cover the sport, and as baseball expanded its geographical reach, the game drew new fans and renewed interest among its old fans.

But football seemed to serve cultural needs most effectively, particularly after the American Football League and the National Football League united in 1967. During the 1960s as well, the Vietnam War became a source of national confusion and distress. Those young men who were chosen to go to Vietnam discovered that that war was not like that fought by their fathers. They were unable to recognize their enemy, and despite their overwhelming advantage in weapons and materiel they were unable to force the enemy to surrender. Meanwhile other young men refused to serve altogether, questioning whether as men they were obligated to support a war in which they did not believe. They also grew their hair long, sometimes pierced their ears, and experimented with their sexuality. Indeed, as late-1960s films like *Easy Rider* demonstrate, traditionalists were afraid that it was becoming harder and harder to tell the boys from the girls.

And so the national championship of professional football, the "Super Bowl," came to be a symbolic representation of that type of masculinity that did support the war and did join the struggle for American success in all endeavors. In describing the early years of the Super Bowl, Warren Farrell has suggested that those athletic encounters served as an opportunity to demonstrate that, in the words of the legendary Green Bay Packers coach, Vince Lombardi, for men "winning is the only thing." Thus, at the Super Bowl, fighter jets fly over the field; the national anthem is sung; red, white, and blue are the colors of the day; and national unity is achieved through dedication to the game.[5] And everybody is assured that it is *men,* and not girls, who are down there on the field.[6]

For the military, the 1970s proved to be a time of substantial change. As the Vietnam War ended, the national draft was abandoned for the first time since 1940, and a system relying on voluntary enlistment was reinstituted. Furthermore, the Second Wave of feminism precipitated by Betty Friedan's book led women to demand entrée into jobs and professions from which they had previously been excluded. By the middle 1970s women were even asking to be admitted to the national service academies, and to be allowed to prepare for careers in the military. As the political scientist Judith Hicks Stiehm argues, the integration of women into the armed forces provided a profound challenge to previously accepted notions about men and women. These officers in training were expected to use their talents in the service of their country wherever possible, and anticipated that they would not be kept in the service positions that had been opened to women during World War II. In studying the experience of women at the Air Force Academy, Stiehm concluded that for the female cadets, strength and agility tests, as well as competitive athletics, were used to prove that they were less likely to be successful air force officers regardless of whether the skills being tested had actual application to military duties. As she points out, young men were required to box at the academy despite the manifest danger to their future career posed by the possibility that they might be knocked out and subsequently denied pilot training. Yet women were exempted from the boxing requirement.[7] As had happened so many times in the past, sports served to divide and alienate those in the military rather than create a unified, fit fighting force.

One century after the crisis in masculinity was first identified, almost one hundred years after troops from the United States arrived in Cuba to begin their global responsibilities, and ten decades after the recognition that modern sports had become a critical part of American culture, the three themes remain bound together. As this is written, soldiers from the Tenth Mountain Division have recently completed a mission to Haiti, while other American soldiers move into Bosnia to serve as peacekeepers. And at the University of Colorado, a major college football coach is offering sports as a means of countering the challenge to masculinity he believes to have been posed by feminism and by the rejection of God.[8] As the people of the planet Earth approach the third millennium, war, sports, and masculinity remain tied together in popular consciousness as they first were at the end of the nineteenth century.

NOTES

1. War and Sports: From the Spanish-American War to 1917

1. Although the general view has been that the war with Spain was undertaken precisely to allow the United States to seize an empire overseas, as for example with G. J. A. O'Toole, *The Spanish War: An American Epic—1898* (New York: W. W. Norton & Company, 1984), David F. Trask provides a compelling argument that President McKinley asked for war only in the face of public demand for the support of the Cuban independence movement, and that events only later led him to conclude that the Philippines should be annexed. See Louis Morton, gen. ed., *The Macmillan Wars of the United States* (New York: Macmillan Publishing Co., 1981), *The War With Spain in 1898,* by David F. Trask. E. Anthony Rotundo identifies the opponents of the United States adventure in empire-building in 1898 as men of an older generation with clear memories of the Civil War, by contrast to those men of Theodore Roosevelt's generation who believed that men needed to fight in order to maintain their masculinity. Rotundo, p. 235.

2. Trask, pp. 158–162.

3. Peter Karsten, "Armed Progressives: The Military Reorganized for the American Century," in *The Military in America: From the Colonial Era to the Present,* ed. Peter Karsten (New York: The Free Press, 1980).

4. Russell F. Weigley *History of the United States Army* (New York: The Macmillan Company, 1967), pp. 296–298, 308.

5. For an unanalytical but still revealing discussion of Army-Navy football, see Gene Schoor, *100 Years of Army-Navy Football: A Pictorial History of America's Most Colorful and Competitive Sports Rivalry* (New York: A Donald Hutter Book, 1989). Geoffrey Perret discusses the introduction of intramurals into the West Point program during the post-World War I superintendency of Gen. Douglas MacArthur and suggests it reflects MacArthur's conviction that the men who dealt best with the war's rigors had been athletes in civilian life in *There's a War to be Won: The United States Army in World War II* (New York: Ballantine Books, 1991). See also Linda Lee Schoonmaker's unpublished dissertation, *The History and Development of the Programs of Physical Education, Intercollegiate Athletics, Intramurals and Recreational Sports for Women at the United States Military Service Academies* (Columbus: The Ohio State University, 1983).

6. Lodge is quoted at page 165 in Robert J. Higgs, "Yale and the Heroic Ideal, Gotterdammerung and the Palingenesis, 1865–1914," in *Manliness and Morality: Middle-Class Masculinity in Britain and American, 1800–1940*, eds. J. A. Mangan and James Walvin (Manchester: Manchester University Press, 1987). For Roosevelt's recruiting policies and his later support of military education for public school children, see J. Thomas Jable, "The Public Schools Athletic League of New York City: Organized Athletics for City Schoolchildren, 1903–1914," in *The American Sporting Experience: A Historical Anthology of Sport in America*, ed. Steven A. Reiss (New York: Leisure Press, 1984).

7. O'Toole, p. 231 and Trask, p. 327.

8. Louis A. Perez, Jr., "Between Baseball and Bullfighting: The Quest for Nationality in Cuba, 1868–1898," *Journal of American History* (September, 1994), pp. 513–515.

9. The history of the Tenth Cavalry's exploits in Cuba has recently been reissued. See Herschel V. Cashin, et al., *Under Fire with the Tenth U.S. Cavalry* (Niwot, Colo.: The University Press of Colorado, 1993; London: F. T. Neely, 1899). For the work of the Twenty-fourth Infantry with disease victims, see Trask, p. 326.

10. Trask argues that despite the chaos on board the ships transporting troops to the Philippines, experience did prove a good teacher, as the soldiers later benefited from the lessons learned in Cuba and were better fed, housed, and entertained, pp. 387–388.

11. Russell Weigley reports that on May 11, 1898, Congress specifically asked for a volunteer force of ten thousand who would be immune to tropical disease. This First-to-Tenth Volunteer Infantry group would include six white and four black regiments. Weigley, p. 297.

12. Arthur R. Ashe, Jr., *A Hard Road to Glory: A History of the African-American Athlete, 1619–1918, Vol. I* (New York: Warner Books, Inc., 1988), p. 14.

13. Ibid., pp. 15, 87.

14. The literature on sports at the turn of the century in the United States and elsewhere is enormous. See, for example, for the ways in which modern sports seemed to permeate the culture, J. Thomas Jable, "The Public Schools Athletic League of New York City: Organized Athletics for City Schoolchildren, 1903–1914," in *The American Sporting Experience: A Historical Anthology of Sport in America*, ed. Steven A. Reiss (New York: Leisure Press, 1984); Donald Mrozek, "From National Health to Personal Fulfillment," and Michael Messner, "The Meaning of Success: The Athletic Experience and the Development of Male Identity," both in *Fitness in American Culture: Images of Health, Sport, and the Body, 1830–1940*, ed. Kathryn Grover (Amherst: The University of Massachusetts Press, 1989); Melvin Adelman "The First Modern

Sport in America: Harness Racing in New York City, 1825–1870," in *The Sporting Image: Readings in American Sport History*, ed. Paul J. Zingg (Lanham, Md.: University Press of America, 1988); and Douglas A. Noverr and Lawrence E. Ziewacz, *The Games They Played: Sports in American History, 1865–1980* (Chicago: Nelson Hall, 1983).

15. For a sense of how character had become identified with athletic success by the end of the nineteenth century, see E. Anthony Rotundo, *American Manhood: Transformations in Masculinity from the Revolution to the Modern Era* (New York: Basic Books, 1993); Harvey Green, *Fit for America: Health, Fitness, Sport and American Society* (Baltimore and London: The Johns Hopkins University Press, 1986); Todd Crosset, "Masculinity, Sexuality, and the Development of Early Modern Sport," in *Sport, Men and the Gender Order: Critical Feminist Perspectivies*, eds. Michael Messner and Donald F. Sabo (Champaign, Ill.: Human Kinetics Books, 1991); (and for Great Britain) Michael C. C. Adams, *The Great Adventure: Male Desire and the Coming of World War I* (Bloomington: Indiana University Press, 1990).

16. Jack C. Lane, *Armed Progressive: General Leonard Wood* (San Rafael, Calif. and London: Presidio Press, 1978), p. 20.

17. Donald J. Mrozek, "The Habit of Victory: The American Military and the Cult of Manliness," in *Manliness and Morality: Middle-Class Masculinity in Britain and America, 1800–1940*, eds. J. A. Mangan and James Walvin (Manchester: Manchester University Press, 1987). In a letter to his son, Kermit, Roosevelt described General Wood as his "playmate," noting that he "comes over every evening and we play singlestick together. We put on heavy padded helmets, breastplates and gauntlets and wrap bath towels around our necks and then we turn to and beat one another like carpets" *Armed Progressive*, pp. 117–118.

18. John K. Mahon, *History of the Militia and the National Guard* (New York: Macmillan Publishing Company, 1983), pp. 146, 147.

19. For a general discussion of the training practices of the U.S. Army and how they have changed over time, see Weigley, *The History of the United States Army*.

20. Maj. Gen. Leonard Wood, Chief of Staff, "Introduction," in *Manual of Physical Training for Use in the United States Army* (Washington, D.C.: Government Printing Office, 1914).

21. *Manual of Physical Training for Use in the United States Army*, p. 5.

22. Ibid., p. 8.

23. Ibid., p. 309.

2. World War I and Military Athletics
at Home and in the Face of Battle

1. For a discussion of the events leading up to the declaration of war on April 2, 1917, see Frederick C. Calhoun, *Power and Principle: Armed Intervention in Wilsonian Foreign Policy* (Kent, Ohio: The Kent State University Press, 1986).

As to why the decision was made to rely on the draft to fill the ranks of the World War I army, see John Whiteclay Chambers II, "The Progressive Era and the Origin of the Modern Military Draft in the United States in World War I," in *The Military in America: From the Colonial Era to the Present,* ed. Peter Karsten (New York: The Free Press, 1980). Chambers discusses the subsequent history of the draft in *To Raise an Army: The Draft Comes to Modern America* (New York: The Free Press, 1987).

2. Russell F. Weigley, *History of the United States Army* (New York: The Macmillan Company, 1967), pp. 354–358.

3. For a discussion of the transformation in American sexual values, including the decline in prostitution as young men turned to young women of their own social class for sexual expression and release, and for the idea of companionate marriage as it developed during the 1920s, see John D'Emilio and Estelle B. Freedman, *Intimate Matters: A History of Sexuality in America* (New York: Harper & Row, 1988).

4. President Woodrow Wilson's "Special Statement," dated April 19, 1918, appears in Edward Frank Allen, *Keeping Our Fighters Fit: For War and After* (New York: The Century Co., 1918).

5. Ibid., pp. 7, 8.

6. D'Emilio and Freedman, p. 212.

7. Harold Seymour, *Baseball: The People's Game* (New York and Oxford: Oxford University Press, 1990), p. 337.

8. United States War Department, Raymond Fosdick, Chairman, *Report of Chairman on Training Camp Activities,* 1918 (Washington, D.C.: Government Printing Office, 1918).

9. A considerable number of these letters survive in the files of the Military History Institute.

10. Allen, p. 26.

11. Fosdick, pp. 3, 4.

12. Ibid., p. 7.

13. Allen, pp. 42, 43.

14. Donald J. Mrozek, "The Habit of Victory: The American Military and the Cult of Manliness," in *Manliness and Morality: Middle-class Masculinity in Britain and America, 1800–1940*, eds. J. A. Mangan and James Walvin (Manchester: Manchester University Press, 1987).

15. For the notion that World War I battlegrounds would serve as a means to repossess lost manliness, see Peter G. Filene, *Him/Her/Self: Sex Roles in Modern America,* 2nd ed. (Baltimore: The Johns Hopkins University Press, 1986).

16. The assumption that virtue and teamwork can be learned through athletics, of course, relates to the Muscular Christianity movement that was an important influence on the YMCA.

17. Weigley, *History of the United States Army,* p. 186.

18. John K. Mahon, *History of the Militia and National Guard* (New York: Macmillan Publishing Co., 1983).

19. For a discussion of Civil War drill, see Russell Weigley, *The History of the United States Army,* p. 231. For a discussion of the sports played by the men in arms during the Civil War, see Lawrence W. Fielding, "War and Trifles: Sport in the Shadows of Civil War Army Life," *Journal of Sport History* 4 (Summer, 1977): 151–168.

20. Sue E. Berryman, "Images and Realities: The Social Composition of Nineteenth and Twentieth Century Enlisted Forces," in *Life in the Rank and File: Enlisted Men and Women in the Armed Forces of the United Sates, Australia, Canada and the United Kingdom,* eds. David R. Segal and H. Wallace Sinaiko, (Washington, D.C.: Pergamon-Brassey's International Defense Publishers, 1986). Berryman points out that the army used different criteria to determine literacy than that used by the census. Nevertheless, she is convinced that the actual percentages of illiterate troops was higher than that of young men outside of the service.

For a discussion of the Civil War-era draft, see, Weigley, *History of the United States Army,* p. 357.

21. Allen, p. 48.

22. According to Russell Weigley, disease casualties during World War I were reduced to fifteen per one thousand per year from the sixty-five per one thousand per year of the Civil War. *History of the United States Army,* p. 371.

23. Donald J. Mrozek, "The Interplay of Metaphor and Practice in the U.S. Defense Establishment's Use of Sport, 1940–1950," *Journal of American Culture* 7 (1984): 54–59. I am indebted to Sue Curry Jansen and Donald Sabo for sharing with me a draft of their paper "The Sport/War Metaphor, Gender Order, and the Persian Gulf War" in which they argue that metaphors of sport and war dominated the discourse surrounding the Persian Gulf War.

24. John J. Pershing, Commander-in-Chief, American Expeditionary Forces, *My Experience in the World War,* vol. i (New York: Frederick A. Stokes Co., 1931), pp. 317–318.

25. Alexander Woollcott, *The Command Is Forward: Tales of A.E.F. Battlefields as They Appeared in the Stars and Stripes* (New York: The Century Co., 1919), Preface.

26. This cartoon appeared in *Stars and Stripes* on June 21, 1918, at p. 7.

27. "Fritz Slams Them Square Over Pan," *Stars and Stripes,* August 16, 1918, p. 7.

28. See the discussion of the transition from the valorization of an individualistic masculinity during the nineteenth century to the developing notion that masculinity demanded subordination for the good of the team in E. Anthony Rotundo, *American Manhood: Transformations in Masculinity from the Revolution to the Modern Era* (New York: Basic Books, 1993).

29. "Baseball Wonders Where It Gets Off," *Stars and Stripes,* July 12, 1918, p. 7; and "237 Baseball Stars Must Work or Fight," *Stars and Stripes,* August 2, 1918, p. 1.

30. Letter from Captain Robert J. Whitfield to his mother, dated October 14, 1918, contained in the Alexander-Whitfield Family Papers collection, at the Military History Institute, Carlisle Barracks, Pennsylvania.

31. For a good general discussion of the decision to continue baseball play during World War II, see Bill Gilbert, *They Also Served: Baseball and the Home Front, 1941-1945* (New York: Crown Publishers, 1992), while Harvey Frommer in *Shoeless Joe and Ragtime Baseball* (Dallas: Taylor Publishing Co., 1992), discusses the national debate about whether to shorten the 1918 season once it had begun.

32. "Many Stars Refuse to Sign Contracts," *Stars and Stripes,* March 1, 1918, p. 1, and "Giants Make Flyers Do Ascension Stunt," *Stars and Stripes,* April 5, 1918, p. 6.

33. "More Baseballs for A.E.F.," *Stars and Stripes,* June 14, 1918, p. 6.

34. Seymour, p. 339.

35. Joseph Durso, *Baseball and the American Dream* (St. Louis: The Sporting News), p. 1986.

36. "Editorial," *Stars and Stripes,* April 12, 1918, p. 4.

37. "Sporting Comment," *Stars and Stripes,* July 19, 1918, p. 6.

38. Arthur S. Link, *American Epoch: A History of the United States Since the 1890s* (New York: Alfred A. Knopf, 1955), p. 202. For a discussion of Americans in battle at the end of May, 1918, see American Battle Monuments Commission, *American Armies and Battlefields in Europe: A History, Guide, and Reference Book* (Washington, D.C.: Center of Military History, 1992; Washington, D.C.: Government Printing Office, 1938), pp. 21–27.

39. "Visiting Airman Breaks Up Meet," *Stars and Stripes*, June 7, 1918, p. 6.

40. Q.M. Sgt. Stuart Carroll, "Star Shells," *Stars and Stripes*, April 12, 1918, p. 6.

41. "Yanks Put Tear in Chateau-Thierry," *Stars and Stripes*, June 14, 1918, at p. 6; and "All-Star Service Teams," *Stars and Stripes*, July 5, 1918, p. 6, represent two among many articles in which the newspaper described the current state of professional baseball by reference to the many players not available to play that summer due to their service responsibilities.

42. "The Sporting Page Goes Out," *Stars and Stripes*, July 26, 1918, p. 6. For the discussion of Ty Cobb and other stars' failure to join up, see the editorial "Sport for Who's Sake?," also on July 26, at p. 4.

43. For discussion of the Secretary of War's "Work or Fight" rule, see "Khaki or Overalls for Ball Players," *Stars and Stripes*, July 26, 1918, p. 6, and the Editorial appearing at P. 4 in the August 30, 1918, issue of *Stars and Stripes*. The proposed all-star tour is discussed in "All Star Nine in Olive Drab May Tour A.E.F.," *Stars and Stripes*, September 6, 1918, p. 1. Harvey Frommer describes in *Shoeless Joe and Ragtime Baseball* how many professional players such as Joe Jackson continued to play baseball in industrial leagues while working in heavy industry for the war effort. According to Frommer, their efforts were not always considered to be equal to those efforts expended by the men in uniform.

44. "For the Good of Baseball," *Stars and Stripes*, September 20, 1918, p. 4.

45. "Playing Baseball Before Battle Helps Make a Soldier Fight," *Trench and Camp*, September 10, 1918, p. 3.

46. "Sailors at San Pedro Stage Furious Bouts," *Trench and Camp*, August 20, 1918, p. 3; and "Twenty-first Has Many Good Athletes," *Trench and Camp*, October 8, 1918, p. 3.

47. "Football Honors Go to Doughboys," *Trench and Camp*, October 29, 1918, p. 1.

48. "Twenty-first Has Many Good Athletes," *Trench and Camp*, October 8, 1918, p. 3.

49. "Injured Men Play Games," *Trench and Camp*, September 3, 1918, p. 1.

50. "Athletic Outlook at Camp Travis Surprisingly Bright," *Trench and Camp*, October 22, 1917, p. 7.

51. Diary of O. W. Lomady, 320th Infantry, Eightieth Division, entry dated June 1, 1918, in the collection of the Military History Institute.

52. Diary of 2d Lt. William F. Todd, Transportation Corps. Nineteenth Grand Division and Nineteenth Engineers-Railway, entries dated August 15 and 18, 1917, in the collection of the Military History Institute.

53. "Military Athletic Outfitters," *Stars and Stripes,* July 19, 1918, p. 7.

54. "First Ball Glove is Made in France," *Stars and Stripes,* June 7, 1918, p. 5; and "Bats and Gloves Being Made Here," *Stars and Stripes,* June 21, 1918, p. 6.

55. Major Harry P. Holt, "A Brief History of the Battalion," *The Whizz-Bang,* February, 1919, p. 2.

56. Steinel's career is described in an article introducing him to the readers appearing in *Stars and Stripes* on February 22, 1918, at p. 6. See also "Put It Up to Us," *Stars and Stripes,* February 22, 1918, p. 6.

57. "Sports Aplenty," *Stars and Stripes,* March 1, 1918, p. 1, and "Mike Donlan Coming Over," *Stars and Stripes,* May 171, 1918, p. 6. According to the Donlan article, Mathewson conferred with YMCA officials to determine whether it would be advisable that he make the trip to France.

58. "Sports Aplenty Will Await Men in Rest Billets," *Stars and Stripes,* March 1, 1918, p. 1.

59. Pershing, p. 151.

60. "Tuileries Sees Its First Ball Game," *Stars and Stripes,* March 1, 1918, p. 6. The similarity between tossing a grenade and throwing a baseball would also be a common theme in sports reporting during the Second World War, as will be discussed in a subsequent chapter.

61. "Gas Mask Game Good as Farce," *Stars and Stripes,* May 31, 1918.

62. "Stalling Banned in Army Matches," *Stars and Stripes,* June 28, 1918, p. 6.

63. "Results from Paris League," *Stars and Stripes,* May 10, 1918, and "Touraine Circuit Is Real Big League," *Stars and Stripes,* July 19, 1918.

64. "Soldier or Sailor? Speak Up, Marine!" *Stars and Stripes,* May 17, 1918, p. 6.

65. Memoirs of Seaver Rice, 1st Eng., 1st Reg., Company C., First Division, in World War I Survey collection.

66. Memoirs of Private Henry K. Carter, 82nd Div., 163rd Inf. Brigade, in World War I Survey collection.

67. Letter to "Mabel and George," dated July 7, 1918, in the Memoirs of Sgt. Maj. Benjamin H. Heath, Eighty-second Div., 163rd Inf. Brigade, in World War I Survey collection.

68. Memoirs of John E. Cooney, Pvt., Charles Van Citters, Clarence O. Pearson, Walter Frei, Herbert C. Smith, Jr., and George McMahon, all of the Transportation Corps., Nineteenth Grand Division and Nineteenth Engineers—Railway, in World War I Survey collection.

69. "Classy Sprinting in Battalion Meet," *Stars and Stripes,* May 31, 1918, p. 6, and "Base Port Athletes Plan Live Holiday," *Stars and Stripes,* May 24, 1918.

70. Diary entry dated July 5, 1918, in papers of Samuel Arthur Devan, Chaplain, AEF, held at the Military History Institute.

71. Memoirs of Allen T. Johnson, Paul C. Meads, William Rufus Mitchell, Howard N. Norton, and James R. Clyburn, all of the Eighty-first Division in the Eighty-first Division, and Mrs. Gladys Dorcy Papers, Military History Institute.

72. For the Secretary of War's directive to Pershing, see *American Armies and Battlefields in Europe: A History, Guide, and Reference Book,* p. 17.

73. For an example of that postwar discourse, see, Thomas Clement Lonergan, *It Might Have Been Lost! A Chronicle from Alien Sources of the Struggle to Preserve the National Identity of the A.E.F.* (New York & London: G. P. Putnam's Sons, 1929). For a recent discussion from the French point of view, see Andre Kaspi, *Le Temps des Americains: Le Concours Americain a La France en 1917–1918* (Paris: Publications de la Sorbonne, 1976).

74. "Engineer Boxers Take Four in Row," *Stars and Stripes,* July 5, 1918, p. 6.

75. "Good Bouts Staged in Base Section 2," *Stars and Stripes,* May 10, 1918, p. 6.

76. "K of C Prize Cup Goes to Gob Nine," *Stars and Stripes,* June 7, 1918, p. 6 and "It's 'Dangereux' but What of It?" *Stars and Stripes,* May 3, 1918, p. 6.

77. "Taplow Canadians Trim London Yanks," *Stars and Stripes,* May 10, 1918, p. 6.

78. "Canadians Blanked by U.S. Naval Air Men," *Stars and Stripes,* May 3, 1918, p. 6, and "Try Out Track Meet Held at A.P.O. 717," *Stars and Stripes,* June 21, 1918, p. 6.

79. Q.M. Sgt. Stuart Carroll, "Star Shells," *Stars and Stripes,* April 26, 1918, p. 6.

80. "As We See Ourselves," *Stars and Stripes,* March 15, 1918, p. 4.

81. "Sioux Chief-to-be Now A.E.F. Captain," *Stars and Stripes,* March 1, 1918, p. 1.

82. For a discussion of the army's attempts to deal with non-English-speaking Slavic troops, see Bruce White, "The American Military and the Melting Pot in World War I," in *The Military in America: From the Colonial Era to the Present.*

150 *Notes*

83. "Sporting News and Comment," *Stars and Stripes,* May 7, 1918, p. 7.

84. "Base Port Athletes Plan Live Holiday," *Stars and Stripes,* May 24, 1918, p. 6.

85. Memoirs of George A. Burton in the Marvin Fletcher Collection, Military History Institute.

86. For a discussion of the so-called crisis in masculinity, see Michael S. Kimmel, "The Contemporary 'Crisis' of Masculinity in Historical Perspective."

3. Playing in the Postwar World and Planning for the Future of Military Sport

1. See Arthur S. Link, *American Epoch: A History of the United States Since the 1890s* (New York: Alfred A. Knopf, 1955) at pp. 235–237 for a discussion of Wilson's demobilization program.

2. According to Frederick S. Calhoun, the last troops from the United States were finally withdrawn from Siberia in the summer of 1920. Frederick S. Calhoun, *Power and Principle: Armed Intervention in Wilsonian Foreign Policy* (Kent, Ohio: Kent State University Press, 1986).

3. David M. Kennedy, *Over Here: The First World War and American Society* (Oxford and New York: Oxford University Press, 1980), p. 206.

4. See my discussion in Chapter 2. Michael C. C. Adams also describes how participation in sport was believed to be a means of preserving virtue in *The Great Adventure: Male Desire and the Coming of World War I* (Bloomington: Indiana University Press, 1990), especially at pp. 41, 42.
See, also, Donald J. Mrodek, "The Interplay of Metaphor and Practice in the U.S. Defense Establishment's Use of Sport, 1940–1950," *Journal of American Culture* 7 (1984): 54–59, in which Mrozek suggests that during the first decade of this century sports were believed to act as a *unique* means of ensuring virtue among those who played them.

5. The fear of alcohol's deleterious effects that informed the prohibition debate and the efforts of social reformers to keep alcohol out of the hands of training soldiers must have had an effect as the World War I veterans responding to the Military History Institute's questionnaire recalled the general unavailability of alcohol while they were in the United States. On the other hand, the same veterans found alcohol to be generally available once they arrived in Europe.

6. Jack Gann, "Athletics in Army Have Made Big Mark," *Amaroc News,* July 13, 1919, p. 7. That Gann emphasizes the cleanness and honesty of Army athletics is

evocative as we remember that a few short months after Gann wrote, the 1919 World Series scandal broke in the newspapers. For a discussion of the 1919 baseball season and the "Black Sox" scandal, see Harvey Frommer, *Shoeless Joe and Ragtime Baseball* (Dallas: Taylor Publishing Company, 1992).

7. "Athletics," *The "Cootie"*, March 29, 1919, p. 3.

8. "Crowds Already Arriving in Coblenz to Attend the Big Third Army Carnival," *Amaroc News*, April 41, 1919, "Monster Carnival Opens Crowds Break All Records," *Amaroc News*, April 23, 1919; and "Hot Shower Baths for Third Division Athletes," *Amaroc News*, May 7, 1919.

9. Photographs of the fields at Heddesdorf and Montabaur appear at p. 12 in *The Indian*'s homeward bound issue, "On the High Seas," published as the troops returned home in 1919.

10. "Athletics," *Whizz-Bang*, February 7, 1919, p. 4.

11. "Athletics," *The Cootie*, March 29, 1919. ("Cooties" were the body lice that plagued the doughboys during World War I, and who made another appearance during the World War II.)

12. See the discussion in the previous chapter about the racial and ethnic makeup of the AEF.

13. "318th Machine Gun Bats Out Some Bull," *The Wildcat*, May 17, 1919, p. 3.

14. The *Whizz-Bang* may be found at Robert L. Harbison, Cpl. Co.F, 320th Infantry, Eightieth Infantry Division. WWIS–485. World War I Survey.

15. "To Teach Frenchies to Toss Baskets," *Amaroc News*, April 21, 1919, p. 3, and "Basketball Will Be Sport with English," *Amaroc News*, July 15, 1919, p. 3.

16. "Americans Teaching Tommies Baseball," *Amaroc News*, June 30, 1919, p. 3 and "Yanks to Demonstrate Their National Game," *Amaroc News*, June 1, 1919, p. 3.

17. Clark Griffith, "When All the World Becomes Baseball Fans," *Trench and Camp*, November 26, 1918, p. 5.

18. "French Athletes Like Yanks' Work," *Amaroc News*, June 4, 1919, p. 1. For a discussion of the army's embrace of boxing during the First World War, see Randy Roberts, "Jack Dempsey: An American Hero in the 1920s," in *The Sporting Image: Readings in American Sport History*, ed. Paul Zingg (Lanham, Md.: University Press of America, 1988).

19. "Like Money from Home," *The Indian*, June 3, 1919, p. 15.

20. "Athletics to the Front," *The Indian*, April 22, 1919, p. 1.

21. "Athletics are Big Factor in Making Fighter," *Amaroc News,* April 23, 1919, p. 3.

22. "Great Variety of Sports for Yankee Forces," *Amaroc News,* August 17, 1919, p. 1; and "Inter-Army Matches Show Form of Yanks Way Below British," *Amaroc News,* October 7, 1919, p. 3.

23. "Yanks Break Even with French and British in Opening of Big Athletic Tournament on Island," *Amaroc News,* September 27, 1919, p. 1; and "Squad of Athletes to Represent Army to Train for Games," *Amaroc News,* October 13, 1919, p. 3.

24. "Rivalry of Units Lends New Feature to Big Sport Show," *Amaroc News,* September 6, 1919, p. 3.

25. Allen Guttmann in *Games and Empires: Modern Sports and Cultural Imperialism* (New York: Columbia University Press, 1994) provides a useful discussion of the ways in which the spread of British sport served the interests of British imperialists, suggesting how sports promoters from the United States might have understood the need to spread American sports as a counterweight to that of the British.

26. W.H.W., Battery E, 146th, letter to the editor, *The Long Range Sniper,* April 17, 1919, p. 2; and "318th Machine Gun Bats Out Some Bull," *The Wildcat,* May 17, 1919, p. 3.

27. "American Spirit," *Amaroc News,* June 17, 1919, p. 2.

28. "Concerning Germans," *The Indian,* July 1, 1919, p. 8. *The Indian* was first published on April 15, 1919, while the Second Division was stationed at Neuwied-on-the-Rhine.

29. Memoirs of Private John E. Cooney are in Transportation Corps. Nineteenth Grand Division and Nineteenth Engineers—Railway. World War I Surveys at Military History Institute.

30. "Yank Boxing Rules Don't Suit British," *Amaroc News,* October 20, 1919, p. 7.

31. Jeffrey Richards, " 'Passing the Love of Women': Manly Love and Victorian Society," in *Manliness and Morality: Middle-class Masculinity in Britain and America, 1800–1940,* eds. J. A. Mangan and James Walvin (Manchester: Manchester University Press, 1987).

32. Thomas J. Knock refers to the "contradictions" that occurred as Wilson tried to negotiate terms that would not utterly destroy Germany financially and politically, while allied leaders and leaders back in the United States continued to demand that Germany be made to pay to the utmost for leading Europe into war. Thomas J. Knock, *"To End All Wars": Woodrow Wilson and the Quest for a New World Order* (New York and Oxford: Oxford University Press, 1992).

33. If British-rules boxing was "ladylike," other sports also were identified as less than masculine. But the validity of those sports could presumably be proven if they were played with sufficient strenuousness. "We Know Tennis Isn't for Effeminate Ones," *Amaroc News,* June 20, 1919, p. 3.

34. "American Girls Have Been Active in Sport Events," *Amaroc News,* July 11, 1919, p. 3.

35. Susan Cahn, *Coming on Strong* (New York: Free Press, 1994) pp. 129, 130.

36. " 'Y' Girls Have Baseball Team," *Amaroc News,* May 25, 1919, p. 1 and " 'Wild Bats' Lose Seven Inning Go to Camouflage Nine," *Amaroc News,* May 26, 1919, p. 1.

37. For a discussion of women's sports during the nineteenth century, see Allen Guttmann, *Women's Sports: A History* (New York: Columbia University Press, 1991). Helen Lefkowitz Horowitz also describes how women's colleges at the turn of the century were building gymnasiums and encouraging young women to participate in sports in *Alma Mater: Design and Experience in the Women's Colleges from Their Nineteenth Century Beginnings to the 1930s* (New York: Alfred A. Knopf, 1984).

38. "Training Bulletin No. 1," in *U.S. Army in the World War, 1917–1919, Vol. 17* (Washington, D.C.: Government Printing Office, 1948).

39. "Training Bulletin No. 2," in *U.S. Army in the World War, 1917–1919* (Washington, D.C.: Government Printing Office, 1948).

40. Ibid., p. 166.

41. See, for example, World War I surveys from Cpl. Fred H. Takes, Eighty-second Division, 163rd Infantry, and PFC George Lokides, 326th Infantry, and the Memoirs of Boldridge Edward Kneece and Samuel Francis Evans of the Eighty-first Division in the Mrs. Gladys Dorcy Papers box, World War I surveys.

42. Major George Whythe, Captain Joseph Mills Hanson and Capt. Carl V. Burger, Eds., *The Inter-Allied Games, Paris, 22nd June to 6th July, 1919* (Paris: The Games Committee, 1919), pp. 17–20.

43. Ibid., at pp. 19, 20.

44. Donald J. Mrozek, "The Habit of Victory: The American Military and the Cult of Manliness," in *Manliness and Morality,* Mangan and Walvin, eds.

45. The decision to add the hand-grenade toss to the program for the Inter-Allied Games may also have been influenced by the adoption during the war of the grenade toss as a part of American intercollegiate sports. However, in the United States the object was not to throw for distance but for accuracy with points awarded for the number of

bull's-eyes hit with a fixed number of grenades. "Sporting Comment," *Stars and Stripes,* June 21, 1918, p. 6.

Although the Baron Pierre de Coubertin had created the Modern Pentathlon in 1912 specifically as a competition involving military skills, no such event was contested at the Inter-Allied Games. See Martin Connors, Diane L. Dupuis, and Brad Morgan, *The Olympics Factbook: A Spectator's Guide to the Winter and Summer Games* (Detroit: Visible Ink, 1992).

46. Richard D. Mandell, *Sport: A Cultural History* (New York: Columbia University Press, 1984), p. 200.

47. William Wambsganss, survey response in Infantry Central Officers Training School, World War I, box. World War I Survey. This is the same William Wambsganss who completed an unassisted triple play while playing for the Cleveland Indians in the 1920 World Series.

48. For Weigley's conclusions on how Americans came to define the object of war as the total defeat of the enemy, see Russell F. Weigley, *The American Way of War: A History of United States Military Strategy and Policy* (New York: Macmillan, 1973).

49. Whythe, et al., eds., pp. 78–83.

50. For one view of the attributes necessary to "modern" sport, see Melvin Adelman, "The First Modern Sport in America: Harness Racing in New York City, 1825–1870," *Journal of Sport History* VIII (Spring, 1981): 5–32.

In *Rites of Spring: The Great War and the Birth of the Modern Age* (Boston: Houghton Mifflin Company, 1989), Modris Eksteins describes the response of the Paris audience to new productions of the Ballet Russe and compares them to the response of the European crowds during the summer of 1914 as they called for assertion of national power.

51. "Allied Horsemen Compete in June," *Stars and Stripes,* April 25, 1919, p. 2. For a discussion of the refusal of many in the British upper classes to recognize that the usefulness of cavalry had ended, and for his suggestions as to why, see Adams, *The Great Adventure.*

After the war the American army, too, still held out hope that cavalry would prove critical to military success and the planning for the Inter-Allied Games reflected the desire to show off military horsemanship at a high level. However, the American army also discovered after the war that they would be unable to sell the horses and mules they had brought to Europe at a competitive price. "Horse Still Good in Modern Warfare," *Stars and Stripes,* May 23, 1919, p. 7.

52. "Overconfidence May Beat U.S. in the Allied Games," *Stars and Stripes,* May 9, 1919, p. 6.

53. "Many Athletes to Return for Games in June," *Amaroc News,* May 11, 1919, p. 1.

54. "Training Bulletin No. 3." In *U.S. Army in the World War, 1917–1919, Vol. 17* (Washington, D.C.: Government Printing Office, 1948).

55. For Kennedy's full discussion of this, see David Kennedy, *Over Here: The First World War and American Society.*

56. Donald J. Mrozek, "The Habit of Victory: The American Military and the Cult of Manliness."

57. For a general history of women from the United States in their nation's military, see Maj. Gen. Jeanne Holm, USAF (Ret.), *Women in the Military: An Unfinished Revolution, Rev. Ed.* (Novato, Calif.: Presidio Press, 1992).

58. Whythe, et al., p. 139. For a short discussion of the experience of navy Yeomanettes during the Great War, see Holm, pp. 12–15.

59. Jack Gann, "Allied Nations Are Together in Sports," *Amaroc News,* June 2, 1919, p. 4.

60. For the team from Czechoslovakia, as well as for other teams from Eastern and Central Europe, the trip to the games was often interrupted by new fighting and by the struggle to obtain transportation under the prevailing chaotic conditions. Thus, the Czechoslovakian team headed for the Games was temporarily detained in Austria by a lack of available railroad stock. "Czecho-Slovakia to be Represented in Allied Games," *Amaroc News,* May 25, 1919, p. 1.

61. "Handsome Statue is Wilson Trophy for Allied Games," *Stars and Stripes,* April 11, 1919, p. 1.

62. For a fuller discussion of the rhetoric surrounding the Olympic Games, see, Allen Guttmann, *The Games Must Go On: Avery Brundage and the Olympic Movement* (New York: Columbia University Press, 1984).

63. See Knock, p. ix.

64. Russell F. Weigley discusses Pershing's struggle to keep the American troops in Europe independent rather than allow them to be subsumed within British and French units in *History of the United States Army* (New York: The Macmillan Company, 1967). For a discussion of Wilson's purposes at Versailles, see John Milton Cooper, Jr., *The Warrior and the Priest: Woodrow Wilson and Theodore Roosevelt* (Cambridge, Mass.: The Belknap of Harvard University Press, 1983). For the French view on the debate about the value of America's entry into the war, see Andre Kaspi, *Le Temps des Americains: Le Concours Americain a La France en 1917–1918* (Paris: Publications de la Sorbonne, 1976).

65. Whythe et al., p. 143.

66. Ibid., p. 334.

67. "The Sportive Realm," *Pittsburgh Courier,* September 20, 1919 (Butler jumped 24 feet 6 inches at Paris, while the national winner jumped just over 22 feet), and "Sol Butler Back from Europe with Five Honor Medals," *Chicago Defender,* August 23, 1919 (which noted as well that the King of Montenegro awarded Butler a knighthood for his achievements).

68. "Haven't Had Enough of France Yet—They're Going Back," *Spokane Washington Chronicle,* August 16, 1919.

69. "Inter-Allied games Will Mark Victory Jubilee," *Stars and Stripes,* May 23, 1919, p. 1.

70. American Battle Monuments Commission, *American Armies and Battlefields in Europe* (Washington, D.C., Center of Military History United States Army, 1992; Washington, D.C., Government Printing Office, 1938), p. 493.

71. MacArthur quoted from his June 22, 1922 Annual Report, included in *A Soldier Speaks: Public Papers and Speeches of General of the Army Douglas A. MacArthur,* Major Vorin E. Whan, Jr., ed. (New York and Washington, D.C.: Frederick A. Preager Publishers, 1965).

72. Brigadier General Edward L. King, "The G-3 Division, War Department General Staff, and Its Present Outstanding Problems," War College Lecture, September 16, 1929, delivered at Washington, D.C. for G-3 Course #5.

73. "Beaucoup Baseballs for Athletic Yanks," *The Amaroc News,* May 24, 1919, p. 3.

74. Raymond B. Fosdick, "Welfare Work," War College Lecture, March 3, 1922, delivered at Washington, D.C.

75. "College Coach Admires Soldier Spirit in Athletics," *The "Cootie",* April 12, 1919, p. 3.

76. Fosdick, "Welfare Work," p. 13.

77. Also at page 13.

78. For a fuller account of the Newport case, and an argument that the case reflects a moment of transition between a definition of homosexuality dependent on the commission of sexual acts, and a definition of homosexuality determined by identity, see George Chauncey, Jr., "Christian Brotherhood or Sexual Perversion? Homosexual Identities and the Construction of Sexual Boundaries in the World War One Era," *Journal of Social History* 19 (1985): 189–212.

79. According to Kevin White, male heterosexuality as a self-conscious part of men's identitites only emerged at the turn of the century as a result of the scientific

study of sexuality. For a further discussion of his theories, see *The First Sexual Revolution: The Emergence of Male Heterosexuality in Modern America* (New York & London: New York University Press, 1993). Michel Foucault pointed out that scientific inquiry led to a self-consciousness about sexuality in general and the enforcement of a discourse about sexuality in *The History of Sexuality: Volume 1: An Introduction* (New York: Pantheon Books, 1978).

4. Building Strong Men and New Facilities for Another War

1. Anthony J. Badger describes the loss of status suffered by many men as they lost their jobs in *The New Deal: The Depression Years, 1933–1940* (New York: The Noonday Press, 1989), pp. 32, 33. According to Badger, the suicide rate in the United States also rose from 14 per 100,000 in 1929 to 17.4 per 100,000 in 1932. Roland Marchand provides an evocative analysis of the impact of visual advertising images on the culture of the 1930s in *Advertising the American Dream: Making Way for Modernity, 1920–1940* (Berkeley, Calif.: University of California Press, 1985). In his discussion of the "clenched fist" parable, Marchand argues that men were encouraged to take charge of their economic lives by their children, who needed them to succeed and refused to let them despair (see, e.g., the illustrations at p. 326, 327). Geoffrey Perret describes the soldiers who fought World War II as having drawn strength from what they had overcome growing up during the Depression in *There's a War to Be Won: The United States Army in World War II* (New York: Ballantine Books, 1991).

2. For General Eisenhower on football, see Gene Schoor, *100 Years of Army-Navy Football: A Pictorial History of America's Most Colorful and Competitive Sports Rivalry* (New York: A Donald Hutter Book, 1989), p. 48.

3. Gen. Douglas MacArthur, in *A Soldier Speaks: Public Papers and Speeches of General of the Army Douglas MacArthur*, Major Vorin E. Whan, Jr., ed. (New York and Washington, D.C.: Frederick A. Praeger, Publishers, 1965), p. 21, 22.

4. As to women's experience, see for example the transcript of Col. Mary A. Halloren's oral interview in the collection at the Military History Institute (MHI), in which she never mentions athletics, sports, or other types of recreation. The MHI also houses transcripts of interviews conducted at a reunion for nurses who served at Pearl Harbor held at San Diego, California in 1991.

5. Senior Officers Oral History Program, Conversations between Lt. Gen. Hobart Raymond Gay and Col. Willard L. Wallace, 1981, Project 81-G.

6. Senior Officers Debriefing Program, Conversations between Gen. James H. Polk, USA, Ret., and Lt. Col. Roland D. Tausch, USA, AWC 1971–1972, and Senior Officers Oral History Program, Conversations between Gen. Robert W. Porter, Jr., and

Lt. Col. John N. Sloan, 1981, Project 81-4. The Charles Gerhardt so much admired by Generals Polk and Porter would later command the Twenty-nineth Division which with the First and Fourth Divisions was chosen to lead the American D-Day invasion forces. For a discussion of Gerhardt's career, see Perret, pp. 299, 318, and 454.

7. Porter interview, pp. 21, 20.

8. Porter interview, p. 72.

9. Senior Officer Oral History Program, Conversation between Lt. Gen. Stanley R. Larsen and Lt. Col. Robert S. Holmes, 1977, pp. 18, 19.

10. Carl Ulsaker, "Memoirs," Carl Ulsaker Papers, Military History Institute, p. 54.

11. Maj. Gen. Earnest L. "Iron Mike" Massad, Senior Officer Oral History Program, 1985.

12. Michael A. Messner, *Power at Play: Sports and the Problem of Masculinity* (Boston: Beacon Press, 1992), pp. 73–75. For a discussion of Eisenhower's knee injury, see Schoor, *100 Years of Army-Navy Football.*

13. Senior Officer Oral History Program, Gen. Andrew J. Goodpaster, interviewed by Col. William J. Johnson and Lt. James C. Ferguson, January 9, 1976, p. 9.

14. Goodpaster interview, p. 3.

15. Massad interview, p. 39.

16. Senior Officer Oral History Report, conversations between Gen. James Alward Van Fleet and Col. Bruce F. Williams, 1973.

17. Drexel McCormack, of the Seventy-fifth Division, recalls that during the Battle of the Bulge a young lieutenant was a particularly effective leader of men, and had been an excellent athlete in civilian life. But McCormack also suggests that this fellow would have been a good leader even without previous athletic experience. Private conversation with author, May, 1994.

18. Russell F. Weigley, *History of the United States Army* (New York: Macmillan Publishing Co., 1967), pp. 396, 401.

19. Ibid., 417.

20. Massad interview, p. 12. General Marshall commanded a CCC camp based at Fort Moultrie, South Carolina, where he found a group of desperately hungry, uncared for young men. For a discussion of that experience see Leonard Mosley, *Marshall: Hero for Our Times* (New York: Hearst Books, 1982), at pp. 103–105.

21. Francis H. Carroll, *Works Progress Administration, District No. 9: Construction Report* (Rochester, New York, January 1, 1938, to December 31, 1938), and Robert G. Hoffman, *Works Projects Administration, District No. 9: Projects Report* (Rochester, New York, January 1–December 31, 1940). Donald S. Howard explains how early WPA policy forbade the application of relief funds to projects involving defense work, and how this policy was terminated in 1940 in *The WPA and Federal Relief Policy* (New York: Russell Sage Foundation, 1943).

22. "Lieut. Douglas Builds Sports at Scott Field," *Scott Field Broadcaster*, March 4, 1941, p. 2. According to the newspaper, Lieutenant Douglas, the Scott Field Athletic and Recreation officer was assisted by Web Henry, a WPA athletic consultant.

23. Weigley, p. 419.

24. Ibid., p. 427.

25. Ibid., p. 431.

26. "Kayo Parade Marks Boxing Championships," *Scott Field Broadcaster*, February 1, 1941, p. 5.

27. "Scott Field Cagers in State Tournament," *Scott Field Broadcaster*, March 4, 1941, p. 5, "Track and Field Meet Set for Last of May," *Scott Field Broadcaster*, April 22, 1941, p. 5; and "Begin Tryouts for Scott Field Baseball Nine," *Scott Field Broadcaster*, May 20, 1941, p. 5.

28. J. Edgar Kirk, "Sport-Pen," *Scott Field Broadcaster*, April 1, 1941, p. 5.

29. The results of the volleyball and Ping-Pong tourneys appear on p. 5 of the *Scott Field Broadcaster*, May 6, 1941, while photographs and stories about the track and field athletes appear on p. 5 of the June 3, 1941 edition.

30. "Plan Extensive Sports Bill for Soldiers Here," *Scott Field Broadcaster*, July 15, 1941, p. 1.

31. "Exercises Begin Here," *Scott Field Broadcaster*, August 26, 1941, p. 5. Apparently, the week before a new order had been issued requiring all men on the base to take two and a half hours of calisthenics a week under the direction of hastily trained men from each squad. "It's True!" *Scott Field Broadcaster*, August 19, 1941, p. 2.

32. "Plan Huge Sport Schedule for Scott Field Men," *Scott Field Broadcaster*, March 18, 1941, p. 5; and "Men Soon Will Bowl on Alleys Here on Field," *Scott Field Broadcaster*, August 12, 1941, p. 5.

33. "Free Smokes," *Scott Field Broadcaster*, September 9, 1941, p. 5.

34. " 'Open Door' Is Policy Between Army and Public," *Scott Field Broadcaster*, March 25, 1941, p. 1.

35. "Track Stars Awaiting Opening Gun of Scott Meet; Entrants Listed," *Scott Field Broadcaster,* July 8, 1941, p. 1. For a discussion of the isolationist challenge to Roosevelt administration policies, particularly that represented by Charles A. Lindbergh, see Richard M. Ketchum, "They Can't Realize the Change Aviation Has Made," in *Experience of War: An Anthology of Articles from MHQ: The Quarterly Journal of Military History,* ed. Robert Cowley (New York: W. W. Norton & Company, 1992).

36. "Joe Louis, Tony Zale to Perform Here on Oct. 11," *Scott Field Broadcaster,* September 30, 1941, p. 5.

37. "Plan Huge Sport Schedules for Scott Field Men," *Scott Field Broadcaster,* March 18, 1941, p. 5; and "Scott Field Men See First Game," *Scott Field Broadcaster,* April 15, 1941, p. 1. Five hundred men from Scott Field attended the Browns' home opener.

38. Pvt. J. Edgar Kirk, "Sport Pen," *Scott Field Broadcaster,* November 11, 1941, p. 4 and Pvt. J. Edgar Kirk, "Sport Pen," *Scott Field Broadcaster,* November 25, 1941, p. 4.

39. "Capt. Siebert to Cross Foils at Missouri Meet," *Scott Field Broadcaster,* February 18, 1941, p. 5, "Plan Fencing Team as Part of Coming Sports Program at Scott Field," *Scott Field Broadcaster,* July 22, 1941, p. 5; and Pvt. J. Edgar Kirk, "Sport-Pen," *Scott Field Broadcaster,* July 29, 1941, p. 5.

40. "2,000 Attend First Post Boxing Bouts," *The Spearhead,* April 4, 1941, p. 8; and "Fort Sam Boxers Best City Men," *The Spearhead,* April 18, 1941, p. 1.

41. "Army Fighters Seek Amateur Titles," *The Spearhead,* May 30, 1941, p. 8, "Local Boxers Ready for All-Army Bouts," *The Spearhead,* April 18, 1941, p. 8.

42. Weigley, p. 432, in which he describes the shock many Americans felt when they saw photographs of the Louisiana maneuvers of September, 1941, in which the soldiers used mock-up rifles. "New Athletic Equipment Ordered for Fort Sam," *The Spearhead,* May 2, 1941, p. 3.

43. "Headquarters Co. D.E.M.L. Enters Softball League," *The Spearhead,* May 2, 1941, p. 5, "Athletic Officer Announces Plans for Post Baseball," *The Spearhead,* May 16, 1941, p. 5.

44. "Finals of Post Baseball Tourney Get Underway," *The Spearhead,* July 4, 1941, p. 3, "Crack Ball Teams Battle for Title," *The Spearhead,* July 11, 1941, p. 1; and Troops Back Their Nines in Hot Tilts," *The Spearhead,* July 11, 1941, p. 1.

45. "Fort Sam Grid Schedule Announced," *The Spearhead,* October 24, 1941, p. 4, "Gunners Hit Ellington in Grid Opener," *The Spearhead,* October 31, 1941, and "All-Star 2nd Division team to Play for 3rd Army Title; Sugar Bowl Goal of Champ.," *The Spearhead,* July 5, 1941, p. 4.

46. For the difficulty the military experienced in training its soldiers during the prewar build-up due to the lack of weaponry (some of which was being transferred overseas pursuit to the Lend-Lease program), see Weigley, pp. 432, 433.

47. "Fort Sam Sports Arena to Open About October 15," *The Spearhead,* July 25, 1941, p. 2 " 'Sportatorium' to be Opened at Early Date," *The Spearhead,* November 21, 1941, p. 4.

48. "Man Needed for Go with Langley Nine," *The Bowman Bomber,* August 15, 1941, p. 3, "Hospital Softballers Rated Base Champs as Play Wanes," *The Bowman Bomber,* October 1, 1941, p. 3; and "Here and There on the Base," *The Bowman Bomber,* October 15, 1941, p. 1. A photograph of the baseball trophy appears on p. 1 of the July 1, 1941 edition of *The Bowman Bomber.*

49. "50th Bomb Builds Miniature Golf Links; Eyes Good Time," *The Bowman Bomber,* August 15, 1941, p. 2, "Basketball Season Merely Awaits Close of Maneuvers," *The Bowman Bomber,* October 15, 1941, and " 'Fit' Army to Be Result of New Training Program," *The Bowman Bomber,* December 1, 1941, p. 1.

50. "Athletic Program Underway in 168th," *The Clarion,* May 24, 1941, p. 3.

51. "34th to Launch Recreation and Athletic Plans," *The Clarion,* June 7, 1941, p. 4.

52. "Division Football Underway," *The Clarion,* October 11, 1941, p. 1, "Football Prospects Bright," *The Clarion,* October 25, 1941, p. 3.

53. "133rd Archers in State Meet," *The Clarion,* November 8, 1941, "Golf Proves Popular Sport in 34th's Artillery Regiments," *The Clarion,* November 15, 1941, p. 6.

54. "367th Captures Negro Baseball Laurels Here," *The Clarion,* November 8, 1941, p. 6, "Boxing Cards Scheduled in 367th Infantry," *The Clarion,* November 22, 1941, p. 6.

55. "Basketball!!!!!" *Clark Field Prop Wash,* October, 1941.

56. For a discussion of the officer cadre of 1940 and 1941 and the decision to establish Officer Candidate Schools during 1941, see Weigley, p. 428.

57. "Col. Ott Keeps Athletic Interests," *The Clarion,* June 21, 1941, p. 3.

58. "Col. Anderson of 185th First Enlisted in 1912, Athletic in Type," *The Clarion,* July 12, 1941, p. 2.

59. Reports on the competitions in the General Daley tournament appear at pp. 7 and 8 in the *Borinquen Bomber* for April, 1941.

60. "44th Bomb Sq. Always Active," *Borinquen Bomber,* August, 1941.

61. "Sports Shrapnel," *Borinquen Bomber,* September 12, 1941, p. 3; "Semi-Pro Circuit Offers Plenty of Action," *Borinquen Bomber,* September 30, 1941, p. 5.

62. "Golf Course Adds Three Holes," *Borinquen Bomber,* September 12, 1941, p. 3; "Horse Shoes to Hold Spotlight October 26th," *Borinquen Bomber,* September 30, 1941, p. 4; "Field Fencers Continue Lead," *Borinquen Bomber,* October 17, 1941, p. 4; and "Island-Wide Talent in Table Tennis Tourney," *Borinquen Bomber,* November 30, 1941, p. 7.

63. "Field Individual Tourney Marked by 5 Knock-Outs," *Borinquen Bomber,* November 17, 1941, p. 5.

5. Creating the Military Sports Machine:
Special Service Officers and World War II

1. Geoffrey Perret, *There's a War to be Won: The United States Army in World War II* (New York: Random House, 1991), p. 63. See also Leonard Mosley, *Marshall: Hero for Our Times* (New York: Hearst Books, 1982), "The next day [after Pearl Harbor] everybody was in uniform, and everybody smelled of mothballs," p. 186.

2. Russell Weigley attributes the ability of the army to field far fewer men to the ultimate success of the millions of men and women the Red Army committed to the defeat of the Germans on the Eastern Front. Russell F. Weigley, *History of the United States Army* (New York: The Macmillan Company, 1967), p. 438. See also Perret, p. 119, who notes that the Red Army was more than twice as large as that of United States. For the navy numbers, see Robert R. Palmer, Bell I. Wiley, and William R. Keast, *The United States Army in World War II: The Army Ground Forces* (Washington, D.C.: Department of the Army, 1948), vol. 2: *The Procurement and Training of Ground Combat Troops,* p. 1.

3. For the social and cultural composition of the armed forces see Sue Berryman, "Images and Realities: The Social Composition of Nineteenth and Twentieth Century Enlisted Forces," in *Life in the Rank and File: Enlisted Men and Women in the Armed Forces of the United States, Australia, Canada and the United Kingdom* eds. David R. Segal and H. Wallace Sinaiko (Washington, D.C.: Pergamon-Brassey's International Defense Publishers, 1986) p. 26. See also Palmer et al., p. 4.

Although the Army General Classification Tests actually measured educational achievement, with black soldiers and white soldiers from the South scoring lower as might be expected given the lower levels of spending on education those groups received, the AGCT was generally interpreted as reflecting *intelligence,* with all of the incorrect assumptions drawn therefrom regarding African-American intelligence in general. For a further discussion of this, see Richard M. Dalfiume, *Desegregation of the U.S. Armed*

Forces: Fighting on Two Fronts, 1939–1953 (Columbia, Mo.: University of Missouri, 1969), at pp. 56–58.

4. Lee Kennett, *G.I.: The American Soldier in World War II* (New York: Charles Scribner's Sons, 1987), p. 27; and Palmer, et al., p. 6.

5. Kennett, p. 47.

6. Weigley, pp. 186, 429. For a discussion of the Louisiana maneuvers and their influence on the careers of many major World War II officers, see Perret, pp. 42–45.

7. Maj. Leon T. David, FA, "Factors Indicating the Status of Morale in a Command," January 20, 1942. In the Leon T. David Papers, Military History Institute, Carlisle Barracks, Pennsylvania.

8. Minutes of Faculty and Staff Conference, April 16, 1942. In "Faculty Minutes of Special Services Branch School March 3 to November 21, 1942," Maj. Leon T. David Papers.

9. The career of Sergeant Bill Keegan, who had previously worked for the Physical Education Department of New York City's Board of Education, and who found himself in the Persian Gulf building athletic fields, distributing athletic equipment, running the library, and putting on shows and movies, suggests the breadth of responsibilities undertaken by the Special Services. "Special Services Men at the Persian Gulf Run Shows, Movies, Books and Fever," *Yank,* May 28, 1943, pp. 6, 7.

10. U.S. War Department, *Special Service Officer, TM 21-205,* May, 1942, p. 11.

11. Ibid., p. 16.

12. The conviction that combat soldiers were motivated by their sense that they were part of the best army fighting for the righteous cause held by Special Service Officers seems not to have reflected reality. As Samuel L. Stouffer and others who surveyed soldier attitudes discovered, most soldiers fought in order to end the task, conclude the war, and get home. For an extended discussion of combat motivation, see Samuel A. Stouffer et al., *The American Soldier: Combat and Its Aftermath , Vol. II* (Princeton: Princeton University Press, 1949), at Chapter 3 "Combat Motivations Among Ground Troops."

13. *TM 21-205,* May, 1942, pp. 24, 25.

14. Kennett, p. 93.

15. *TM 21-205,* May, 1942, pp. 85, 86.

16. Ibid., pp. 67–75.

17. "U.S. Lists Huge Sums for Sports," *Bomb Bay Messenger,* July 18, 1943, p. 2.

18. Jary, "Sports Review," *Cochran Communique,* March 2, 1945, p. 8.

19. *TM 21-205,* May, 1942, p. 84.

20. See, for example, "817th Teams Battle to 6-6 Tie in Camp's Football Opener," *Armodier,* November 5, 1942, p. 5.

21. "Softball Leads Spring Parade," *The Spearhead,* March 6, 1942, p. 4;and "Athletic Department Plans Track and Swimming Meets," *Cochran Communique,* May 22, 1943, p. 8.

22. The prevention of venereal disease was made the responsibility of the commanding officer. To emphasize the importance of disease prevention, Secretary of War Stimson ordered that unusually high VD rates be noted on the commanding officer's efficiency reports, which would effectively destroy the commander's possibility of promotion. Overseas, individual officers met this challenge by setting up brothels, such as the one established for the First Armored Division in Oran. Training films describing the horrors of infection and the availability of condoms also helped keep the amount of disease down. Perret, pp. 470, 471. To further ensure that GIs would not pick up venereal diseases, post newspapers occasionally carried advertisements for condoms and cartoons encouraging their use, such as the one which appeared in *Bom Bay* on April 22, 1943, assuring the soldiers that they were free and readily available.

23. Perret, pp. 453, 454.

24. See the discussion in Perret at p. 530 of the projected cost of an invasion of the Japanese mainland. According to Geoffrey Perret, in many theaters of operation the Special Services officer was provided with as many as eight trucks filled with boxing gloves, basketballs, and other paraphernalia. Perret, p. 93.

25. "Sports Program Important in Redeployment Training," *Armored News,* June 18, 1945, p. 7; and "European Sports Program Opens," *Cochran Field Communique,* May 12, 1945, p. 3.

26. Darrel Holland, survey of World War II veterans from American Legion Post, Newton, Illinois.

27. According to an article in *Yank,* Special Services expected at least 60 percent of the GIs in Europe to participate in the planned sports program that was to follow the defeat of Germany. "Unmilitary Training," *Yank,* October 6, 1944, p. 10. For the special program for potential professional athletes, coaches and managers, see "Sports Plans for Occupation GIs Revealed," *George Field News,* February 17, 1945, p. 7.

28. U.S. War Department, *The Special Services Officer (Athletic and Recreation), TM 21-205,* September, 1944, p. 21.

29. For an extensive discussion of the messages received by sports spectators, see Katherine McCrone, "Play Up! Play Up! and Play the Game!: Sport at the Late Victorian Girls Public Schools." In Mangan and Park, *From "Fair Sex" to Feminism.*

30. *TM 21-205*, September, 1944, pp. 24, 25.

31. Ibid., p. 29. According to the *Sourdough Sentinel*, for example, soldiers stationed in Alaska were treated to a Winter Carnival in February, 1944, which featured boxing, all disciplines of skating, skiing, ski jumping, and ice hockey, with a special appearance by the Oxford Rifles, Canada's Army Hockey Team. "Alaska's Sports Stars Ready for Carnival," *Sourdough Sentinel*, February 10, 1944, p. 1, in Box "AAF Bases—Alpha by Base," Military History Institute collection.

32. "Soldier Sports Have Doubled Since March," *Armored News*, July 31, 1944, p. 11.

33. *TM 21-205*, September, 1944, p. 50–52. As Colonel Delbert points out in the fictionalized treatment of army life, *From Here to Eternity*, "Every soldier knows that good athletics make good soldiering." James Jones, *From Here to Eternity* (New York: Charles Scribner's Sons, 1951), p. 55.

34. According to Geoffrey Perret, the North African editions of *Stars and Stripes* are generally considered to be the best and most honest of the newspapers which were published in the many theaters of operations during the war. Perret, p. 481.

35. "Bonura Gets Award," *Stars and Stripes*, October 27, 1943, p. 3; and "Navy to Stage MBS Allied Swimming Meet," *Stars and Stripes*, July 5, 1944.

36. See "B.B. Leagues Now Being Organized," May 4, 1943; "Four Oran Baseball Leagues are Organized," June 1, 1943; "Oran Football Goes into Gear Sunday," November 19, 1943; "Sports Had Good Year in North Africa," January 10, 1944; "3,000 Attend Hoop Openers," January 26, 1944; "Volleyball Tournament Gets Underway Tuesday," April 17, 1944; and "276 Entered in MBS Track Finals," June 15, 1944, all in *Stars and Stripes.*

37. "Baseball School," *Stars and Stripes*, May 18, 1944, p. 7.

38. "Casa Yanks Get Eisenhower Award," *Stars and Stripes*, October 7, 1943, p. 3.

39. "Basketball Finals Ready for MBS," *Stars and Stripes*, March 9, 1944, p. 7.

40. For the "Poi Bowl," see "Down the Runway," *Brief*, December 26, 1944, p. 16; for the Spaghetti Bowl, see "Moody, Spaghetti Bowl Star is Former Knox Armoraider," *Armored News*, January 8, 1945, p. 6; and for the Lily Bowl, see "Lily Bowl Dilemma," *B.B.C. News*, December 18, 1943, p. 2. Stephen Ambrose discusses the anticipated participation of football players from the 101st Airborne Division in the

Champagne Bowl in *Band of Brothers: E Company, 506th Regiment, 101st Airborne from Normandy to Hitler's Eagle's Nest* (New York: Simon & Schuster, 1992), p. 169. That "bowl" games did not have to coincide with the traditional New Year's day date is reflected in the August 1, 1944 game played in Panama between representatives of the Coast Artillery and the Mobile Forces, and the game scheduled for November, 1944, in China, described in "On the Gridion," *Brief,* September 12, 1944, p. 16. In the postwar movie, *Battleground,* practices for the members of the 101st Airborne preparing for a big football game are interrupted by their call to Bastogne.

41. "Rabchasers Win North Africa's Grid Crown," *Stars and Stripes,* January 3, 1944, p. 3, "Moody, Spaghetti Bowl Star is Former Knox Armoraider," *Armored News,* January 8, 1945, p. 6, and "Navy Beats AAF, Dobbs in Poi Bowl Game, 14–0," *Brief,* January 16, 1945, p. 17.

42. "Yank About Town," *Stars and Stripes,* December 29, 1943, p. 2.

43. "Arab Bowl Tops New Year," *Stars and Stripes,* December 31, 1943, p. 1 and "Notre Dame Unable to Play in Arab Bowl," *Stars and Stripes,* December 31, 1943, p. 3.

44. "Arab Bowl Tops New Year."

45. "Gridiron Training is Preparing Men to Battle Enemy," *The Real McCoy,* October, 30, 1942, p. 5. In Papers of the 601st Ordnance Battalion, Military History Institute, Carlisle Barracks, Pennsylvania.

46. Both the Arab Bowl and Mustard Bowl programs are contained in the Papers of the 601st Ordinance Battalion.

47. According to *Stars and Stripes,* Bonura received his Legion of Merit in recognition of his work as "Czar of North African Baseball." "Bonura Gets Award," *Stars and Stripes,* October 27, 1943, p. 3.

48. Geoffrey Perret describes in detail the many times in which American and British commanders came into conflict, from planning the Torch landings in North Africa through the final push into Germany. For Perret's view, see his description of the command given to the American Gen. William H. Simpson by Field Marshal Bernard Law Montgomery to stop his Ninth Army's advance as they reached the Rhine. As Perret put it, the "British were planning a grand-opera Rhine crossing, clambake and media fun fest. Nobody was going to plunder Monty of his moment. The men of the Ninth Army drew up to the Rhine and gazed across, wondering what might have been." Perret, p. 438.

See also the discussion of the efforts made by Montgomery to seize command of all allied troops during the Battle of the Bulge, and subsequent attempts by Prime Minister Churchill to soothe the consequent bad feelings engendered by Montgomery's implication that it was the British who had saved the day during the Bulge rather than the Americans in Gerald Astor, *A Blood-Dimmed Tide: The Battle of the Bulge by the Men Who Fought It* (New York: Donald I. Fine, 1992), pp. 338, 382, 383.

49. "Boxing," *B.B.C. News,* July 10, 1943, p. 1. For the relatively favorable view of British command during the Battle of the Bulge see J. Lawton Collins, *Lightning Joe: An Autobiography* (Baton Rouge & London: Louisiana State University Press, 1979), pp. 282–297.

50. "Army Boxers Triumph," *B.B.C. News,* July 17, 1943, p. 1.

51. "Knockouts Feature Thrilling ARC Bouts," *Stars and Stripes,* May 13, 1943, p. 1, "Fifth Army Boxing Bouts Draw 4,000," *Stars and Stripes,* July 15, 1943, p. 3 (featuring bouts between GIs and French civilians as well); "Navy to be Host for Allied Bouts," *Stars and Stripes,* p. 3; "Allied Net Tourney Opens Tonight," *Stars and Stripes,* April 3, 1944, p. 3; "Allied Track Stars Capture MBS Inter-Allied Zone Finals, *Stars and Stripes,* June 20, 1944, p. 3, and "Allied Track and Field Meet Scheduled for July," Stars and Stripes, March 29, 1944, p. 3. Another series of Inter-Allied boxing matches were held at the Palais de Sport in Paris at the beginning of December, 1944, drawing entries from military men in England, Italy, France, and Africa. For an announcement of those contests, see "Sports Service Record," *Yank,* October 20, 1944, p. 23.

52. "Toney Trains Hard for Title Match Against Cerdan," *Stars and Stripes,* December 14, 1943, p. 3. See also Johnny McCoy Hale Fights Cerdan at Petain Stadium," *Stars and Stripes,* August 5, 1943, p. 3, "Cerdan K.O.s Hale in 1:35 of 2nd, *Stars and Stripes,* August 10, 1943, p. 3 and "Cerdan by TKO in Second," *Stars and Stripes,* December 27, 1943, p. 3.

53. "Allied Track & Field Meet Scheduled for July," *Stars and Stripes,* March 29, 1944, p. 3. Under the caption "Roman Holiday," *Yank* published a series of photographs of the Inter-Allied Track and Field Meet at pp. 12 and 13 in the August 25, 1944 issue.

54. "Sports Service Record," *Yank,* June 9, 1944, p. 23, "Sports Service Record," *Yank,* March 16, 1945, and "Nevius Breaks High Jump Record," *The B.B.C. News,* June 5, 1943, p. 13.

55. Captain Tom Shehan, "The Soccer Situation," *Yank,* June 8, 1945, p. 23.

56. "Sports Service Record," *Yank,* March 3, 1944, p. 23.

57. "Soccer Teams on Station Organized; Plan Unit Games," *Gosport,* September 11, 1942, p. 5.

58. For the cricket match, see "Plan Cricket Match at Legion Field Sunday Afternoon," *Gosport,* September 18, 1942, p. 5. As had been the case during the First World War, Americans and Canadians played baseball at London's Hyde Park. An

illustration of such a game appeared at p. 6 of the April 14, 1944, issue of *Yank*. See also "Corry British Men Eke Out Victory in Swimming Meet," *Gosport*, August 4, 1944, p. 2, and "70 Limeys Try-Out for Softball Squads," *Gosport*, April 14, 1944, p. 3.

59. For a discussion of the extent to which bitterness was directed against the Japanese, and not to the Germans or Italians, see Stouffer, et al., p. 158. The Japanese were also apparently intrigued by the American character during the war, finding it remarkable that American POWs surrendered and equating that with the U.S. belief that war is like sports. See *Hochi Shimbun*, February 8, 1942, reprinted in *POW Camps During the Great Asiatic War (Overseas)*, Yochio Chaen, ed. (Tokyo: Fuji Publications, 1987), p. 57.

60. "Expert Likes Ju-Jitsu Over Boxing for Army," *The Armodier*, March 3, 1943, p. 6; "Medic Teaches Pals Jui Jitsu," *The Spearhead*, March 20, 1942, p. 4; and "CAC's Receive Extensive Physical Training," *Banana Peelings*, April 18, 1945, p. 10. See also the announcement that judo classes were being formed in *Bomb Bay*, November 17, 1943, p. 7. The *Drew Field Echoes* devoted a multi-issue series to photographs demonstrating how judo moves could disarm an attacker, as for example those which appear at p. 14 of the March 9, 1944 issue.

61. "Veteran Matman Says Wrestling Beats Jui-Jitsu," *Bomb Bay Messenger*, June 13, 1943, p. 11; and Sgt. Frank DeBlois, "Bench Warming," *Amphibian*, March 2, 1944, p. 7 (describing the arrival in the army of Fritzie Zivic an "old cauliflower commando [for whom] jui jitsu holds fewer terrors than mah jong [who will give] the first Jap who mixes it [with him] the old elbow, knee and eye thumb treatment so fast he'll think he tackled a giant squid").

62. "Sports Service Record," *Yank*, April 21, 1944, p. 23.

63. "Baseball Makes 16th Grenade Tossers Expert," *Armodier*, March 30, 1944, p. 1.

64. "47th A.R. Grenade Golf Course Trains GIs," *Armodier*, April 15, 1943, p. 2.

6. Strong Men, Strong Bodies, Off to War, 1941–1945

1. According to Stephen E. Ambrose this is the message of D-Day when "the soldiers of democracy showed that they could outfight and outthink the soldiers of totalitarianism." Ambrose "Foreword" in *Voices of D-Day: The Story of the Allied Invasion Told by Those Who Were There*, ed. Donald J. Drez (Baton Rouge and London: Louisiana State University Press, 1994), p. xiii.

2. See, for example, "Sports," *Bom Bay*, April 15, 1943, in which Cpt. Jack Sweetland announced the opening of the enlisted men's swimming pool and "New Pool Opened for Enlisted Men," *Cochran Communique*, May 22, 1943, p. 1. At the Pensacola Naval Air Station a heated pool was installed for the use of the enlisted men and restricted to their use, while the officers' pool was closed while an enclosure was built. "Station Pools Remain Open; Beaches Closed," *Gosport*, November 6, 1942, p. 5.

3. See, for example, "16th Officers in Hot Table Tennis Tournament," *Armodier*, April 20, 1944, p. 6; "335th Tennis Tournament Under Way," *Bom Bay*, March 4, 1943, p. 7; "A Few Dribbles from the Hardwood," *Bom Bay*, October 29, 1942, p. 12; "477th Wins Championship in 335th Softball League," *Bom Bay*, May 20, 1943, p. 5; and "Lt. McCloud Announces Officers' Tennis Tournament," *The Bomb Bay*, May 5, 1943, p. 7.

4. Harry Pruzan Questionnaire, Tenth Mountain Division Surveys box, Military History Institute, Carlisle Barracks, Pennsylvania.

5. "Tennis Contests for Enlisted Men Will Begin Soon," *Banana Peelings*, October 18, 1944, p. 8. "Golf Matches to Replace Handball in Competition," *Gosport*, June 4, 1943, p. 5, "Tennis Coach Plans General Program for Officers, Cadets"; *Gosport*, March 17, 1944 (since, according to the article, tennis could likely be a "social" recreation for the cadets once they became officers); and "45-Game Baseball League Announced for Inter-Unit Play," *Gosport*, March 24, 1944, p. 7.

6. "ASF to Have Golf Tourney," *Armodier*, September 28, 1944, p. 6; "Golf Course Open to Enlisted Men 5 Days a Week; Order Clubs" *Gosport*, April 23, 1943, p. 5 (enlisted men were allowed on the course on Monday, Wednesday, and Friday mornings, and Tuesday and Thursday afternoons); "George Golfers Get Real Break on City Greens," *George Field News*, April 28, 1944, p. 6; "Bowling Tournament for Cochran Personnel," *Cochran Communique*, May 29, 1943, p. 1; and "George Golfers to Play Local Vincennes Team," *George Field News*, July 7, 1945, p. 6. See, also, "Golf Tournament on Drew Course Begins Next Month," *Drew Field Echoes*, January 27, 1944, p. 15.

7. "Tickets on Sale at Athletic Office for Alabama Game," *Gosport*, October 2, 1942, p. 5.

8. "ASF To Have Golf Tourney," *Armodier*, September 28, 1944, p. 6.

9. Regulation quoted in "Tankers Not Expected to Match Last Season's Record," *Armodier*, November 23, 1944, p. 6 to explain that although most of the players from the previous year's excellent basketball team were still at Camp Chaffee, the majority were officers and were not going to be allowed to play.

10. "New Rules Set for Comdt's Cup Play," *Gosport*, November 19, 1943, p. 4.

11. "AAFE FTC Tennis Championships to be Played on Post Courts August 7–12," *Cochran Communique,* July 12, 1944, p. 1; and "Cochran Wins Net Doubles Title," *Cochran Communique,* August 16, 1944, p. 1.

12. "Laff of the Week," *Bom Bay,* February 18, 1943, p. 4.

13. "At Ease!" *Armodier,* October 8, 1942, p. 4.

14. See the discussion of the problems faced by African-American troops while serving in the South in Stetson Conn, general editor, *United States Army in World War II* (Washington, D.C.: Office of the Chief of Military History) *Special Studies: The Employment of Negro Troops* by Ulysses Lee, at pp. 104–105.

15. "Chaffee Merry-Go-Round," *Armodier,* October 1, 1942, p. 5.

16. "The Breezer," *Armodier,* January 20, 1944, p. 7.

17. "Bakery Basketeers Kayo 889th Ord. in Speedy Fort Smith Feud Game," *Armodier,* December 10, 1942, p. 5; "Town Grizzlies Trip Flashy QMers," *Armodier,* February 4, 1943, p. 6, "16th Div. Tankers and Arkansas Razorbacks Play Monday Night," *Armodier,* December 16, 1943, p. 6, "CCA Defeats Bruins 29–20," *Armodier,* January 18, 1945, p. 6, "Polo Grounds," *Double Deucer,* July 23, 1943, p. 10 (this is the Polo Grounds that served as home to the New York Giants baseball team); "396th Bomb Group Cagers Outscore Weatherford Five," *Drew Field Echoes,* December 16, 1943, p. 2, "Athletics Have Boom Season; Enlarged Program Is Planned," *The Bowman Bomber,* March 6, 1942, p. 11 (announcing that thanks to the donation of some land by the Kort Brothers, the soldiers would have diamonds on base the following year); and "Basketeers Open HF League Play," *Bomb Bay,* November 3, 1943, p. 2.

18. "Down the Runway," *Brief,* July 18, 1944, p. 17.

19. "Powerful Chaffee Quintet Takes a 72–29 Decision," *Armodier,* February 8, 1945, p. 6; "AWUTC 5 Plays Coast Guard," *Drew Field Echoes,* December 16, 1943, p. 15 (after first scrimmaging against the team from Plant City High School); "RTG Enters GI League," *Amphibian,* April 8, 1944, p. 7 (a Tallahassee softball league that included Army teams and industrial teams), "8-A Softball Teams Begin Workouts," *Gosport,* March 10, 1944, p. 3; "Squadron C Maintains Unbroken Record in Mount Carmel Victory" *George Field News,* November 18, 1944, p. 6; "Corpus Christi Softball Team Will Play Here," *Gosport,* August 13, 1943, p. 1; "Post Baseball Team Meet Waycross This Saturday in Season's Opener," *Cochran Communique,* April 26, 1944, p. 1; "Boston Braves Pitcher Sparks 1850th SU," *The Armodier,* May 6, 1943, p. 6; "Civilian Group Downed by Base Kegler Experts," George Field News, January 20, 1945, p. 6, and "Crack Mobile Softball Team Wins Over NAS in 13th Frame; Huler Fans 19 Men," *Gosport,* June 29, 1945, p. 3.

20. Sunday's Ball Games to Be Free to Servicemen," *Armodier*, June 15, 1944, p. 7.

21. "A.E.R. Benefit Game Big Success," *Bomb Bay Messenger*, August 8, 1943 (at which 8,500 fans turned out to see Joe Dimaggio play for the Santa Ana Army Air Base team); "Bombers, McClellan Clash in Series This Weekend for NonCom Fund," *The Bomb Bay*, July 14, 1943, p. 1; "Baseball Can Help," *Armored News*, July 31, 1944, p. 6; "Muderski Hits Ball and Jackpot at Same Time," *Armored News*, July 10, 1944; "Center Boxers Will Feature in Local Bouts," *Gosport*, July 23, 1943, p. 5; and "Chinese Citizens Sponsor Series," *Bomb Bay*, August 18, 1943, p. 5.

22. "Service Men to See Plenty of Football at Special Prices," *Armodier*, September 23, 1943, p. 7, "Free Swimming For Service Men," *Bom Bay*, November 12, 1942, p. 5; "Unit Baseball," *Double Deucer*, May 20, 1943, p. 2; and "Home Town Team Sends a Gift," *Armodier*, July 13, 1944, p. 6.

23. "Golf Attracts Many Army and Navy Men," *Armodier*, November 11, 1943, p. 6.

24. "The Breezer," *Armodier*, June 3, 1943, p. 6; and "Fort Smith Players Guests of 59th AFA at Baseball Party," *Armodier*, July 29, 1943, p. 6; and "Station Pugs to Fight Army at Barrancas," *Gosport*, October 2, 1942, p. 5. See also "Casaba Game, Dance Scheduled Saturday," *Armodier*, February 24, 1944, p. 1, in which the sportswriter comments, "All civilians of Fort Smith and vicinity to be the guests of the division to thank the civilians of this area who have generously aided in the welfare of the men of the 16th."

25. "Aniko, Logsden Win in Slow Semi-Finals in Amphitheater," *Armodier*, May 20, 1943, p. 7; "Boxers Preparing for State Meet," *Armodier*, March 2, 1944, p. 6; "Navy Fighters Win 10 to 16 Tilts in Golden Gloves Meet," *Gosport*, March 23, 1945; "Stewart Wins Title," *Cochran Communique*, February 26, 1944, p. 1; "Drew Boxers in Garden," *Drew Field Echoes*, March 9, 1944, p. 15; and "594th Takes 544th Again," *Amphibian*, February 12, 1944, p. 7.

26. "Swim Team Flies to AAU Tourney," *Gosport*, August 21, 1942, p. 5; "Swim Mark Set at AAU Meet," *Gosport*, August 28, 1942, p. 5; and "Post Team Enters SEAAU Swim Tourney," *Cochran Communique*, July 26, 1944, p. 8.

27. "NATC Machinist's Mate Seeks Florida State Open Championship This Weekend," *Gosport*, July 21, 1944, p. 3; "Chaffee Linksman Set to Sweep UTC Golf Tournament," *Armodier*, September 9, 1943, p. 6; and "Navy Golfers Enter Pensacola's $6,500 Open Tournament," *Gosport*, February 2, 1945, p. 6. See, also, "Tankers Place Four Men on Arkansas All-State Hoop Team," *Armodier*, March 23, 1944, p. 1.

28. "Raiders Capture U.S. Softball Title," *Bomb Bay*, September 22, 1943, p. 1.

29. "Louisiana State Cagers Meet Goslings Tonight," *Gosport,* January 21, 1944; and "Bombers Open S.F. Loop Play Sunday," *Bomb Bay,* December 15, 1943, p. 7.

30. For football, see "Air Base Represented on Wright Team," *Bomb Bay Messenger,* October 4, 1942, p. 7; "2nd Air Force Pigskin Toters Will Play Here Oct. 17th," *Bomb Bay Messenger,* October 11, 1942, p. 8; "4th Air Force Boasts Topnotch Football Club," *Bomb Bay,* October 14, 1943, p. 7.

31. "Servicemen in Sports," *Brief,* November 16, 1944, p. 16; "Writer Rates 220th Team 40th Among Service 11's," *Armored News,* October 23, 1944.

32. See, for example, discussions in "'Varsity' Basketball Dropped, Inter-Mural Leagues Formed," *Gosport,* December 11, 1942, p. 5; and "The Breezer," *Armodier,* September 30, 1943, p. 7.

33. "Raiders Seek U.S. Title," *Bomb Bay,* September 8, 1943, p. 1. See also, "No Bowl Games for Pre-Flight Teams," *Gosport,* December 4, 1942, p. 6.

34. "NATC Will Not Have Football Team This Fall," *Gosport,* August 27, 1943, p. 5.

35. "Off-Base Sports Bow to War Needs," *Drew Field Echoes,* March 9, 1944, p. 14.

36. Pvt. Owen Smith, "Down the Middle," *Bomb Bay Messenger,* May 9, 1943, p. 11.

37. Clipper, "On the Bench," *Cochran Communique,* May 15, 1943, p. 8.

38. "Perfect Physical Fitness Will Help Keep 'Em Flying," *Bom Bay,* October 29, 1942, p. 5; and "Boxing Lessons in Hanger Nine for All G.I. Fighters," *Bom Bay,* June 17, 1943, p. 5.

39. See, for example, Pfc. Jack Ellis, sports editor for the *Bomb Bay Messenger,* who predicted in "War Puts Sports on Wane: Attention of U.S. Youth Focused on Patriotism," that baseball moguls were likely to be "booed into bankruptcy" should they try to maintain the game during the war. *Bomb Bay Messenger,* December 20, 1942, p. 12.

40. Sgt. Bill Davidson, "Sports During the War?" *Yank,* April 27, 1945, p. 23.

41. The letter from the "Two College Men" appears in "Mail Call," *Yank,* July 13, 1945, p. 18.

42. "Sports Service Record," *Yank,* March 17, 1944, p. 23, "Sports Service Record," *Yank,* March 2, 1945, p. 23; and "Barney Ross Says Nix to Sports Cancellation," *The Bomb Bay,* June 9, 1943, p. 3. Pfc. Karl M. Dreir to Miss Leah Reynolds, October

24, 1944, in The Leah and Lena Reynolds Papers, Military History Institute, Carlisle Barracks, Pennsylvania.

43. Eldon Wakefield and Howard Riley surveys in the collection of the author, conducted during August, 1993. Thomas Gannon and Thomas Alexander Questionnaires in Bomb Squadron #1–#421 Surveys, Military Institute, Carlisle Barracks, Pennsylvania.

44. "Prop Notes," *Bomb Bay Messenger*, April 4, 1943, p. 8.

45. "Golden Gloves Boxer Packed Punch for 3rd," *Armored News*, June 18, 1945, p. 5.

46. "Former Chicago White Sox Outfielder Limbers Up to Take Swing at Axis," *Armored News*, February 28, 1945, p. 12.

47. See, "Big League War," *Brief*, May 22, 1945, p. 3, subheaded "European War Over, AAFPOA's New Chief Gives Air Assault Master Plan for V-J Day." Earlier a Colonel Philbrook had been quoted to the effect that the Axis was a bunch of "bush leaguers," "On the Ball," *Broadcaster*, May 31, 1943, p. 2.

48. "Team Plays Score in Battle, Says Former Grid Star," *Armored News*, July 3, 1944, p. 1.

49. "In the Service the World Over," *Brief*, December 12, 1944, p. 17.

50. "Baseball Slide Saves Private from Nazi Plane," *Armored News*, May 2, 1945, p. 4.

51. John Downs Questionnaire, in Bomb Squadron #1–#421 Surveys, Military History Institute, Carlisle Barracks, Pennsylvania.

52. "Grid Tactics Helped New 3FC Tac Inspector Shoot Down Nazi Ace," *Drew Field Echoes*, December 15, 1944, p. 8. See, also, the photograph of George Franck, a football player at the University of Minnesota, said to be ready "to score on Axis," at p. 5 of the *Bomb Bay Messenger*, October 4, 1942.

53. Lawrence Myers Questionnaire, Bomb Wings/Groups Surveys, Military History Institute, Carlisle Barracks, Pennsylvania.

54. "Bench-Warmer," *Brief*, March 28, 1944, p. 8. See, also, "U.S. 'Tigers' Claw at Japs," *The Bowman Bomber*, March 6, 1942, pp. 4, 6.

55. "Physical Training Program Widespread," *Bomb Bay Messenger*, February 14, 1943, p. 1.

56. "Strictly Off the Cuff," *Armodier*, April 15, 1943, p. 4.

57. "These Men Will Fight for George," *George Field News*, February 24, 1945, p. 6.

58. James Jones, *From Here to Eternity* (New York: Charles Scribner's Sons, 1951), p. 44.

59. For example, the phrase is quoted in "Commandant's Cup award," *Gosport*, January 8, 1943, p. 2, and "Offense Is Our Game," *The Bowman Bomber*, April 1, 1942, p. 2.

60. "544th T-5 Waitkus Hit .350 for Cubs in 1942," *Amphibian*, March 25, 1944, p. 5; "22nd Medics," *Double Deucer*, November 26, 1943, p. 5; and "Pitcher More, 174th IR, Sustains Broken Jaw," *Armodier*, May 4, 1942, p. 6. For a discussion of the 101st Airborne wrestling match—and of the response by First Lt. Schmitz's men to his injury, see Ambrose, p. 63.

61. "On the Ball," *Broadcaster*, May 31, 1943, p. 2.

62. Donald W. Romiger, "From Playing Field to Battleground: The United States Navy V-5 Preflight Program in World War II," *Journal of Sport History* 12 (Winter, 1985): 252–264.

63. "It's Not Football," *Armored News*, January 29, 1945, p. 8.

64. Cpn. David Alexander, "First Echelon," *Armored News*, June 18, 1945, p. 7.

65. " 'Big Game' Next on Schedule of Center Graduates," *Armored News*, January 15, 1945, p. 12; and " 'Ghost' Division Maps Places That It Haunted," *Armored News*, July 9, 1945, p. 16.

66. "Lethal Bowling," *Yank*, April 7, 1944, p. 12.

67. "Officer Plays Golf on Pillbox Course, Goes Around in Par," *Armored News*, November 14, 1944, p. 15.

68. "Less Bitching, More Pitching," *Bom Bay*, April 15, 1943, p. 2.

69. "Athletic Facilities Improved for New Year," *Bom Bay*, January 7, 1943, p. 9; "Gymnasium a Reality as Work Begins on Recreation and Athletic Building," *Cochran Communique*, June 5, 1943, p. 1; "Gala Festivities Open New Rec. Hall," *Bomb Bay Messenger*, February 21, 1943, p. 1; "New Gymnasium Be Opened for Use Next Month," *Banana Peelings*; March 24, 1943, p. 1; "Super Rec. Hall for SC Soldiers at Bldg. No. 1911," *Armodier*, December 31, 1942, p. 3, "Gigantic HF Athletic Field Planned," *Bomb Bay*, October 27, 1943, p. 7, and "The Breezer," *Armodier*, February 17, 1944, p. 6 (discussing the construction of a pool and a tennis court).

70. S. Sgt. Ben Kaplan, "Sports Chatter," *Cochran Field Communique*, June 2, 1945, p. 3.

71. "Shapiro Takes Handball Lead," *George Field News*, September 30, 1944, p. 6; "PFC Greene Foul Shooting Winner," *George Field News*, September 23, 1944,

p. 6; "Champs of Tournaments to Get Gold Baseballs," *Armodier,* May 27, 1943, p. 6; "Field Day! Depot Athletes to Compete for Prizes Saturday," *The Bomb Bay,* April 28, 1943, p. 1 (with cigarettes and cigars the prizes); "Hundred Dollar $$ Ball Game," *Double Deucer,* June 11, 1943, p. 6; "Bums Win Hoop Tourney, Awarded Keg of PX Brew," *Cochran Communique,* February 23, 1945, p. 8; and private letter to author from Orville T. Murphy, Professor of History, SUNY University at Buffalo, April 24, 1994.

72. "Every Soldier in Sports is Aim of Spring Program," *Bomb Bay Messenger,* April 4, 1943, p. 11; "Athletic Council Formed to Plan Squadron Sports," *Cochran Communique,* October 30, 1943, p. 8; "Personnel Spend Half-Million Hours in Athletics Here," *Gosport,* April 6, 1945, p. 5; "Platoon Training Does Wonders to Men of 571st," *Drew Field Echoes,* December 2, 1943, p. 10; and "4 Games Slated in Sqd. 7 Intraunit Tag Football Meet," *Gosport,* November 3, 1944.

73. "Intra-Outfit Basketball Program Launched; Leagues Tee Off Tuesday," *Cochran Communique,* December 8, 1944, p. 1; "The Breezer," *Armodier,* March 16, 1944, p. 6; "786th Tankers Victorious Over 787th Jabs, 33 to 29," *Armodier,* February 10, 1944, p. 6; "3-Day Boxing Meet Set Here to Begin Tuesday," *Gosport,* September 17, 1943, p. 1; and "Wildcat League Planned in Basketball Competition," *Gosport,* November 19, 1943, p. 4. See also "Rams Pro Star Heads Football Hopefulls at Knox," *Armored News,* August 28, 1944, p. 10.

74. "Crusaders Face Police Today in Return Game," *George Field News,* November 4, 1944, p. 6.

75. "GI Hoopsters Urged to Come out for Post Basketball Squad Practice," *Cochran Communique,* October 13, 1944, p. 8.

76. "Softball Chatter," *Banana Peelings,* June 28, 1944, p. 8. See, also, "Gosling Boxers Win 6 Bouts to Trounce Corpus Battlers," *Gosport,* May 14, 1943, p. 5; "Sqd. 7's Nine Wins 2 from Corpus Christi," *Gosport,* August 20, 1943, p. 4, "Base Nine Defeats C's Team Second Time in Six-Inning Mid-Week Fray by Score 7-2," *George Field News,* April 14, 1945, p. 6; "Tennis Matches Scheduled for This Afternoon," *Banana Peelings,* September 20, 1944, p. 8; "Cage Quintet of 903d QM Bends Joints," *Drew Field Echoes,* December 9, 1943, p. 6; and "322rd Basketball Team Is Fighting for League Title," *Cochran Communique,* January 1, 1944, p. 5.

77. "Bush League," *Brief,* March 6, 1945, p. 16.

78. Wayne F. Dudley Questionnaire, World War II surveys, "AAF Bases—Alpha by Base," Military History Institute, Carlisle Barracks, Pennsylvania.

79. Ernest Stolper, QM Bakery Co., Questionnaire, World War II surveys, "Quartermaster Corps," Military History Institute, Carlisle Barracks, Pennsylvania.

80. "Down the Runway," *Brief,* March 6, 1945, p. 17; and Sgt. Jim Harrigan, "Sports Stars," *Stars and Stripes,* June 12, 1944, p. 3.

81. Robert L. Shawver to his parents, dated March 19, 1944, in World War II surveys, "Bomb Squadrons #1-#421," Military History Institute, Carlisle Barracks, Pennsylvania.

82. "Old Shoes, Red Cross String Make Baseball," *Bomb Bay,* January 12, 1944, p. 5.

83. Perret.

7. WACs, WAVEs, "SISSIES," and the "Negro Soldier:" Military Sports for the Maginalized

1. Only 3,640 African-American men were in the army on August 31, 1939, out of a total strength of 189,839. These soldiers were concentrated in the segregated units that had traditionally absorbed black enlistees, although the Ninth and Tenth Cavalries that had so distinguished themselves in the Indian Wars and in the Spanish-American War had deteriorated into little more than service units. Because of the army's determination to continue segregation within its ranks, those African-Americans who were drafted or who enlisted entered the military with no guarantee of units, billets, or training groups. For a discussion of the expansion of African-American numbers within the army, see Stetson Conn, gen ed., *U.S. Army in World War II: Special Studies,* 8 vols. (Washington, D.C.: Department of the Army, 1966), vol. 8. *The Employment of Negro Troops,* by Ulysses Lee, pp. 88–97 and Richard M. Dalfiume, *Desegregation of the U.S. Armed Forces: Fighting on Two Fronts, 1939–1953* (Columbia, Mo.: University of Missouri Press, 1969). See, also, for total army numbers, Russell F. Weigley, *History of the United States Army* (New York: The Macmillan Company, 1967).

2. See, for example, the discussion of military recruitment efforts and explanations for their failure in D'Ann Campbell, *Women at War with America: Private Lives in a Patriotic Era* (Cambridge: Harvard University Press, 1984). Susan M. Hartmann also describes the varied experiences of American women during the Second World War in *The Home Front and Beyond: American Women in the 1940s* (Boston: Twayne Publisher, 1982).

3. Stetson Conn, gen. ed., *U.S. Army in World War II: Special Studies*, 8 vols. (Washington: Department of the Army, 1954), vol. 5, *The Women's Army Corps*, by Mattie E. Treadwell, p. 639.

4. Ibid., pp. 639, 640, 666. "Physical Program for WAVES to Begin Here Monday," *Gosport,* March 3, 1944, p. 3.

5. "Hospital WAVES Win in Badminton Opener," *Gosport,* September 24, 1943, p. 4 and "WACs vs SPARS Again Swimming," *WACtivities,* September 2, 1943, p. 6. See, also "Hancock Trophy Planned for WAVE Athletic Competition, *Gosport,* July 16, 1943, p. 5, and "Ping-Pong Tournament," *WAAC-tivities,* December 11, 1942, p. 1. (*WAAC-tivities* changed its name to *WACtivities* when the status of women in the Army was regularized in 1943).

6. "Versatile Sports Program Being Organized in A & R," *Gosport,* January 5, 1945, p. 3. Mattie E. Treadwell discusses at length the rumor campaign against the WACs and the Army's response to it in *The Women's Army Corps.*

7. The game between Private Grossman and Seaman Carlin is described in the caption to a photograph appearing at p. 8, *Cochran Communique,* May 1, 1943. See, also, "Tennis Meet May 29," *Drew Field Echoes,* May 11, 1944, p. 14. The War Department directive is noted in "Line News in Brief," *Brief,* April 11, 1944, p. 7. Military women were also allowed out of uniform when in a group of less than three people.

8. See, for example, "Ky Champions Win by Only 2–1 Over NCO Team," *Armored News,* July 10, 1944 (ARTC WAC softball team versus a team from the West Louisville Girls' Club), "NAS WAVES Trounce Mobile Civlian Team," *Gosport,* July 27, 1945, p. 3, "Macon Gals to Oppose WAC's in Softball," *Cochran Communique,* July 10, 1943, p. 8, "GI Josephines Drop Third in Row," *Drew Field Echoes,* January 29, 1945, p. 15, and "Three Post Teams Play in Ga. Softball League," *Cochran Communique,* May 17, 1944, p. 8 (with the women's softball games preceding men's games as part of nightly tripleheaders at the post).

9. For a discussion of the military's response to rumors of homosexual acitivity, see Allen Berube, *Coming Out Under Fire: The History of Gay Men and Women in World War Two* (New York: The Free Press, 1990), pp. 225, 226.

10. "Splashes from the Waves," *Banana Peelings,* February 7, 1945, p. 5.

11. "WAC PT Instructor," *Drew Field Echoes,* June 22, 1944, p. 10. Further suggesting the extent to which female athleticism might be understood as sexual is the account given by Mattie E. Treadwell of the response to the photographs in the WAC physical training manual. She says that the manual "contained a number of careful photographic illustrations which for some cause proved extremely popular with the male personnel." Treadwell, *The Women's Army Corps,* p. 639.

12. The photographs appear at p. 14 of *Banana Peelings,* April 4, 1945.

13. The photograph appears at p. 3 of *Gosport,* July 27, 1945. The definition for pulchritudinous comes from Charles Earle Funk, Editor, *Funk and Wagnalls New Practical Standard Dictionary of the English Language* (New York and London: Funk and Wagnalls Company, 1946), p. 1,060.

14. The photograph appears at p. 7 of *Cochran Communique,* September 13, 1944.

15. Camp Chaffee's golf club was for officers' wives who therefore were immune from sexual speculation, but the bowling and basketball leagues were for WACs who were often the subject of rumor, innuendo, and gossip. "Ladies Golf Club Organizes," *Bom Bay,* March 31, 1943, p. 5, and "WAC Cage, Bowling Loops Set," *Drew Field Echoes,* October 27, 1944, p. 15.

16. See, for example, the notices announcing the enlistment of Ida Hanchett, 1943 National Archery Champion and the presence at Hammer Field of Jean "Flash" Gordon, who played first base for the 1939 Southern Counties (California) softball champions, *Bomb Bay Messenger,* April 11, 1943, p. 11 and April 18, 1943, p. 3. See also "WAC Sarge Used to Be Champ Softball Pitcher," *George Field News,* September 30, 1944, p. 6. On the other hand, the enlistment of softball pitcher Kitty Sinkwich was recognized by pointing out her relationship to her brother Frankie, former Georgia All-American in football and commenting that she thought football was "silly." "Sport Slants," *Bomb Bay,* December 22, 1943, p. 7 and "Sports Service Record," *Yank,* January 5, 1945, p. 23.

17. "WAC Softball Team Invades NAS Monday for Tilt with WAVES," *Gosport,* October 6, 1944, p. 3.

18. "WACS' Baseball team Develops Expert Skills," *George Field News,* April 14, 1945, p. 6 (although the title of the article refers to a WAC baseball team, the content makes clear that the WACs were actually playing softball) and "WAVE Sets Bowling Mark," *Gosport,* August 6, 1943, p. 4.

19. "Whiting Ace," *Gosport,* March 3, 1945, p. 3 (Dorothy Duchers, AMM2c, averaging more than twenty points per game for her basketball team) and "Queen of Swat," *Gosport,* May 4, 1945, p. 2.

20. Sgt. Dorothy Auman maintained a 140 average, sufficient to beat men three times in Kessler Field bowling tournaments, "Sports Slants," *Bomb Bay,* December 1, 1943, p. 7. At Fort Knox, a WAC team was successful in a mixed bowling league. "WAC Keglers Take Two of Three Games," *The Armodier,* March 8, 1945, p. 6. Also at Fort Knox, WAC Vernett Claus participated in a twenty-four person table tennis tournament, won by Pvt. Richard C. Willson, "School Crowns Ping Pong Champ," *Armored News,* February 28, 1945, p. 10.

21. "WAC Doings," *George Field News,* October 7, 1944, p. 4, "Bowling Alleys in Welfare Building Now in Operation," *Banana Peelings,* December 2, 1942, p. 5 and "Physical Program for WAVES to Begin Here Monday," *Gosport,* March 3, 1944, p. 3.

21. "New Gym to Open Soon," *Bomb Bay,* August 18, 1943, p. 7 (the gymnasium had seating for one thousand spectators, a basketball court, room for boxing and wrestling matches, space in the balcony for judo classes and one set of lockers and showers).

23. "NAS Swim Meet Slated for Pool June 21; Open to All," *Gosport*, June 16, 1944, p. 3.

24. "Nurse's Pitching Causes Defeat of Medical Det. Ten," *Scott Field Broadcaster*, August 26, 1941, p. 1.

25. "Sports Service Record," *Yank*, January 5, 1945, p. 23.

26. "WACs Lose to WAVES in Mad Ball Scramble," *Cochran Communique*, September 20, 1944, p. 1.

27. "Lady Rasslers Display Talents," *Drew Field Echoes*, November 24, 1944, p. 14.

28. "AWUTC '5' to Play WACS with Soldiers in Gas Masks," *Drew Field Echoes*, December 23, 1943, p. 15.

29. Jamieson, "Strictly Personnel," *Double Deucer*, July 16, 1943, p. 7.

30. "WACS Works," *Bom Bay*, November 3, 1943, p. 4.

31. "WAC Cheerleaders Add Color to Grid Games," *Drew Field Echoes*, October 13, 1944, p. 2.

32. A photograph of the WAC cheerleaders who joined some GIs in raising enthusiasm during the 1945 Spaghetti Bowl in Florence, Italy, appears in *Yank*, February 9, 1945, p. 22. Army women also led the cheers at the New Year's Day, 1943, Arab Bowl at Oran in North Africa.

33. Robert B. Westbrook, " 'I Want a Girl, Just Like the Girl That Married Harry James': American Women and the Problem of Political Obligation in World War II," 42 *American Quarterly* (December, 1990): 587–614.

34. See, for example, p. 12 of the *Drew Field Echoes*, for February 10, 1944. The photograph of the Buffalo baseball team appears on p. 7 of the May 11, 1944 issue of *The Armodier*, published for the soldiers stationed at Camp Chaffee, Arkansas.

35. Poole's photograph appears at p. 3, *Banana Peelings*, January 12, 1944. Poole's picture would turn up again according to *Banana Peelings* in the July 1944 edition of SEE "which is usually filled from cover to cover with photos of gorgeous girls." "What? Poole, Again?" *Banana Peelings*, May 3, 1944, p. 5.

36. "Pratt-Side to the Ice," *George Field News*, January 6, 1945, p. 6.

37. As Allan Berube has shown, some lesbians did indeed serve in the military during World War II, but other women surely joined because their husband, brother, and other loved ones were also involved in the fight. Allan Berube, *Coming Out Under Fire: The History of Gay Men and Women in World War Two* (New York: The Free Press, 1990).

38. "The WACS' Works," *The Bomb Bay,* July 7, 1943, p. 4.

39. As Captain Joe Fernandes, head coach of the George Field football team said in September, 1944, "Football is not a game for sissies and any man who is afraid of getting hurt or going through some vigorous training periods need not come out for the team. "Here's the Lowdown on Football Team Being Organized at George," *George Field News,* September 30, 1944, p. 6. Boxing was often referred to as an especially manly sport. See, for example, "Boxer Goodwin Argues Legality of his Right-Cross-Rabbit Hook," *The Armodier,* October 15, 1942, p. 5. See also the discussion in Chapter 4 concerning the training of officers between the two world wars.

40. James Jones, *From Here to Eternity* (New York: Charles Scribner's Sons, 1951), p. 13.

41. According to Jim Estep, former captain of the Naval Academy's fencing team, that sport was "looked down upon as being effeminate . . . [since it was] more about strategy and subtlety, and these traits were considered feminine and inferior." Estep is quoted at p. 105 in Michael A. Messner and Donald F. Sabo, *Sex, Violence and Power in Sports: Rethinking Masculinity* (Freedom, Calif.: The Crossing Press, 1994).

42. Charles Earle Funk, Editor, *Funk and Wagnalls New Practical Standard Dictionary of the English Language* (New York and London: Funk and Wagnalls Company, 1946), p. 1,221.

43. Allan Berube, *Coming Out Under Fire: The History of Gay Men and Women in World War Two* (New York: The Free Press, 1990).

44. Robert Fleisher quoted at p. 94, Berube, *Coming Out Under Fire.*

45. Badminton equipment appeared on the War Department's 1943 approved list of sporting equipment, along with footballs, basketballs, volleyballs, handballs, horseshoes, and fishing tackle. "U.S. Lists Huge Sums for Sports," *Bomb Bay Messenger,* July 18, 1943, p. 2.

Badminton tournaments were played on the Naval Air Station at Banana River, Florida, at the Fourth Air Force Replacement Depot, at Fort Chaffee, Arkansas, on the Pensacola, Florida, Naval Air Station, at Barksdale Field, Louisiana, and at Fort Bell in Bermuda. "Personnel Starts Training Classes in New Gymnasiums," *Banana Peelings,* May 19, 1943, p. 14, "Field Day! Depot Athletes to Compete for Prizes Saturday," *The Bomb Bay,* April 28, 1943, p. 4, "Super Rec Hall For S.C. Soldiers at Bldg. No. 1911," *The Armodier,* December 31, 1942, p. 3, "Sport's Intramural Program on NAS Planned for 1945," *Gosport,* December 1, 1944, p. 3, "Tournaments Scheduled for Enlisted Men During July," *The Bowman Bomber,* July 2, 1942, p. 5, and "Badminton Tournament," *B.B.C. News,* October 23, 1943, p. 9.

46. "Expert Likes Ju-Jitsu Over Boxing for Army," *The Armodier,* March 4, 1943, p. 6.

47. "Top Badminton Exponent Booms Sport on Drew," *Drew Field Echoes,* August 17, 1944, p. 15.

48. Captain Norman R. Hart, "Behind the Brassard News," *The Weekly Salute,* May 17, 1943, p. 9, "Personnel Starts Training Classes in New Gymnasiums," *Banana Peelings,* May 19, 1943, p. 14.

49. "Pfc. Kurt Wins Camp Table Tennis Title," *The Armodier,* January 14, 1943, p. 5.

50. J. Edgar Kirk, "Sport Pen," *Scott Field Broadcaster,* July 29, 1941, p. 5, and "Champ AWUTC Fencer Likes to be Foiled," *Drew Field Echoes,* October 17, 1944, p. 2 (Captain Goodstein was not only a fencer but a lightweight finalist in his college boxing tournament).

51. "Athletic Wilson of 4th SAW Knows His Stuff," *Drew Field Echoes,* December 2, 1943, p. 14.

52. "Heavyweight Sid Gets Scared, Kayoes Opponent," *The Armodier,* June 10, 1943, p. 6.

53. In From Here to Eternity, remember, the boxing champion, Cpl. Isaac Nathan Bloom, kills himself after being caught up in the "Queer Investigation" for fear that he himself was homosexual.

54. For a comparison of the composition of the armies of the two world wars, see Sue E. Berryman, "Images and Realities: The Social Composition of Nineteenth and Twentieth Century Enlisted Forces." In David R. Segal and H. Wallace Sinaiko, eds., *Life in the Rank and File: Enlisted Men and Women in the Armed Forces of the United States, Australia, Canada and the United Kingdom* (Washington, D.C.: Pergamon-Brassey's International Defense Publishers, 1986).

55. According to Richard M. Dalfiume, although the army guaranteed that blacks would serve in the same percentage as their percentage in the general population, and that black units would be placed in every branch of the army, combat or not, the War Department's policy not to "intermingle colored and white enlisted personnel" undercut efforts to ensure full participation. Dalfiume, pp. 38, 39.

56. A full discussion of the position taken by African-American leaders in demanding that their constituents be permitted to participate in the national defense and of the response to those demands by Congress and the army appears in Stetson Conn, gen. ed., *United States Army in World War II: Special Studies,* 8 vols. (Washington, D.C.: Office of the Chief of Military History, 1966), vol. 8: *The Employment of Negro Troops,* by Ulysses Lee, Chapter 3, The Negro Position Defined. For a full discussion of the efforts to force the Army Air Force to utilize black personnel in all positions,

see Stanley Sandler, *Segregated Skies: All Black Combat Squadrons of WWII* (Washington, D.C., and London: Smithsonian Institution Press, 1992). The color barrier to full participation in the war effort by black seamen began to be broken when a mess boy grabbed a gun and began shooting at the Japanese during the Pearl Harbor bombardment. Neverthless, there were no African-American ensigns in the navy as late as August 1942. For a fuller discussion of mess attendant Doir Miller's experiences at Pearl Harbor, see Gordon W. Prange, *At Dawn We Slept: The Untold Story of Pearl Harbor* (New York: Penguin Books, 1982), p. 514. (Perhaps not coincidentally, Miller was West Virginia's heavyweight boxing champion before the Pearl Harbor attack.) See also "If Negro's Good Enough for Navy, He's Good Enough For Majors,'—Parker," *Pittsburgh Courier,* July 25, 1942, and Fay Young, "Through the Years," *Chicago Defender,* August 1, 1942. As Bernard C. Nalty demonstrates in *Strength for the Fight: A History of Black Americans in the Military* (New York: The Free Press, 1986), black sailors served in many capacities in the nineteenth-century Navy.

57. Although African-American women also served in the military during World War II, their numbers were extremely small. I have been unable to find any information as to whether the program of sports provided for them was more reflective of the experience of their sisters or their black brothers.

One particular postal directory battalion made up of African-American women, commanded by Maj. Charity Adams did achieve great fame for the efficiency with which they kept mail flowing to the men following the Normandy break-out. Perret, p. 444.

58. Brig. Gen. Benjamin O. Davis, Sr., letter, October, 23, 1942, in Benjamin O. Davis, Sr., Papers, Military History Institute.

59. Lt. Gen. Leslie J. McNair as quoted at p. 105, Ulysses Lee, *The Employment of Negro Troops*. For another discussion of the use of black troops during World War II and in Korea, see J. Lawton Collins, *Lightning Joe: An Autobiography* (Baton Rouge and London: Louisiana State University Press, 1979).

60. Sandler, pp. 124–127.

61. Lt. Col. Marshall S. Carter, undated letter, in Benjamin O. Davis, Sr., Papers, Military History Institute.

62. Sandler, p. 134.

63. General Andrew J. Goodpaster interviewed by Col. William D. Johnson and Lt. Col. James C. Ferguson, Senior Officer Oral History Program, January 9, 1976, archives of Military History Institute, p. 3. For a general discussion of the effect of the Great Depression on America's African-American population, see Anthony J. Badger, *The New Deal: The Depression Years, 1933–1940* (New York: The Noonday Press, 1989), p. 25.

64. The official history of the African-American soldiers' place in the army suggests that the War Department, and the army, believed that although "separate units continued segregation . . . segregation was a practice which it [the army] had found in the civilian community and which it had no right to alter until the civilian community had changed its own methods or had given the Army, through the Congress, a clear mandate to do so." Nevertheless, the army acknowledged that the policy of separation served to prevent freedom of movement for African-Americans and also produced "inequalities of facilities and opportunities for the minority." Ulysses Lee, *The Employment of Negro Troops*, p. 83.

65. Jules Tygiel, *Baseball's Great Experiment: Jackie Robinson and His Legacy* (New York: Vintage Books, 1983), p. 38.

66. Ulysses Lee, *The Employment of Negro Troops*, pp. 302, 303. A typical recreational facility for African-American troops is described in "Camp De Soto Activities Dedicate Service Club," *Drew Field Echoes*, April 27, 1944, p. 2.

67. "Swimming Classes for Colored Men Held at East Beach," *Gosport*, April 28, 1944, p. 3.

68. "Colored Squads to Begin Softball Tilts," *Gosport*, April 21, 1944, p. 3, "Malden Beats George Section Boys in 8–5 Win," *George Field News*, October 7, 1944, p. 6, and "367th Planning Sport Program of Seven Events," *The Clarion*, December 20, 1941.

69. "Squad Seven Colored Men to Form Softball Team," *Gosport*, March 17, 1944, p. 8, "ATTG Boxers Take Five of Nine Matches Against Tallahassee Airmen," *Amphibian*, April 8, 1944, p. , "MacDill Negro Gridders to Meet 'Hawks,' " *Drew Field Echoes*, January 13, 1944, p. 15, and "Bronson, Whiting Colored Fighters Divide Four Bouts," *Gosport*, June 1, 1945, p. 3.

70. Walter R. Chivers, "Walter Chivers Says," *Atlanta Daily World*, March 8, 1942 ("Saying Total War Needs Total Time Commitment"), and "Tuskegee-Wilberforce Game for Army Relief," *Chicago Defender*, October 3, 1942.

71. "Tuskegee Relays to be Entered by Army Camps, Naval Bases," *Atlanta Daily World*, April 8, 1942, "K.C. Youth Leads 'Kegee Track Stars to Win," Kansas City *Call*, May 28, 1943, "Service Men Dominate Lists in Millrose Games Renewal," *Daily Worker*, February 5, 1943 (played for United Seamen's Service) and the photograph captioned "Congratulations, Joshua," showing Cpl. Joshua Williamson shaking hands with Col. John D. Markey, post commander, and being recognized for having won the Penn Relays high jump competition, in the Norfolk *Journal and Guide*, April 8, 1943.

72. "Base Athletes Turn Out for First Field Day," *Bomb Bay Messenger*, October 25, 1942, p. 5, "This Isn't a B-17 . . . It's Triplett," *The Bomb Bay*, July 28, 1943,

p. 7, "Airbees, 438th Clash Tonight to Decide Cage Lead," *Bomb Bay*, December 15, 1943, p. 7, and "Softball Trophy Tourney Starts," *The Bomb Bay*, April 23, 1943, p. 6. Reid's golf triumph is described in Arthur R. Ashe, Jr., *A Hard Road to Glory: A History of the African-American Athlete, 1919-1945, Vol. 2* (New York: Warner Books, 1988), at p. 67.

73. See the discussion of barnstorming exhibitions before the war in Jules Tygiel, *Baseball's Great Experiment: Jackie Robinson and His Legacy* (New York: Vintage Books, 1984).

74. Ibid., p. 91.

75. Photographs of the integrated baseball and basketball teams appear at p. 11 of the May 16, 1943 and December 25, 1942 issues of *Bomb Bay Messenger*, respectively. See also " 'Big Ike' Does It Once More—Gets his 26th No-Hit Softball Game," *Bomb Bay Messenger*, May 2, 1943, p. 11.

76. "George Eleven Plays Indianapolis Police Tonight," *George Field News*, October 21, 1944, p. 6.

77. "Boxing Team Bows In," *Brief*, March 21, 1944, p. 16.

78. Ashe, Jr., especially at p. 98.

79. See the Kansas City *Call*, "A Forward Step for Missouri U.," October 8, 1943, and Nat Low, "Inter-Racial Stars Beat Diesels 13–0," *Daily Worker*, November 8, 1943.

80. "Army Brings Democracy to Virginia on Mixed Grid Team," *Afro-American*, October 30, 1943, "Lee's Mixed Team to Play Seven Games," Norfolk *Journal and Guide*, October 23, 1943, "All Stars on Camp Lee Mixed Grid Team," Kansas City *Call*, September 17, 1943, "Sepia Grid Stars to Play on Powerful Camp Lee Team," Pittsburgh *Courier*, September 18, 1943.

81. "No Baseball Color Line at Grenier Field," Baltimore *Afro-American*, June 12, 1943, and "Camp Upton's Ball Team Glorified by Two Negro Soldiers," New York *Age*, September 18, 1943.

82. Lucious Jones, "The Sports Roundup," *Pittsburgh Courier*, September 18, 1943.

83. "Joe Brings Check to Navy Relief, Visits Negro Paralysis Victims," *Daily Worker*, January 14, 1942. See also, for a general discussion of Louis' early career, Dominic J. Capeci, Jr., and Martha Wilkerson, "Multifarious Hero: Joe Louis, American Society and Race Relations During World Crisis, 1935-1945," in *The Sporting Image: Readings in American Sport History*, ed. Paul J. Zingg (Lanham, Md.: University Press of America, 1988).

Andrew Young, former Mayor of Atlanta, argues that Louis's victory over Schmeling represented an advance victory over Hitler's ideas about a master race, in Joe Louis Barrow, Jr., and Barbara Munder, *Joe Louis: Fifty Years an American Hero* (New York: McGraw-Hill Book Companmy, 1988), p. 101.

84. "I Am An American Day," *Pittsburgh Courier*, May 30, 1942. The drawing was advertised in the January 31, 1942 issue of the *Pittsburgh Courier*, selling for fifty cents. For more on the African-American response to the war and for the *Courier*'s Double-V campaign, see Sandler, pp. 63–69.

85. "Joe Louis and the Army," Atlanta *Daily World*, June 12, 1942, "The Case of Joe Louis," New York *Age*, June 13, 1942, and "Louis-Conn Fight Irks Congressman," *Courier-Journal*, September 24, 1942. Westbrook Pegler's "Fair Enough," is reprinted in the *Amsterdam Star-News*, June 20, 1942.

86. "Louis-Conn Fight is Definitely Off," *New York Times*, September 27, 1942.

87. Sam McKibben, "Segregated Seating Plans Fail at Dinner for Louis' Boxers," Atlanta *Daily World*, February 1, 1943.

88. Barrow, Jr. and Munder, pp. 142, 144.

89. Joe Williams, "Dempsey vs. Louis? Soldiers Take Old Manassa Mauler!" *Birmingham Post*, February 16, 1943.

90. Fay Young, "Through the Years," *Chicago Defender*, January 31, 1942.

8. Conclusion

1. Betty Friedan, *The Feminine Mystique* (New York: Dell Publishing Co., 1984). For another discussion of women's return to the home in the postwar era, see Elaine Tyler May, *Homeward Bound: American Families in the Cold War Era* (New York: Basic Books, 1988).

2. Although many commentators point to the 1950s situation comedies *Father Knows Best* or *Leave It to Beaver* as suggesting the extent to which a cultural consensus had been reached by which women were confined to the home and men were sent out into the world, I would recommend close attention be paid to the implications in early episodes of *I Love Lucy*. Lucy's struggle to find some broader meaning to her life, and to create a career for herself, although subject to ridicule, reflects the ongoing debate about what men and women should be doing with their lives.

3. For the cultural response to the bomb, see Paul Boyer, *By the Bomb's Early Light: American Thought and Culture at the Dawn of the Atomic Age* (New York: Pantheon Books, 1985).

4. For Jackie Robinson's career, see Jules Tygiel, *Baseball's Great Experiment: Jackie Robinson and His Legacy* (New York: Vintage Books, 1984).

5. Warren Farrell, "The Super-Bowl Phenomenon: Machismo as Ritual," in *Jock: Sports and Male Identity*, eds. Donald F. Sabo, Jr., and Ross Runfulo (Englewood Cliffs, N.J.: Prentice-Hall, 1980).

6. For a view from the playing field, see David Kopay's memoir of his time as a professional football player and his struggle to understand how he could be both a professional football player and a gay man in a homophobic society. David Kopay and Perry Deane Young, *The David Kopay Story: An Extraordinary Self-Revelation* (New York: Arbor House, 1977).

7. Judith Hicks Stiehm, *Bring Me Men and Women: Mandated Change at the U.S. Air Force Academy* (Berkeley: University of California Press, 1981), pp. 97, 98.

8. Kenneth L. Woodward with Sherry Keene-Osborn, "The Gospel of Guyhood," *Newsweek,* August 29, 1994, pp. 60, 61.

BIBLIOGRAPHY

Adams, Michael C. C. *The Great Adventure: Male Desire and the Coming of World War I*. Bloomington: Indiana University Press, 1990.

Adelman, Melvin. "The First Modern Sport in America: Harness Racing in New York City, 1825–1870." *Journal of Sport History* VIII (Spring, 1981): 5–32.

Allen, Edward Frank. *Keeping Our Fighters Fit: For War and After*. New York: The Century Co., 1918.

Ambrose, Stephen E. *Band of Brothers: E Company, 506th Regiment, 101st Airborne from Normandy to Hitler's Eagle's Nest*. New York: Simon & Schuster, 1992.

American Battle Monuments Commission. *American Armies and Battlefields in Europe: A Histoy, Guide, and Reference Book*. Washington, D.C.: Center of Military History, 1992; Washington, D.C.: Government Printing Office, 1938.

Army Service Forces. *Logistics in World War II: Final Report of the Army Service Forces*. Washington, D.C.: Government Printing Office, 1993; Washington, D.C.: Government Printing Office, 1948.

Ashe, Arthur, R., Jr. *A Hard Road to Glory: A History of the African-American Athlete, 1619–1918, Vol. 1*. New York: Warner Books, 1988.

Ashe, Arthur, R., Jr. *A Hard Road to Glory: A History of the African-American Athlete, 1919–1945, Vol. 2*. New York: Warner Books, Inc., 1988.

Astor, Gerald. *A Blood-Dimmed Tide: The Battle of the Bulge by the Men Who Fought It*. New York: Donald I. Fine, 1992.

Ayteo, Don. *Blood and Guts: Violence in Sports*. New York: Paddington Press, 1979.

Badger, Anthony J. *The New Deal: The Depression Years, 1933–1940*. New York: The Noonday Press, 1989.

Banner, Lois. *American Beauty*. New York: Alfred A. Knopf, 1983.

Barrow, Joe Louis, Jr., and Barbara Munder. *Joe Louis: Fifty Years an America Hero*. New York: McGraw-Hill Book Company, 1988.

Berube, Allen. *Coming Out Under Fire: The History of Gay Men and Women in World War Two*. New York: The Free Press, 1990.

188   *Bibliography*

Boyer, Paul. *By the Bomb's Early Light: American Thought and Culture at the Dawn of the Atomic Age.* New York: Pantheon Books, 1985.

Brod, Harry, ed. *The Making of Masculinities: The New Men's Studies.* Boston: Allen & Unwin, 1987.

Cahn, Susan. *Coming on Strong.* New York: The Free Press, 1994.

Calhoun, Frederick C. *Power and Principle: Armed Intervention in Wilsonian Foreign Policy.* Kent, Ohio: The Kent State University Press, 1986.

Campbell, D'Ann. *Women at War with America: Private Lives in a Patriotic Era.* Cambridge: Harvard University Press, 1984.

Carroll, Francis H. *Works Progress Adminstration, District No. 9: Construction Report.* Rochester, New York: January 1, 1938 to December 31, 1938. Unpublished report held in the archives of the Monroe County, New York, County Historian's Office.

Cashin, Herschel V., et al. *Under Fire with the Tenth U.S. Cavalry.* Niwot, CO: The University Press of Colorado, 1993; London: F.T. Neely, 1899.

Chambers II, John Whiteclay. *To Raise an Army: The Draft Comes to Modern America.* New York: The Free Press, 1987.

Chauncey, George, Jr. "Christian Brotherhood or Sexual Perversion? Homosexual Identities and the Construction of Sexual Boundaries in the World War One Era." *Journal of Social History* 19 (1985): 189–212.

Clinton, Catherine and Nina Silber, eds. *Divided Houses: Gender and the Civil War.* New York and Oxford: Oxford University Press, 1992.

Collin, Richard H. *Theodore Roosevelt, Culture, Diplomacy, and Expansion: A New View of American Imperialism.* Baton Rouge & London: Louisiana State University Press, 1985.

Collins, Gen. J. Lawton. *Lightning Joe: An Autobiography.* Baton Rouge & London: Louisiana State University Press, 1979.

Conn, Stetson, gen. ed., *U.S. Army in World War II: Special Studies.* Vol. 5, *The Women's Army Corps,* by Mattie E. Treadwell. Washington, D.C.: Department of the Army, 1954.

Conn, Stetson, gen. ed., *U. S. Army in World War II: Special Studies.* Vol. 8, *The Employment of Negro Troops,* by Ulysses Lee. Washington, D.C.: Department of the Army, 1966.

Connell, R. W. *Gender and Power: Society, the Person and Sexual Politics.* Stanford: Stanford University Press, 1987.

Connors, Martin, Diane L. Dupuis, and Brad Morgan. *The Olympics Factbook: A Spectator's Guide to the Winter and Summer Games*. Detroit: Visible Ink, 1992.

Cooper, John Milton, Jr. *The Warrior and the Priest: Woodrow Wilson and Theodore Roosevelt*. Cambridge, Mass.: The Belknap Press of Harvard University, 1983.

Cowley, Robert, ed. *Experience of War: An Anthology of Articles from MHQ: The Quarterly Journal of Military History*. New York: W. W. Norton & Company, 1992.

Dalfiume, Richard M. *Desegregation of the U.S. Armed Forces: Fighting on Two Fronts, 1939–1953*. Columoia, Mo.: University of Missouri Press, 1969.

Danzig, Allison. *Oh, How They Played the Game: The Early Days of Football and the Heroes Who Made It Great*. New York: The Macmillan Company, 1971.

Dijkstra, Bram. *Idols of Perversity: Fantasties of Feminine Evil in Fin-de-Siecle Culture*. New York: Oxford University Press, 1986.

Dos Passos, John. *Nineteen Nineteen*. London: Constable and Company, 1932.

Drez, Donald J. *Voices of D-Day: The Story of the Allied Invasion Told by Those Who Were There*. Baton Rouge and London: Louisiana State University Press, 1992.

Dunning, Eric and Kenneth Sheard. *Barbarians, Gentlemen and Players: A Sociological Study of the Development of Rugby Football*. New York: New York University Press, 1979.

Durso, Joseph. *Baseball and the American Dream*. St. Louis: The Sporting News, 1986.

Dyer, Thomas G. *Theodore Roosevelt and the Idea of Race*. Baton Rouge and London: Louisiana State University Press, 1980.

Eksteins, Modris. *Rites of Spring: The Great War and the Birth of the Modern Age*. Boston: Houghton Mifflin Company, 1989.

Fielding, Lawrence W. "War and Trifles: Sport in the Shadows of Civil War Army Life." *Journal of Sport History* 4 (Summer, 1977): 151–168.

Filene, Peter G. *Him/Her/Self: Sex Roles in Modern America,* 2nd ed. Baltimore and London: The Johns Hopkins University Press, 1986.

Fosdick, Raymond B., Chair. *Report of Chairman on Training Camp Activities, 1918.* Washington, D.C.: Government Printing Office, 1918.

Fosdick, Raymond B. "Welfare Work," Army War College Lecture, March 3, 1922.

Foucault, Michel. *The History of Sexuality. Volume I: An Introduction*. New York: Pantheon Books, 1978.

Freedman, Estelle and John D'Emilio. *Intimate Matters: A History of Sexuality in America*. New York: Harper & Row, 1988.

Friedan, Betty. *The Feminine Mystique*. New York: Dell Publishing, Co., 1984.

Frommer, Harvey. *Shoeless Joe and Ragtime Baseball*. Dallas: Taylor Publishing Company, 1992.

Funk, Charles Earle, ed. *Funk and Wagnalls New Practical Standard Dictionary of the English Language*. New York and London: Funk and Wagnalls Company, 1946.

Fussell, Paul. *The Great War and Modern Memory*. New York and London: Oxford University Press, 1975.

Gilbert, Bill. *They Also Served: Baseball and the Home Front, 1941-1945*. New York: Crown Publishers, 1992.

Gilmore, David D. *Manhood in the Making: Cultural Concepts of Masculinity*. New Haven: Yale University Press, 1990.

Green, Harvey. *Fit for America: Health, Fitness, Sport, and American Society*. Baltimore and London: The Johns Hopkins University Press, 1986.

Grover, Kathryn, ed. *Fitness in American Culture: Images of Health, Sport, and the Body, 1830-1940*. Amherst: The University of Massachusetts Press, 1989.

Guttmann, Allen. *Games and Empires: Modern Sports and Cultural Imperialism*. New York: Columbia University Press, 1994.

Guttmann, Allen. *Women's Sports: A History*. New York: Columbia University Press, 1991.

Guttmann, Allen. *A Whole New Ball Game: An Interpretation of American Sports*. Chapel Hill, N.C.: The University of North Carolina Press, 1988.

Guttmann, Allen. *Sports Spectators*. New York: Columbia University Press, 1986.

Guttmann, Allen. *The Games Must Go On: Avery Brundage and the Olympic Movement*. New York: Columbia University Press, 1984.

Hanson, Capt. Joseph Mills, ed. *The Inter-Allied Games: Paris, 22nd June to 6th July, 1919*. Paris: Ste. Ame de Publications Periodiques, 1919.

Hartmann, Susan M. *The Home Front and Beyond: American Women in the 1940s*. Boston: Twayne Publisher, 1982.

Hearn, Jeff and David Morgan, eds. *Men, Masculinities and Social Theory*. London: Unwin Hyman, 1990.

Higgonet, Margaret Randolph, et al., eds. *Behind the Lines: Gender and the Two World Wars.* New Haven and London: Yale University Press, 1987.

Hoberman, John M. *Sport and Political Ideology.* Austin: University of Texas Press, 1984.

Hoffman, Robert G. *Works Projects Administration, District No. 9: Projects Report.* Rochester, New York: January 1–December 31, 1940. Unpublished report held in the archives of the Monroe County, New York, County Historian's Office.

Holm, Maj. Gen. Jeanne, USAF (Ret.). *Women in the Military: An Unfinished Revolution,* Rev. Ed. Novato, Calif.: Presidio Press, 1992.

Holt, Richard, ed. *Sport and the Working Class in Modern Britain.* Manchester and New York: Manchester University Press, 1990.

Horowitz, Helen Lefkowitz. *Alma Mater: Design and Experience in the Women's Colleges from Their Nineteenth Century Beginnings to the 1930s.* New York: Alfred A. Knopf, 1984.

Howard, Donald S. *The WPA and Federal Relief Policy.* New York: Russell Sage Foundation, 1943.

Jansen, Sue Curry and Donald Sabo, "The Sport/War Metaphor, Gender Order, and the Persian Gulf War." Unpublished draft, October, 1991.

Jeffords, Susan. *The Remasculinization of America: Gender and the Vietnam War.* Bloomington: Indiana University Press, 1989.

Jomini, Clausewitz, and Schlieffen. West Point: Department of Military Art and Engineering, 1943.

Jones, James. *From Here to Eternity.* New York: Charles Scribner's Sons, 1951.

Karsten, Peter, ed. *The Military in America: From the Colonial Era to the Present.* New York: The Free Press, 1980.

Kaspi, Andre. *Le Temps des Americains: Le Concours Americain a La France en 1917–1918.* Paris: Publications de la Sorbonne, 1976.

Kaufman, Michael, ed. *Beyond Patriarchy: Essays by Men on Pleasure, Power, and Change.* Toronto: Oxford University Press, 1987.

Keegan, John. *The Second World War.* New York: Viking Penguin, 1990.

Keegan, John. *The Price of Admiralty: The Evolution of Naval Warfare.* New York: Viking, 1988.

Keegan, John. *The Mask of Command.* New York: Elizabeth Sif ton Books, Viking, 1987.

Keegan, John. *The Face of Battle: A Study of Agincourt, Waterloo and the Somme.* New York: Viking Penguin, 1978.

Kennedy, David M. *Over Here: The First World War and American Society.* Oxford and New York: Oxford University Press, 1980.

Kennett, Lee. *G.I.: The American Soldier in World War II.* New York: Charles Scribner's Sons, 1987.

King, Brig. Gen. Edward L. "The G-3 Division, War Department General Staff and Its Present Outstanding Problems," Washington, D.C., G-3 Course #5, 1929.

Kirsch, George B. *The Creation of American Team Sports: Baseball and Cricket, 1838–72.* Urbana: University of Illinois Press, 1989.

Knock, Thomas J. *"End All Wars": Woodrow Wilson and the Quest for a New World Order.* New York and Oxford: Oxford University Press, 1992.

Kopay, David and Perry Deane Young. *The David Kopay Story: An Extraordinary Self-Revelation.* New York: Arbor House, 1977.

Kuklick, Bruce. *To Every Thing a Season: Shibe Park and Urban Philadelphia.* Princeton, N.J.: Princeton University Press, 1991.

Lane, Jack C. *Armed Progressive: General Leonard Wood.* San Rafael, Calif. and London: Presidio Press, 1978.

Leinbaugh, Harold P. and John D. Campbell. *The Men of Company K: The Autobiography of a World War II Rifle Company.* New York: William Morrow and Company, 1985.

Leslie, W. Bruce. *Gentlemen and Scholars: College and Community in the "Age of the University," 1865–1917.* University Park: Pennsylvania State University Press, 1992.

Link, Arthur S. *American Epoch: A History of the United States Since the 1890s.* New York: Alfred A. Knopf, 1955.

Lonergan, Thomas Clement. *It Might Have Been Lost! A Chronicle from Alien Sources of the Struggle to Preserve the National Identity of the A.E.F.* New York and London: G. P. Putnam's Sons, 1929.

Mahon, John K. *History of the Militia and the National Guard.* New York: Macmillan Publishing Company, 1983.

Mandell, Richard D. *Sport: A Cultural History.* New York: Columbia University Press, 1984.

Mangan, J.A. and James Walvin, eds. *Manliness and Morality: Middle-Class Masculinity in Britain and America, 1800–1940.* Manchester: Manchester University Press, 1987.

Mangan, J.A., ed. *Pleasure, Profit, Proselytism: British Culture at Home and Abroad, 1700–1914*. London: Frank Cass, 1988.

Mangan, J.A. and Robert S. Park. *From 'Fair Sex' to Feminism: Sport and the Socialization of Women in the Industrial and Post-Industrial Eras*. London and Totowa, N.J.: Frank Cass, 1987.

Manual of Physical Training for Use in the United States Army. Washington, D.C.: Government Printing Office, 1914.

Marchand, Roland. *Advertising the American Dream: Making Way for Modernity, 1920–1940*. Berkeley, Calif.: University of California Press, 1985.

Mason, Tony. *Association Football and English Society, 1863–1915*. Sussex: The Harvester Press, 1980.

May, Elaine Tyler. *Homeward Bound: American Families in the Cold War Era*. New York: Basic Books, 1988.

Mee, Charles L., Jr. *The End of Order: Versailles, 1919*. New York: E. P. Dutton, 1980.

Messner, Michael. *Power at Play: Sports and the Problem of Masculinity*. Boston: Beacon Press, 1992.

Messner, Michael and Donald F. Sabo. *Sex, Violence and Power in Sports: Rethinking Masculinity*. Freedom, Calif.: The Crossing Press, 1994.

Messner, Michael and Donald F. Sabo, eds. *Sport, Men and the Gender Order: Critical Feminist Perspectives*. Champaign, Ill.: Human Kinetics Books, 1991.

Meyer, Robert, Jr., ed. *The Stars and Stripes Story of World War II*. New York: David McKay Company, 1960.

Miller, Nathan. *Theodore Roosevelt: A Life*. New York: Quill: William Morrow, 1992.

Mormino, Gary Ross. "The Playing Fields of St. Louis: Italian Immigrants and Sports, 1925–1941." *Journal of Sport History* 9 (Summer, 1982): 5–19.

Mosley, Leonard. *Marshall: Hero for Our Times*. New York: Hearst Books, 1982.

Mrozek, Donald J. *Sport and American Mentality, 1880–1910*. Knoxville: University of Tennessee Press, 1983.

Mrozek, Donald J. "The Interplay of Metaphor and Practice in the U.S. Defense Establishment's Use of Sport, 1940–1950." *Journal of American Culture* 7 (1984): 54–59.

Nalty, Bernard C. *Strength for the Fight: A History of Black Americans in the Military*. New York and London: The Free Press, 1986.

Nelson, Keith L. *Victors Divided: America and the Allies in Germany, 1918-1923.* Berkeley, Calif.: University of California Press, 1975.

Notes on Bayonet Training, No. 2. Washington, D.C.: Government Printing Office, 1917.

Noverr, Douglas A. and Lawrence E. Ziewacz. *The Games They Played: Sports in American History, 1865-1980.* Chicago: Nelson Hall, 1983.

O'Connell, Robert L. *Sacred Vessels: The Cult of the Battleship and the Rise of the U.S. Navy.* Boulder, Colo.: Westview Press, 1991.

O'Toole, G. J. A. *The Spanish War: An American Epic—1898.* New York: W. W. Norton and Company, 1984.

Palmer, Robert R., Bell I. Wiley, and William R. Keast. *The United States Army in World War II: The Army Ground Forces. Vol. 2: The Procurement and Training of Ground Combat Troops.* Washington, D.C.: Department of the Army, 1948.

Perez, Louis A., Jr. "Between Baseball and Bullfighting: The Quest for Nationality in Cuba, 1868-1898." *Journal of American History* (September, 1994): 493-517.

Perret, Geoffrey. *There's a War to Be Won: The United States Army in World War II.* New York: Ballantine Books, 1991; New York: Random House, 1991.

Pershing, John J., Commander-in-Chief, American Expeditionary Forces. *My Experience in the World War, Vol. I.* New York: Frederick A. Stokes, Co., 1931.

Pleck, Elizabeth and Joseph H. Pleck. *The American Man.* Englewood Cliffs, N.J.: Prentice-Hall, 1980.

Pope, Steven W. "An Army of Athletes: Playing Fields, Battlefields, and the American Military Sporting Experience, 1890-1920." *Journal of Military History* (July, 1995): 435-456.

Prange, Gordon W. *At Dawn We Slept: The Untold Story of Pearl Harbor.* New York: Penguin Books, 1982.

Pronger, Brian. *The Arena of Masculinity: Sports, Homosexuality, and the Meaning of Sex.* New York: St. Martin's Press, 1990.

Riess, Steven A., ed. *The American Sporting Experience: A Historical Anthology of Sport in America.* New York: Leisure Press, 1984.

Romiger, Donald W. "From Playing Field to Battleground: The United States Navy V-5 Preflight Program in World War II." *Journal of Sport History* 12 (Winter, 1985): 252-264.

Rotundo, E. Anthony. *America Manhood: Transformations in Masculinity from the Revolution to the Modern Era.* New York: Basic Books, 1993.

Ryan, Mary P. *Cradle of the Middle Class: The Family in Oneida County, New York, 1790–1865*. Cambridge and New York: Cambridge University Press, 1981.

Sabo, Donald F., Jr. and Ross Runfulo. *Jock: Sports and Male Identity*. Englewood Cliffs, NJ: Prentice-Hall, 1980.

Sandler, Stanley. *Segregated Skies: All-Black Combat Squadrons of WWII*. Washington, D.C. and London: Smithsonian Institution Press, 1992.

Schoonmaker, Linda Lee. *The History and Development of the Programs of Physical Education, Intercollegiate Athletics, Intramurals and Recreational Sports for Women at the United States Military Service Academies*. Columbus: The Ohio State University, 1983, unpub. diss.

Schoor, Gene. *100 Years of Army-Navy Football: A Pictorial History of America's Most Colorful and Competitive Sports Rivalry*. New York: A Donald Hutter Book, 1989.

Segal, David R. and H. Wallace Sinaiko, eds. *Life in the Rank and File: Enlisted Men and Women in the Armed Forces of the United States, Australia, Canada and the United Kingdom*. Washington, D.C.: Pergamon-Brassey's International Defense Publishers, 1986.

Seymour, Harold. *Baseball: The People's Game*. New York and Oxford: Oxford University Press, 1990.

Shilts, Randy. *Conduct Unbecoming: Gays and Lesbians in the U.S. Military*. New York: Fawcett Columbine, 1994.

Special Service Officer, TM 21-205. Washington, D.C.: War Department, 1942.

The Special Service Officer (Athletics and Recreation), TM 21-205. Washington, D.C.: War Department, 1944.

Stiehm, Judith Hicks. *Bring Me Men and Women: Mandated Change at the U.S. Air Force Academy*. Berkeley: University of California Press, 1981.

Stouffer, Samuel A., et al. *The American Soldier: Combat and Its Aftermath, Vol. II*. Princeton, N.J.: Princeton University Press, 1949.

Theweleit, Klaus. *Male Fantasies, Vol. 2: Psychoanalyzing the White Terror*. Minneapolis: University of Minnesota Press, 1989.

"Training Bulletin No. 1." In *U.S. Army in the World War, 1917–1919, Vol. 17*. Washington, D.C.: Government Printing Office, 1948.

"Training Bulletin No. 2." In *U.S. Army in the World War, 1917–1919, Vol. 17*. Washington, D.C.: Government Printing Office, 1948.

"Training Bulletin No. 3." In *U.S. Army in the World War, 1917–1919, Vol. 17*. Washington, D.C.: Government Printing Office, 1948.

Trask, David. *The War With Spain in 1898.* New York: Macmillan Publishing Co., 1981.

Tygiel, Jules. *Baseball's Great Experiment: Jackie Robinson and His Legacy.* New York: Vintage Books, 1983.

Weigley, Russell F. *The American War of War: A History of United States Military Strategy and Policy.* New York: The Macmillan Company, 1973.

Weigley, Russell F. *History of the United States Army.* New York: The Macmillan Company, 1967.

Westbrook, Robert B. " 'I Want a Girl, Just Like the Girl That Married Harry James': American Women and the Problem of Political Obligation in World War II." *American Quarterly* 42 (December, 1990): 587–614.

Whan, Major Vorin E., Jr., ed. *A Soldier Speaks: Public Papers and Speeches of General of the Army Douglas MacArthur.* New York and Washington, D.C.: Frederick A. Praeger, Publishers, 1965.

White, Kevin. *The First Sexual Revolution: The Emergence of Male Heterosexuality in Modern America.* New York and London: New York University Press, 1993.

Woollcott, Alexander. *The Command is Forward: Tales of A.E.F. Battlefields as They Appeared in the Stars and Stripes.* New York: The Century Co., 1919.

Zingg, Paul J., ed. *The Sporting Image: Readings in American Sport History.* Lanham, MD: University Press of America, 1988.

Newspapers

During both world wars, newspapers were published at various Army posts and naval stations in the United States and overseas. Many of these have been preserved on microfilm in the collection of the Military History Institute. In addition to those newspapers, *Stars and Stripes* began publication in Europe as the American buildup moved forward in 1918. That newspaper ceased publication at the end of the war, but returned during World War II. The solders' newspaper, *Yank,* began publication during the Second World War as well. For this project newspapers representing the black press were also consulted, as was the *New York Times.*

For World War I

Amaroc News
The Camp Garrett Camouflager
Chicago Defender
The Cootie
The Gold Bar

The Indian
The Long Range Sniper
New York Times
Pittsburgh Courier
Spokane Washington Chronicle
Stars and Stripes
Trench and Camp
The Whizz-Bang
The Wildcat

For World War II

Amphibian
Amsterdam Star-News
The Armodier
Armored News
Atlanta Daily World
Baltimore Afro-American
Banana Peelings
The B.B.C. News
Birmingham News
Birmingham Post
Bom Bay
The Bomb Bay
Bomb Bay Messenger
Borinquen Bomber
Boston Guardian
The Bowman Bomber
Brief
Broadcaster
Chicago Bee
Chicago Defender
Chicago Tribune
The Clarion
The Clark Field Propwash
Daily Worker
Double Deucer
Drew Field Echoes
George Field News
Gosport
Kansas City Call
New York Age
New York Times

Norfolk Journal and Guide
Pittsburgh Courier
The P.M. Daily
The Real McCoy
Scott Field Broadcaster
The Sourdough Sentinel
The Spearhead
Spindrift
Spokane Chronicle
Stars and Stripes
Topeka Capital
WACtivities (aka *WAAC-tivities*)
Washington Post
The Weekly Salute
World Telegram
Yank

Soldier Surveys and Memoirs

Beginning in the 1970s, the Military History Institute at Carlisle Barracks in Pennsylvania began distributing surveys first among surviving veterans of World War I, and recently among surviving veterans of World War II. Many veterans have chosen merely to answer the questions posed by the relevant surveys, but some veterans have also provided the Institute with written memoirs, diaries, and other memorabilila from their time in the service. These documents are an invaluable resource fo historians. In this project, I used survey responses and other material from the following individuals or units, which are identified as they appear in the archival record at the Institute.

From World War I

Reg. Bugler Sgt. Roy H. Amidon
Col. Abbott Boone
Charles L. Boyd
Philip Brooks
Wiiliam Burley
George A. Burton
Pvt. Henry K. Carter
A. W. Chilton
James R. Clyburn
Judson Colburn
Pvt. John E. Cooney
James Corne
Albert A. Dockery

2d Lt. William F. Dodd
Guytress Eley
Henry Ellsworth
Asa Eubank
Arthur Evans
Samuel Francis Evans
1st Lt. Francis H. Farnum
Robert John Fleming
Frank J. Franek
Walter Frei
Wade Gardner
Albert Gulli
Cpl. Robert L. Harbison
David E. Harris
Sgt. Major Benjamin H. Heath
Guy V. Henry, Sr.
John M. Hester
Benjamin F. Hoge
Gordon Coble Hunter
Thomas F. Ingraham
Olin Jenkins
Allen T. Johnson
Peter W. Kegeries
Boldridge Edward Kneece
August Knowles
Col. Edson A. Lewis
Julian Robert Lindsey
Brig. Gen. Clarence Linniger
Diary of O. W. Lomady
Pvt. George Loukides
George McMahon
Harry Maltby
Paul C. Meads
William Rufus Mitchell
George L. Morgan
Howard W. Norton
John M. Palmer
Clarence O. Pearson
Joseph Peterson
Howard Petz
Wallace C. Philoon
Lawrence Radloff

Benjamin Reeder
Memoirs of Seaver Rice
Mark Richmond
Kerr T. Riggs
Gustav Risch
W. O. Ryan
Fred Shelley
Arthur Smith
Herbert C. Smith, Jr.
Nelson Souder
James Stocking
Cpl. Fred H. Takes
Charles Van Citters
E. R. Van Deusen
John D. Wagner
Raymond Waldron
George Wayne Walker
William Wambsganss
Orlando Ward
Lester Warner
Morris D. Weisman
Edward Williams
Raymond Wright

From World War II
Tenth Mountain Division

Eric Carl Anderson
Herman F. Appel
Kenneth Bergren
Charles Bradley
Gerard Brueders
Fred Burke
Casper Cowan
Ralph Crawford
Warren Cusick
Thomas Deming
C. L. Eichman
Marvin Fishman
Henry Forner
Paul F. Gerads
Lloyd Gordon
Joe E. Green

Joseph M. Green
William Gribble
Earl Griffin
James Hadley
Herman Holthaus
Robert Hooker
Frederick Hoppe
Avril Jenson
Hersel Jones
Andrew Kadie
Vernon Keslar
Harold Krause
Delmar Kubley
Kermit Moore
Robert Neimeyer
Walbert Nelson
Charles H. Parr
Attil Pasquini
Roy Peterson
Felix Poletti
Harry Pruzan
Steve Swencki
Paul Szecsey
August Reborek
Sam Tocco
Lorenzo Voisine
Robert Weiler
Raymond Welch
L. W. Wellington
Orris White

Service Forces

Walter Baues
Elbert Friend
Duane Kirssin
Jack Maltby
Clyde Miller
Robert Rupprecht
Raymond Stevens

Camps/Forts

Robert Bulmore
Gerald Corwin

William Holly
Henry Leerkamp
William Maholet
Frank Meyers
James Muscara
Robert Rex
Carl Richie
Floyd Stigler
Edmond Ward

First Division Headquarters

Christopher Alster
Dorris Barickman
Robert Bogart
Vernon Broom
Michael Colgan
William Cozad
Joseph Donnelly
David Englander
Raymond Huntoon
George Hutnick
John Lagrutta
Kenneth Lord
Harold Milne
Emerald Ralston
Armando Rosa
Henry Ruge
Robert Ryan
John Savarino
Paul Skogsberg
George Stathern
Philip Varden
Edward Wiejaczka

First Division/Sixteenth Infantry Regiment

William Behlmer
Isodore Berkowitz
Ralph Berry
Everett Booth
Robert Brand
Warren Briescher

Henry Buettner
John Carroll
Paul Coffer
Richard Cole
Daniel Curatola
Bryce Denno
William Dillon
Wilbur Dinsmore
Earl Eigabroadt
Theodore Lazarakis
Herbert Longrelt
Joseph Mancino
Ronald Martin
Carmen Meduri
Roy Millard
Albert Nendza
Andrew Nesevitch
Joseph Nichols
William Nimmo
Richard Odyers
Joseph Pilck
Richard Ricioppo
Richard Rivard
Edward Sackley
Dale Sinciair
Allen Smith
Warren Sweetman
Stanley Taylor
Sylvester Tighe
Arthur Tozar
Thaddeus Tragarz
Vincent Tuetken
Albert Wells
Wilson Young

First Division/First Eng. Batt./First Eng. Combt Batt.

Raymond Bidleman
Herbert Browning
Zigmond Czarnecki
Oreste DelGallo
Leo DesChamps
William Flynn

Geoffrey Keyes
Mike Klaich
Theodore Mishkel
Henry Rowland
Edward Stanton

First Division/Fifth FA/Seventh FA

Alfred Alvarez
Charles Bradbury
Nicholas Chelenza
Bernard Clark
Stephen Coupe
Donald Curtis
Theodore Dedowitz
Thomas Lancer
Richard Lindo
Oscar Rich
Thomas Toterhi
Robert Veit

First Division/Thirty-second/Thirty-third FA

William Chamberlin
James Deverell
George Doucette
William Faust
Malcolm Marshall
Douglas Murray

Chaplain's Corps

Frank Dennis
Judah Nadich

Morale Services Division

Irving Cutler

Base Section Garrison Forces Base Command

Edward Barnes
Frank Lock

AAF Bases

Ralph Borsa
Edison Breckenridge

Arthur Brownlee
Rudolph Bors
Raymond Chariton
Robert Chatlain
Wayne F. Dudley
George Hall
Floyd Hall
Reuben Herr
Elmer Kesslin
Robert Logan
Edwin Preston
Alfon Quitta
Ralph Summy
Gobie Trail

Bomb Wings/Groups

Alvin Anderson
Kenneth Applegate
Joseph Arndt
Richard Boulay
Henry Burman
Martin Chavez
Denzel Clark
Joseph Conlon
Fred Cormier
Frank Crooks
Henry A. Diehl
Arthur Droegmeier
Robert Edwards
Philip Ervin
William Gardin
Ernest Gustafson
William Hill
David Horner
George Kanefsky
Bernard Lapp
Oreste Leto
Neil Liahtner
Sam Liner
Clair Marlatt
Lawrence Myers
Earl Payne

Francis Payne
Clifford Peterson
Frank Petrash
John Pluckhahn
Eli Pronchick
Leonard Raterman
Richard Roudebush
Harry Schulz
Sylvester Stanley
Paul Wright

Bomb Squadrons #1–#421

Thomas Alexander
Merle Bolen
James R. Cole
John Downs
Donald Dukeman
Joseph Dyblee
Frank Dziengowski
Louis Fliegelman
Alfred Flocke
Thomas Gannon
Joel Griffin
Charles A. Harris
James Hill
Ervin Huebner
S. Thomas Jacobs
Lewis Knight
Howard Koepke
John Krug
Dell McIntyre
Glen McQueen
Clyde Marshall
Reynolds Merritts
George Miles
Robert L. Shawver
Webster Singer
William Spaienza
Edward Spalding
Robert Stein
James Thompson

Quartermaster Corps

Oliver Barraclough
Carle Blackman
Clarence Brink
Leslie Brown
Charles Butte
Bruce Farr
David Field
Moses Gossett
Robert Harrison
Robert Higley
Charles Jackson
Albert Legg
John Little
Albert McGraw
Thomas McLouglin
Dee Mathews
William Mullen
David Newsam
Wallace Poole
James Robertson
Richie Schackelford
Benjamin Schneiderman
Lyman Schwarzkopf
Henry Shumamker
Ernest Stolper
George Thornton
Victor Troy
Warren Wirebach

Ninety-second Infantry Division

John Hunter
Spencer Moore
Homer Somers

Other Contributors

Darrel Holland
Drexel McCormack
Orville T. Murphy
Howard B. Riley
Eldon Wakefield

Papers

The Military History Institute also has accepted for preservation the papers of many officers and men who served in the U.S. military, as well as the collected papers of civilians whose relationships with men in the armed forces serve to illuminate their wartime experiences.

For the purposes of this project, the papers of the following individuals have been quite useful.

Alexander-Whitefield, Family Papers
Leon T. David, Papers
Benjamin O. Davis, Sr., Papers
Mrs. Gladys Darcy, Papers
Samuel Arthur Devan, Chaplain, Papers
Dugway Proving Group Papers
Marvin Fletcher Collection (especially with regard to African-American soldiers from
    the Philippines through World War I)
Walter Galson, Papers
Leah and Lena Reynolds, Papers
James H. and Adeline Gorder Richards, Papers
Carl Ulsaker, Papers
James Alward Van Fleet, Papers
601st Ordnance Battalion, Papers

Oral Histories

Since the 1970s, a program for the debriefing of senior officers has been conducted under the auspices of the Army War College. Transcripts of those conversations are kept in the collections at the Military History Institute.

Those officers whose memories were used for this project include the following.

Conversations between Lt. Gen. William P. Ennis, Jr., and Lt. Col. Miquel E.
    Monteverde, Sr., 1984.
Conversations between Lt. Gen. Hobart Raymond Gay, and Col. Willard L. Wallace,
    Project 81-6.
Conversations between Gen. Andrew J. Goodpaster, and Col. William D. Johnson and
    Lt. James C. Ferguson, January 9, 1976.
Interview with Col. Mary A. Hallaven.
Conversations between Lt. Gen. Stanley R. Larsen and Lt. Col. Robert S. Holmes, 1977.
Conversations with Maj. General Earnest L. "Iron Mike" Massad, 1985–1986
Conversations between Gen. James H. Polk, USA, Ret., and Lt. Col. Roland D. Tausch,
    AWC 1971–72.

INDEX

Index